YOUNG PEOPLE LEAVING STATE CARE IN CHINA

Xiaoyuan Shang and Karen R. Fisher

First published in Great Britain in 2017 by

Policy Press
University of Bristol
1-9 Old Park Hill
Bristol
BS2 8BB
UK
t: +44 (0)117 954 5940
pp-info@bristol.ac.uk
www.policypress.co.uk

North America office:
Policy Press
c/o The University of Chicago Press
1427 East 60th Street
Chicago, IL 60637, USA
t: +1 773 702 7700
f: +1 773-702-9756
sales@press.uchicago.edu
www.press.uchicago.edu

© Policy Press 2017

British Library Cataloguing in Publication Data
A catalogue record for this book is available from the British Library

Library of Congress Cataloging-in-Publication Data
A catalog record for this book has been requested

ISBN 978-1-4473-3669-3 hardcover
ISBN 978-1-4473-3670-9 ePdf
ISBN 978-1-4473-3671-6 ePub
ISBN 978-1-4473-3672-3 Mobi

Cover design by Qube Design Associates, Bristol
Front cover image: istock
Printed and bound in Great Britain by CPI Group (UK) Ltd, Croydon, CR0 4YY
Policy Press uses environmentally responsible print partners

Contents

Contents

List of tables and figures

List of tables

List of figures

Glossary and abbreviations

All names used in the book are aliases unless the case is in the public media or the person agreed to be named.

Affordable housing
> Government low-cost housing available to disadvantaged families to purchase for home-ownership.

Alternative care
> Care for children away from their birth parents, including state care, kinship care and other informal care.

BNU
> Beijing Normal University.

Carer
> Informal carers, including family, kin and friends, caring for children in alternative care.

Children and young people with disabilities
> The book uses person-first language consistent with the UNCRPD style, that is child first, disability second.

De facto adoption
> Informal adoption or foster care families without registration of the relationship or the child.

DPF
> Disabled Persons' Federation.

Hukou
> Resident card registration.

Inclusive education
> The book refers to inclusive education as supported education within a mainstream classroom or school. It contrasts with special education in a segregated environment.

Informal carer
> Unpaid carers and kinship carers (contrasted with paid support workers). It includes informal or de facto adoption and foster care families, where the child is often an unregistered citizen.

Institutional care
> Residential care in institutions, approximately 50–500 children in each institution. See also state child welfare institution.

Kinship care
> Informal alternative care within the extended family of the orphan.

Low rental housing
> Government public housing.

MCA
> Ministry of Civil Affairs. Provincial and local levels of civil affairs are referred to as a department or bureau.

MLS
> Minimum living security – social security for low-income households, *dibao*.

NGO
> Non-governmental organization.

Orphans allowance
> Basic living security allowance for orphans.

RMB
> Chinese dollar (Yuan, *renminbi*), 10 RMB = £1.1.

State care
> Government alternative care of state wards, which is the responsibility of local city state child welfare institutions.

State child welfare institution
> Local government organization responsible for state wards, including organizing adoption and usually providing institutional care, and sometimes also other forms of alternative care in the community, such as foster care.

State guardianship or state ward
> Child without known birth family or extended family in the guardianship of the state.

UNCRC
> United Nations Convention on the Rights of the Child 1990.

UNCRPD
> United Nations Convention on the Rights of Persons with Disabilities 2008.

Wubao
> Income support in rural areas guaranteeing five supports, now replaced with MLS.

Authors

Dr Xiaoyuan Shang is a Professor at Beijing Normal University, and Associate Professor, Social Policy Research Centre, UNSW Sydney, Australia. Her research interest is social security reforms and child welfare and protection in China, focusing on the alleviation of poverty and social services for vulnerable groups, including children, older people and people with disabilities. She is an international leader in Chinese child welfare research and has published extensively on Chinese social policy (email: x.shang@unsw.edu.au).

Dr Karen R. Fisher is a Professor at the Social Policy Research Centre, UNSW Sydney, Australia. She conducts social policy research in Australia and China about the organization of community services, particularly: disability and mental health policy; programme and service evaluation; and the policy process. She applies participatory methods with people with disabilities, disability policy officials and service providers. She researches with Xiaoyuan Shang on Chinese disability policy (email: Karen.fisher@unsw.edu.au).

Acknowledgements

Thank you to the participants in the research who shared their stories. The research was funded by the Australian Research Council and Right To Play China and conducted by researchers from UNSW Sydney and Beijing Normal University. Ethics approval was from UNSW. Thank you to the directors and other staff in the child welfare institutions, the young people, and the foster parents for their contribution to the fieldwork. Thank you to the fieldwork researchers Yu Jie, Dou Zhenfang, Yang Xi, Xie Xin and Li Zhe.

The following publications are adapted for chapters in this book with permission from the journals:

- Chapter material about Daxing foster care is from a previous study: Shang, X. (2008) *Chinese vulnerable children protection system*. Beijing: Social Sciences Academic Press, pp 139–43 (in Chinese).
- Chapter Ten is modified from a related publication: Shang, X. and Fisher, K.R. (2017) 'Everything for the children: the case of orphans growing up in de facto adoption families', *Journal of Social Service Research*.

ONE

Introduction to leaving state care in China

Context of young people leaving care in China

In the 1980s, the mortality rate and living conditions of children in Chinese state child welfare institutions shocked the world through the BBC documentary film *The dying rooms*. Many orphaned children, mostly healthy girls, who were living in state child welfare institutions died of poor care or inadequate medical treatment. At that time, the death rate was 50–80% in some welfare institutions.

The documentary triggered strong reactions from child welfare organizations throughout the world, as well as from the Chinese government. The state changed the policy to allow donations to the welfare institutions and permitted domestic and international adoption. The state also increased funding for children's welfare institutions. Some institutions in poorer cities already had a history of foster care. Now, in response to public concern, other major cities, including Beijing and Shanghai, also began to accept the internationally recognized benefits of family-based foster care as a better alternative to institutional care.

These efforts of international organizations and the Chinese government have since radically improved the way in which state care in China operates. Changes in policy, funding and alternative care types substantially changed the care of children who are in the guardianship of state welfare institutions. This book is about that first generation of children and young people who grew up in Chinese state child welfare institutions after the scandal of *The dying rooms*. It explores their childhood experiences, their transition to adulthood and how these experiences affect their adult life.

According to the Ministry of Civil Affairs (MCA, 2013a), China had about 615,000 Chinese children aged under 18 years whose parents had died or could not be found in 2012. They included 109,000 children in the guardianship of child welfare institutions operated by civil affairs departments, and over 500,000 children raised by relatives, other guardians, other people or non-governmental organizations.

It is estimated that roughly 20% of the children and young people in state care are aged over 16 years old (MCA, 2013b), with about 10,000 orphaned young people reaching adulthood each year. In this book, we generally refer to them as young people in state care, rather than orphans, because their circumstances are often that their families cannot be found rather than they have died (Heaser, 2016).

Only children without any known family connections are eligible for state care – other orphans are cared for within their extended family. Unlike high-income countries, the only children in the guardianship of the state are these orphans without known family because China is still taking early steps to develop a child protection system that can remove children who are subject to abuse or neglect within their family (Shang and Wang, 2013; Shang and Katz, 2014).

China has many children who are orphaned each year, when either both parents die or cannot be found, or one dies and the other parent cannot be found. Annually, tens of thousands of children are left without their birth parents. Most of them are cared for within their kinship family. Some children without family connections end up in local state welfare institutions, which assume legal guardianship responsibility as the public agency subordinate to the Bureau of Civil Affairs.

The institutions attempt to arrange adoption for children in their care, usually within China. Most of the children have disabilities because, like other countries, alternatives to state care are more likely to be found for children without disabilities. If they are not adopted, the state continues to care for them during their childhood and perhaps adulthood. Children in state care are registered as urban residents and are entitled to comprehensive social welfare, including free education, social assistance, health care and therapy. This level of social protection is higher than that of people living in most rural areas or who move to urban areas.

Most formal alternative care for children without families in China is institutional care (Shang and Fisher, 2014a). If children in state care are not adopted, most of them (86%) live in state child welfare institutions. The remainder live in foster care arranged by the institution or the local civil affairs department. A small number of non-governmental organizations also care for some children. These proportions are similar to other post-communist transition countries (Stein, 2014). Irrespective of where the state wards live, the welfare institution is the legal guardian of all children in state care unless they become adopted. Alternative care is discussed further in Chapter Two.

The children in formal foster care are either in very poor areas, where the government cannot afford expensive institutional care and foster care is regarded as a cheap alternative, or in big cities, where international organizations have supported pilot projects since the late 1990s (Shang, 2008a). Some children move between institutions and foster care as their circumstances change. Given this current predominant practice of institutional care, if children are in state care, they are likely to spend their childhood in an institution. As a result, they face serious challenges to establishing an independent life, employment, housing and social connections when they enter adulthood. Children who grow up in foster care at least have the opportunity to form foster-family relations, but are these relationships sufficient for adult independence?

About 20% of children in state care are aged above 16 years (Shang, 2008b). Young adults in state care reach the age when their peers would expect to gain economic and social independence, which this book refers to as young people leaving state care. Children in institutional care grow up without connections to a family or community. They lack the community-based education, skills and social contact usually needed to achieve independent adult lives. They lack the broader formal and informal social support available to other citizens to facilitate their social inclusion. These circumstances pose serious challenges to establishing an independent life, employment, housing and social networks when they enter adulthood.

The rapid social, economic and demographic changes in China have affected all aspects of the living environment of children and young people in China, particularly children in state care (Shang and Wu, 2003). Positive developments are the growth of the mixed welfare state and the relaxation of the family planning requirements, so that all families can now choose to have more than one child and they are more likely to receive free social services. These trends imply that fewer children will be left in state care in the future (Blaxland et al, 2015; Fisher et al, 2016). On the other hand, whereas the government once arranged jobs for young people leaving care or other young people with disabilities, it now relies on the developing labour market to fulfil this function (Shang, 2003, 2009).

Without the social connections of their peers in the community, when young people in state care reach adulthood, many of them continue to rely on state welfare provision, including employment, institutional care, subsidized housing and income support. Most young people remain in state care even when they are adults because they do not have the connections and support to gain independence. They remain the responsibility of the state, usually condemned to a life in an institution for their entire life. Despite these dire outcomes for many young people in state care in China, evidence about their experiences has not been systematically researched until now.

Leaving state care in China

The book is the result of international collaborative research to learn more about and improve this transition to adulthood of young people leaving state care in China. It addresses difficult questions about whether socio-economic outcomes are different for young people who have lived in foster care compared to those who have only lived in institutional care. It examines how children in state care, particularly children with disabilities, experience their transition to adulthood, and the impact of their childhood on that experience, particularly the use of foster care and other alternative care. It is hoped that the findings influence policies and promote alternative care, which has the best outcomes for children.

The consequences of a childhood of state care that does not support and prepare a child for independence can be lifelong. It is therefore important to understand what contributes to positive outcomes when they reach adulthood. The book examines questions about the young people's experiences, such as: what is the impact of becoming orphaned and growing up without care in a family? How do these young people view themselves and their community? What is the impact on their sense of their adulthood and capacity to live in the community? How do they achieve independent income and housing? Are they able to find love, friendship and marriage?

Chinese state child welfare institutions implement several types of alternative care. The type of alternative care affects the childhood and transition of young people. This raises a second set of questions, such as: how do the different types of alternative care affect the transitions of young people leaving care in China? What aspects of the alternative care types support young people's capacity for transitioning to independence? These two sets of questions are critical to understanding how to improve the childhood and adulthood of the many children in state care.

Descriptions from research with young people in an institution and in foster care illustrate the stark difference in the living conditions of young people in state care (all names are aliases). The first example is from a social work researcher speaking with eight young women in a welfare institution. They were aged 15–18 years. Xiaomei was the oldest in the group and when she came in, she shouted: "What are we going to talk about? Be quick". The other girls laughed, two of them slept on chairs. Xiaomei spoke aggressively and occasionally swore. Xiaoling watched the researcher out of the corner of her eyes and said, "Why do you want to interview us? Where are you from?". The girls would not answer questions individually. When one spoke, the others followed suit. Only Xiaomei spoke independently. The researcher noted:

> "The children at the welfare institution exhibited serious psychological problems. The staff said Xiaomei is a headache for every staff of the welfare institution. She does not trust anybody or open her heart to anybody. Nevertheless, this simply shows how the teenager protects herself. Among all the children there, Xiaomei has the strongest awareness of taking precautions and self-protection. In essence, she is vulnerable. The more vulnerable the heart, the more she needs to protect herself through a variety of ways. She needs intense psychological support."

In contrast, the researchers interviewed another young woman who had grown up in foster family. Ying was 22 years old. When she was three years old, she became a state ward and was cared for in a welfare institution, which sent her to a foster family. Her third older brother in the foster family drove her to the research interview and waited outside until the interview finished. Ying had a strong sense of belonging in the foster family and a clear vision for a future independent life without unusual reliance on the family. She said: "My mom treats me like her other children". Speaking of when she left the foster family to attend high school, she said: "At the beginning, I didn't want to leave home…. Now that I experienced social interactions and competition, I feel even more warmth in the family". The close foster-family relations had enabled Ying to be generous. The school has a donation box. She said she thought that the money donated might be distributed to children in disaster areas, and so she donated money that could be used to pay for two dinners. She also indicated that if she could, she would definitely help children with similar experiences as hers.

  These stories of young people in state care demonstrate disparate childhoods – one in an institution and one in foster care. Only the latter had opportunities for family relationships. Even from these brief descriptions, the implications are clear that the type of alternative care during childhood affects options for leaving care and future independent lives. The young people had very different views about the community and their future. The children growing up in institutions had limited life experience in the community; they exhibited fear and distrust towards community members and feared what it meant to leave the institution, even if there were no direct obstacles. They faced many challenges, even just from their behaviour and confidence. In contrast, the young woman who grew up in a family environment faced challenges similar to other children who grow up with their parents – she had a home, a family, and trust and goodwill towards the community and other people. Her only additional challenge was not knowing her birth family.

The book examines whether, in the Chinese context, the type of alternative care that a child experiences affects social and economic outcomes in their adulthood. A starting assumption is that children growing up in family care could be expected to be better integrated in their communities compared to children in institutional care, and would be more likely to have social networks to help them achieve their goals.

International framework to understand the problem of leaving state care

Leaving state care is an important international policy area for two reasons – for all young people, entering adulthood is a time of great change, usually with the support of family members to embark on steps towards independence in choices about current and future living arrangements, economic participation and social relationships. Children who have grown up in state care face an additional set of challenges as they leave their full dependence on state support (Mendes and Snow, 2016). The success of managing these two transitions to adulthood and out of state care depends on: their childhood experiences; support from the state and other social connections during childhood and young adulthood; and the opportunities in their wider community to enact their choices (Anghel, 2011; Stepanova and Hackett, 2014). Whether the transition experiences of children in state care are positive is therefore dependent on a supportive policy environment. International research shows that they are likely to have experienced traumatic experiences during their childhood, compounded by any inadequacies in the quality of state care that they received (Mendes, 2009).

Orphaned children leaving institutional care face the added disadvantage that they have grown up in relative social isolation from their peers (Anghel, 2011). Even when state wards live in family-based care, they face many disadvantages when seeking social and economic independence. In a country of diversity and social change such as China, learning from experiences where young people had good support during childhood and young adulthood is important so that others can benefit from policy directions that seek to improve their lives.

Children's rights and social inclusion

The book uses a children's rights and social inclusion framework to understand how state institutional or foster care facilitates young people's social inclusion and the socio-economic outcomes for young people leaving care. Social inclusion and social exclusion are multidisciplinary concepts, involving economic, social, political, cultural and specific aspects of disadvantage and deprivation (Hills et al, 2001; Levitas et al, 2009).

Social inclusion is also internationally recognized as a key goal of children's and disability rights. The rights in a social inclusion framework are civil, economic, developmental and social rights. These rights are exemplified in the United Nations Convention on the Rights of the Child (UNCRC, 1989) and the most recent United Nations Convention on the Rights of Persons with Disabilities (UNCRPD, 2008), which aims to achieve 'full and effective participation and inclusion in society'. The United Nations Guidelines for the Alternative Care of Children (UNGACC, 2009) includes specific guidance for policies on leaving care, emphasizing the need to plan the transition out of care with the active participation of the child early in the child's life. In fact, the affiliates to the International Research Network on Transitions to Adulthood from Care (INTRAC) have used a UNCRC framework to critique the current limits to states' policies on leaving care (Munro et al, 2011). China was among the first signatories to the conventions.

Three aspects of social inclusion are important in framing analysis of the disadvantages for young people leaving care in countries in economic transition (Hobcraft, 1998; Kamerman, 2002; Levitas et al, 2009). First, social exclusion is a concept of multidimensional disadvantage, more comprehensive than just income poverty or unemployment, in which children and young people are more vulnerable than adults. Second, the dynamic dimension of social exclusion is particularly devastating for children and young people in institutions because of the temporal and duration effect of early childhood experiences on later capabilities and social networks in their transition to adulthood. Third, social exclusion encompasses the concept of deprivation of human rights, which is particularly useful in countries in transition, where vulnerable children and young people are denied basic rights.

When these three aspects are theorized in the positive, a concept of social inclusion that encompasses aspects of multidimensional, dynamic and human rights has the potential to reframe analysis of the transition experiences of young people leaving care. Social inclusion implies facilitating full citizenship, including dimensions of civil, economic, developmental and social participation, rather than merely focusing on material supply or survival. Conceptualized this way, social inclusion is an important theoretical framework for policy analysis of childhood disadvantage and the impact on the transition to adulthood.

Compared to other children, young people leaving care or with disabilities face greater obstacles to social inclusion during childhood and adulthood. Unsuitable care and support during childhood limits their options as they enter adulthood. The difficulties are even greater for young people living in institutional care due to an absence of contact with formal and informal support networks in the community, such as a local school, family, friends, neighbours and other children (Hillan, 2008). Examining the experiences of these young people in China can contribute to understanding how social policies can respond to their rights to social inclusion through childhood and young adulthood.

As the lifetime impact of disadvantage is particularly devastating for children and young people, governments pay special attention to policies designed to combat childhood exclusion (Micklewright, 2002; Frazer and Marlier, 2007). International experience of children's social inclusion in different forms of alternative care reveals that family-based care is usually the most conducive environment for most children, especially young children. This position is represented in UNGACC (2009), which promotes that children should be placed within families whenever possible. Family-based care is the preferred form of alternative care for most state wards for many reasons, in part, because it can reduce isolation during childhood and can facilitate social connections. In China, however, which type of alternative care should be the dominant is still disputed and institutional care remains the most common. If these disputes cannot be resolved with international and national evidence of the impact on the social inclusion of children,

children in state care will continue to reach adulthood disadvantaged compared to their peers who grew up with their families. This book aims to contribute to that process.

Transition to adulthood

The transition to adulthood, particularly that of children leaving alternative care, crosses many disciplines in research (Harder et al, 2011). It encompasses: psychological well-being, independence and development in psychology; employment, housing and economic independence in economics; and social networking and independence in responsibilities, marriage and family relationships, as well as social integration, in sociology. This book touches on each of these areas.

Social policy about alternative care is concerned with support for the transition of children to adulthood and the implications for successfully leaving care. Transition to adulthood is a social construction about young people shifting towards more independent roles and the social responsibilities expected in adulthood (Goodkind et al, 2011). Transition implies a change from one stage to another, whereas, of course, children and young adults actually live their lives as a continuity of their identity and a dynamic social interaction with the people and social structures around them. In this sense, transition is a falsely linear label that describes the imperceptible changes that most young people experience over many years. Most young people continue to rely on their families for support in many aspects of their lives throughout these years, without an abrupt point of transition from one stage to the next.

For some young people with disabilities, even conceptualizing a culturally and personally relevant understanding of adulthood independence is contested (Murphy et al, 2011). Using a social model of disability, independence in this context means receiving the support they need to live where and with whom they choose (Wiesel et al, 2015). Achieving these goals or accessing the support to do so is often difficult, especially if their childhood experience in state care has added to their support needs (Mendes et al, 2011; Mendes and Snow, 2014; Malvaso et al, 2016). Other young people with disabilities in China would usually expect to be living with their families or with friends in tertiary education, work accommodation or private rental (Fisher and Li, 2008; Fisher et al, 2011). In contrast, young people with disabilities who grew up in state care are unlikely to have these supports or to have witnessed the norms of support and independence that peers in the community might expect.

The lives of children in state care can be subjected to greater age categorization than their peers because the implication of their age and stage can be a trigger for bureaucratic eligibility. Transition of state wards to high school, vocational training, tertiary education, employment or housing can rely on formalized decisions and support from a welfare institution. These markers of young adult independence that their peers in the community might take for granted in the context of their family can become bureaucratized steps at the discretion of the institution. Most high-income countries now recognize this and provide additional support to young people leaving state care because of the disadvantages that they could experience as young adults (Mendes, 2009; Pinkerton, 2011; Mendes and Snow, 2016).

This book explores four aspects of the transition to adulthood, namely: establishing self-identity; employment and economic independence; independent housing; and social participation, friends, family and social networking. In the Chinese system, a measure of transitions is whether they obtain registered permanent residence separate from the state welfare institution. They are only able to achieve this status if they have independent housing, economic means, social security and identity.

Research approach

The research focused on whether children and young people in state care received the support they needed to live independently in adulthood. This focus includes several dimensions: the needs of the children; the type of state care; the support they received in state care; the attitudes of people and opportunities in their community; and the support they received when they reached young adulthood. The elements of the question are summarized in Box 1.1.

Box 1.1: Research questions about leaving state care

Does the Chinese state support children and young people in care to achieve social inclusion in their young adulthood and to experience their rights to transition towards independent living in the same way as their peers in their communities? Including:
- Support to young people to avoid risks of social exclusion:
  - multidimensional disadvantage of children and young people with disabilities;
  - dynamic temporal and duration effect of early childhood experiences on later capabilities and social networks in their transition to adulthood; and
  - deprivation of human rights – civil, economic, developmental and social participation, not just material supply or survival.
- Support to achieve social inclusion and full citizenship when they leave care:
  - establishing self-identity; employment and economic independence; independent housing; and social participation, friends, family and social networking.

The research was conducted over five years from 2009 to 2013. Four areas were included in the research – Beijing, Shanxi, Xinjiang and Guangxi – with multiple sites in each area (see Figure 1.1). The locations were chosen randomly from places that had implemented transition policies for young people leaving care. In-depth research was also conducted in Datong (Chapter Eight) because Dr Shang's research team has conducted research at the site since 2001 (Shang, 2003). Their in-depth understanding and relationships with the Datong Welfare Institution managers, workers, families, children and young people enabled the data collection and critical analysis of the material.

The study was primarily qualitative, including a policy review, interviews, focus groups and observations, applying intercultural methodologies by Chinese and Australian researchers (Fisher et al, 2015). The research team was led by Dr Shang and included social work graduate students from Beijing Normal University (BNU) and the Chinese Academy of Social Sciences (CASS). In each city, province and region, local policies about support for young people in care were examined. The team conducted a preliminary Internet search first to discover all public information. The team also asked local government officials and staff in the child welfare institutions to provide non-confidential documents during field investigation. The

Figure 1.1: Young people leaving state care research sites – provinces, regions and cities

Note: Shaded and bold indicates research sites from 2009 to 2013.

collected public data were analysed for preliminary findings before the interviews and focus groups, and analysed in-depth after the team returned to Beijing. In addition, the policies and procedures of each child welfare institution were also collected and analysed, including a description of the size and history of the institution, how children are supported, how foster care is organized, and support for leaving care. These policies and practices are presented in Chapters Three and Four.

In addition, research was conducted with relevant people, including young people in care or leaving care, their foster families, and child welfare institution staff and managers. The interviews and focus groups included the directors, teachers, childcare workers, other local staff and officials, and national policy officials who volunteered to participate. Young people who had grown up in care were interviewed. In most locations, young people were contacted through the institution to ask for voluntary participation. In Beijing, because many young people had left care, they were approached through a snowballing method to establish contact with them. Focus group discussions were also held with staff at institutions and with young people if they were still associated with an institution. Sometimes, institution staff observed a focus group of young people in order to offer support if necessary. All interviews with young people were conducted privately without the presence of staff. No noticeable difference was observed between the findings of the group discussions and those of the in-depth interviews. Ethical considerations about interviewing young people leaving care or still in care meant that the research process was adapted to the young person's preferences, including: where, when and with whom the interview was conducted; how the interview proceeded, following an interview structure or open discussion; and follow-up support (Keller et al, 2016).

Prior to the interviews, the study team explained the purpose of the study and gained written consent from the participants and guardians as necessary. With the consent of the interviewees, the interviews were recorded. In addition to the interviews and focus groups, 17 young people wrote their own biographies about their past experience and expectations (16 of whom also participated in other research activities). Interviews were also conducted with staff at the welfare institutions, local social policymakers and staff at other relevant agencies, older adults who had previously been state wards, and foster parents.

Profiles of young people in care

A total of 54 young people participated in the in-depth interviews and focus groups (see Table 1.1). Full details about the participants are given in Appendix 1. The participants lived in Beijing, Shanxi, Xinjiang and Guangxi. Their characteristics were spread approximately evenly between male and female, with and without disabilities, and school age and young adults. To protect the young people's privacy, aliases are used in place of their real names. The name of the child welfare institution is also usually omitted when referring to the stories from the young people unless it is relevant to the story.

Most of them had secondary schooling or above, though one person had never attended any school. The highest education was secondary technical school or vocational school, and two had attended university. Most of them had grown up in foster care or institutional care, or both. Eight young people had shifted from institutional care to foster care. Some (17%) had grown up in their own family but had entered state care after their parents died or had lived in an informal care family in the community.

Table 1.1: Characteristics of the young people in care research participants

	Young people	%
All	54	100
Age group		
18 years or less	12	22
19 to 25 years	28	52
26 years or more	14	26
Sex		
Male	34	63
Female	20	37
Disability		
Yes	25	46
None or corrective surgery	29	54
Education		
Primary school or lower	8	15
Junior or senior high school, secondary technical school or vocational school	33	61
Technical college or above	13	24
Main alternative care		
Institutional	24	44
Foster care	11	20
Institutional care then foster care	8	15
Informal kinship or non-kinship care (then institutional)	11	20

Notes: Data from 2013 (full details in Appendix 1). Young people aged 16–40.

The experience of the young people in their transition to adulthood was not encouraging (see Table 1.2). Most of them still lived in dormitories at a welfare institution or other group housing owned by their school, employer or the military. Only 11% lived in a private rental property or owned their own home (a welfare-subsidized house purchased from the welfare institution). Place of residence and home-ownership is a critical condition for independent living and independent residential registration in China, as described in Chapter Four.

Most of them were in education or employment, but one third who were adults and no longer attending school were unemployed. Some of them were engaged in odd jobs in the welfare institutions to earn petty cash. Without the basic conditions of housing and employment for independent living, most of the young people were unmarried. Five of the six young people who had married were women. The one man, Bing, aged 28 years at the time of the research, was a successful military retiree who had married a staff member of the welfare institution. His family unit apartment was provided by the welfare institution and the money for the marriage was donated by people in the community.

Table 1.2: Profile of the transition to adulthood of the young people in care research participants

	Young people	%
All	54	100
Housing		
Welfare institution (3 one-bed apartment; 30 dormitory)	32	59
Dormitory housing (school, employer or military)	10	19
Foster families	6	11
Housing in market (5 rental, 1 ownership[a])	6	11
Employment		
Children or attending school	19	35
Employed	16	30
Odd jobs at welfare institution	6	11
Unemployed	13	24
Marital status		
Unmarried	48	89
Married	6	11
Registered permanent residence (*hukou*)		
Collective welfare institution	53	98
Independent	1	2

Notes: Data from 2013 (full details in Appendix 1). Young people aged 16–40.
[a] Purchased welfare-subsidized house from the welfare institution.

Structure of the book

The book is divided into two parts. The first part is about the policy context of alternative care in China. Chapter Two introduces alternative care options in China by presenting the profile of children in state care and where they live. Chapter Three adds detail about the policies and practices in child welfare institutions, which have responsibility for the guardianship and care of children who are state wards. Chapter Four rounds out this part by moving to the more specific policies about the transition out of care of children who are state wards and other orphaned children once they reach young adulthood.

The remaining chapters are structured around the four aspects of transition to adulthood: establishing self-identity; employment and economic independence; independent housing; and social participation, friends, family and social networking. Each chapter examines the experience of the young people in their transition to adulthood and leaving care against the child rights and social inclusion framework. Does the Chinese state support young people in state care to achieve social inclusion in their young adulthood and experience their rights to transition towards independent living in the same way as their peers in their communities? The final chapter draws conclusions for policy and theory about young people leaving state care in China.

TWO

Children in alternative care

In most high-income countries, the main reasons that children are in alternative care are family abuse and neglect. In China, due to the absence of an effective child protection system, very few children receive alternative care for these reasons. In China, children receiving alternative care provided by the state are mainly children without parents. Most children who are orphaned live with extended family. If they become state wards, the child welfare institution tries to arrange adoption. Otherwise, the most common forms of alternative care are institutional care or foster care.

   This chapter describes who is in care and the forms of care. These questions are important because the way in which alternative care is organized affects the childhood experience of the young people and their future opportunities. The qualities of the alternative care that they encounter might contribute to their current and future social inclusion by addressing and anticipating their current and potential disadvantages, for example, by forming family connections in adoptive or foster families. Alternatively, the arrangements might aggravate their disadvantages by layering further experiences of social exclusion, such as segregation from other children and families throughout their childhood.

Children in state care

Alternative care in China includes extended family care, adoption, institutional care and foster care. The first two forms of care are not normally referred to as alternative care in high-income countries. The data released by the Chinese Ministry of Civil Affairs (MCA) in 2005 based on a census of orphans in China are the most complete data available about alternative care in the country. Although the data were collected more than a decade ago, the types of alternative care have not changed. Excluding adoption, when children become part of a new family, most children in alternative care are cared for in their extended family (kinship care, 62.3%), followed by foster care (12.6%) and institutional care (11.8%).

Table 2.1: Main approaches to alternative care

Approach to care	Percentage of orphans
Extended family, kinship care	62.3
Foster care	12.6
State welfare institution	11.8
Other approaches	12.6

Note: Total orphans = 563,625.

Source: Shang (2008a).

In most rural areas of China, kinship is still central to social life. Extended families, particularly those in the patrilineal line, remain the central social relationship among many farming communities. Following tradition, children have the surname of their father and inherit the paternal line. Therefore, when children lose their parents, the paternal extended family first assumes responsibility for raising them. Only when the paternal extended family members cannot assume such responsibility should the maternal extended family members assume such responsibility. In the families researched for this book, very few orphans were homeless due to an absence of care either from their extended family or the state. Most children in state care were raised within institutions.

Recently, the child protection system in China has begun developing in ways that will change the future profile of children in state care. A significant change in legislation is only now coming into effect, whereby the state can remove guardianship from parents who abuse their children. The *Opinions on Several Issues Concerning the Management of Violations by Guardians Against Rights and Interests of Minors According to Law 2014* is a turning point for child protection in China. It heralds a new beginning for the government and community to act against serious harm to children within families. It will enable the establishment of a system of child protection in China. In the future, it is likely that children in state care and young people leaving care will have had quite different experiences in their childhood compared to children who were orphaned, affecting their capacity to transition to an independent adulthood.

Children with disabilities in state care

Most children in state care are children with disabilities whose families cannot be found. The estimate of all Chinese people with disabilities is 6.34% of the total population (82.9 million people) (CDPF, 2007), including 5 million children aged under 18 years and 3.8 million children aged 0–14 years (Chen and Chen, 2008). This is a decrease of about 50% since the same survey 20 years earlier, most likely due to a lower proportion of children born with noticeable disabilities as China's health system and living conditions improve (5.6% of all newborns, approximately 250,000 children per year) (Ministry of Health, 2012). Another reason might be that some children born with disabilities were abandoned or received poor care and died.

Some parents make the difficult decision that leaving their children with disabilities to be found and put in state care is the only way in which their child will receive the expensive health care and therapy that they need since universal public health or free disability support is not available in most of the country, particularly rural areas (Fisher and Shang, 2013, 2014; Shang and Fisher, 2014b, 2016; Fisher et al, 2016). Currently, over 90% of children admitted to state welfare institutions each year are children with disabilities (Shang, 2012). These children are likely to face greater challenges when they reach adulthood because of their need for disability support and having grown up in state care.

Alternative care for children in state guardianship

The administrative responsibility for alternative care lies with city-based welfare institutions, which are part of the MCA. The state's obligations are to provide care and support for children in their guardianship, that is, children who have no known extended family. The institutions first try to find and to return the child to the extended family before state guardianship is accepted. The next step for welfare institutions is to try to end state guardianship by arranging national or international adoption into another family.

If a child is not adopted, the usual option is institutional care. In some poorer provinces, local child welfare institutions have a long history of foster care to manage the high cost of institutional care (Shang and Fisher, 2014a). Since 1997, many other cities have introduced foster care and small group family care. However, debates between welfare institutions about state preferences for institutional or foster care continue. The MCA has not declared that family-based care is a preferred care type (field research, Beijing 2014), despite the international evidence and United Nations (UN) guidelines (UNGACC, 2009).

In the course of the development of state child welfare institutions in China, international child welfare service organizations played a major and positive role in promoting changes to approaches to alternative care and providing supplementary funding. These resources helped accelerate the modernization of the Chinese child welfare system and introduce international good practice to China where relevant. Examples of this engagement are described in later chapters.

The main types of alternative care currently provided can be grouped into four simplified categories: adoption, foster care, institutional (residential) care and family care units. They are described later as background to the findings about young people's experiences of leaving care in the remainder of the book.

Adoption

Family adoption transfers the rights and obligations for the care of children from the state to alternative parents completely and irreversibly. Such placement is designed to provide children with permanent, continuous family relationships (UNGACC, 2009). Family adoption is the preferred policy response for children in state guardianship in China. Annually, tens of thousands of children receive permanent adoption (see Table 2.2). Adoption is the major practice diverting children out of state care. In this policy area, the main disputes are about the practice of international adoption and whether the demand from Chinese and international families wanting to adopt children distorts the number of children entering state care (Dowling and Brown, 2009; Johnson, 2016; Wang, 2016). Most children who are adopted do not have disabilities or their disabilities are minor or remedied with surgery. Most children who remain in state care have disabilities.

The 1996 International Conference of the International Council on Social Welfare (ICSW) ratified the rules on the implementation of domestic and transnational adoption and foster care, which stressed that all children have the right to grow up in a family environment and, as the preferred option, receive care from their biological parents. The rules also emphasized that children should receive adoptive care, as the first resort, within their native country. Only when children cannot receive satisfactory care within their native country should international adoption be considered as a solution. China adheres to the principle of prioritizing domestic adoption over international adoption and the principle of the best interests of children, as established in the UN Convention on the Rights of the Child. Domestic adoption has become the primary approach to the placement of children in state care in China, both registered and de facto adoption.

Domestic adoption

Adoption is referred to in various laws and regulations. The *Marriage Law 1950* stipulates that the rights and obligations of adoptive parents and adoptive children are the same as those of biological parents and their children. The *Marriage Law 1980* stipulates that the state protects lawful adoption relationships. *Opinions on Several Issues Regarding Adoption Relationship 1951* states that the adoption agreement signed between biological parents who are unable to raise their children and the adoptive parents should prioritize the children's interests. *Interim Measures for Handling Several Major Notarial Matters 1982* and *Opinions on Issues Regarding Implementing Civil Policies/Laws 1984* include provisions on the notarization of adoption and protection of lawful adoption relationships, including de facto adoptions.

The *Adoption Law 1991* was the first national law to standardize adoption and protect lawful adoption relationships. The *Adoption Law 1998* revised the law to lower the threshold for adoption and enhance adoption procedures. *Measures for Registration of Adoption of Children by Chinese Citizens 1999* and the *Provisions on Jurisdiction and Documents Necessary for Certification of Adoption by Overseas Chinese and Chinese Citizens Residing in Hong Kong, Macau or Taiwan 1999*, from the MCA, stipulate the procedures for registering adoptions. The *Notice on Addressing Issues Concerning Informal Adoption of Children by Chinese Citizens 2008*, from the MCA and four other ministries, addresses the irregularity of Chinese citizens adopting children without using the official registration procedure. Its purpose is to safeguard the lawful rights and interests of children by establishing legal provisions on the notarization and permanent residence registration of children who had been the subject of de facto adoption. More detail is discussed in Chapter Ten.

Table 2.2: Registered domestic and international adoptions, 1996–2012

Year	Number of registered adoptions	Adoptions by Chinese citizens (%)	Adoptions by foreign citizens (%)
1996	18,896	78	22
1997	21,548	80	20
1998	26,498	78	22
1999	38,074	84	16
2000	55,802	88	12
2001	44,706	81	19
2002	45,336	78	22
2003	54,159	83	17
2004	52,603	76	24
2005	49,506	72	28
2006	48,178	80	20
2007	45,192	82	18
2008	42,550	87	13
2009	44,260	90	10
2010	34,529	86	14
2011	31,424	88	12
2012	27,278	85	15

Note: Recording of information on registered adoption began in 1996. The children adopted included orphans and abandoned children at social welfare institutions or in the community and whose parents could not raise them. For instance, in 2012, 23,157 cases of adoption by Chinese citizens were registered, including 9,883 orphans and abandoned children from social welfare institutions, while the rest were children abandoned in the community; 4,121 cases of adoption by citizens were registered, including 4,079 children from social welfare institutions and 42 children whose parents could not raise them.

Source: MCA (1996–2012).

International adoption

The few international adoptions that occurred soon after 1949 were under the provisions of the Marriage Law, and the practice increased after the late 1970s. The Ministry of Justice recorded around 10,000 cases of the notarization of international adoptions from 1981 to 1989, including adoptions by foreigners, citizens of other countries and with Chinese heritage, overseas Chinese, and citizens of Hong Kong, Macau and Taiwan (Jiang, 2005).

Article 20 of *Adoption Law 1991* provides standards and the documentation required for international adoption. China ratified the UN Convention on the Rights of the Child in 1992, committing to international provisions on child protection and adoption. In 1993, China also ratified the UN Convention on Protection of Children and Co-operation in Respect of Intercountry Adoption, which created a framework for inter-country cooperation to protect children and ensure the best interests of children and respect for children's basic rights in inter-country adoption. The *Measures for Adoption of Children by Foreigners in China 1993* detail the measures for international adoption. Cases of international adoption increased continuously during this time.

The China Centre of Adoption Affairs was established in 1996 as the sole Chinese government organization responsible for all international adoptions. International adoption was gradually scaled up at this time. The *Measures for Registration of Adoption of Chinese Children by Foreigners 1999* formalized the previous implementation measures. The *Notice on Further Strengthening Placement of Children for Foreign Adoption 2000* recognized that international adoption was an appropriate approach for the placement of orphaned children but stressed the sensitivity and importance of effective management and supervision. The *Provisions on Placement of Children by Social Welfare Institutions for International Adoption 2003* standardized the placement of children for adoption.

China became a major origin of children who were internationally adopted due to the standardized, simple adoption procedure and lower costs. It established international adoption relationships with many countries, including the US, UK, Spain, Canada and Australia. From 1996 to 2005, the cases of international adoption increased year on year, from 4,092 registered international adoptions in 1996 to 14,036 cases in 2006 (MCA, 1996–2012; see also Table 2.2), which hit the highest record in the *China civil affairs' statistical yearbook*.

The trend decreased from 2007 when the China Centre of Adoption Affairs raised the requirements and prioritized the quality of the applications from people wanting to adopt. The changes were to comply with the principles in the Hague Convention protecting the best interests of children and ensuring an appropriate family environment. The new practices reduced the cases of adoption as a large proportion of applicants did not meet the eligibility criteria for adoption. As the global recognition of domestic adoption increased (Dowling and Brown, 2009; Selman, 2012) and the relative economic situation in foreign countries weakened, the cases of international adoption from China decreased year on year. In 2012, the registered cases of international adoption decreased to 4,121, which was 15% of all adoptions (MCA, 1996–2012; see also Table 2.2).

Institutional care provided by state child welfare institutions

Children in state guardianship are administratively the responsibility of state welfare institutions. Most children in care live in the institutions, at least temporarily, before they are adopted or shifted to foster care. Others remain in institutional care throughout their childhood and even into adulthood. Institutional care is care provided to multiple children residing at the same place and cared for by paid workers. Institutional care is sometimes referred to as 'residential' care internationally to avoid negative connotations. In China, 'institutional care' is the term preferred by the government, which does not recognize the derogatory label.

Institutional care by state welfare institutions is a comprehensive accommodation arrangement for children under state guardianship who temporarily or permanently do not live with their birth or adoptive parents because their parents cannot be found, or the children cannot, are not allowed or are unwilling to live with them. The care arrangements include protection, control, behaviour management, and medical and physical care for disability, chronic illness and mental health. Residential care institutions are generally intended to meet any special needs of children in alternative care.

In China, institutional care is still the dominant form of care provided by the government. Care services are primarily provided by state child welfare institutions. In the early 1990s, state child welfare institutions were criticized by international human rights organizations due to serious child maltreatment and high mortality rates. Over the following 15 years, most facilities and staffing of child welfare institutions were improved as a result of the public criticism and as public expectations and concepts about the care of children changed. As a result, the material conditions in many institutions have improved. Most of the young people in the research said that they were satisfied with their living conditions because: they had a small living allowance; they received education at schools within welfare institutions or nearby depending on their ages; and their medical and disability therapy costs were paid for by the welfare institutions. For example, Zhong, a 26-year-old young man with disabilities who had grown up in foster care in Beijing and now worked and lived independently in a private rental, spoke positively about the material development support he received from the welfare institution:

"[In the institution school,] we were divided into senior, middle and junior classes according to ages … courses such as maths, Chinese language and general knowledge were provided by in-house teachers. In addition to these courses, there was therapy training, such as physical movement training and speech therapy. In terms of living, there were routine meals and regular physical exercise."

After 30 years of economic development starting in the 1980s, the government accumulated public financial resources that improved the financial situation of child welfare institutions in developed areas. At the same time, in the context of a commitment from the central government for orphan basic living protection, Chinese regional areas received substantial central funds to develop new child welfare institutions. Although the intention of the policymakers was to establish local child welfare resource centres, most areas used the funds to build new welfare institutions. In such a context, institutional care received greater emphasis. The policy choice of institutional care or foster care as the best type of alternative care for child outcomes is still disputed by officials (field research, Beijing 2014). All the young people discussed in this book grew up in this period. The issues in the state child welfare institutions and the subsequent changes affected their childhood and teenage years.

Family group care

Family group care or group homes are a variation on institutional care. Each family group consists of a single residential apartment, usually caring for up to 10 children. Paid carers serve as the parents of the children to create a family environment. This type of care is referred to in China as family group care.

Small group families are configured in two ways: discrete families and congregate families. Discrete family care units are operated by the same institution in separate communities but are independent family care groups. Congregate family care units are operated by the same institution, too, but are composed of families or family-like care groups proximate to each other. Many family care groups operate in different parts of China. Chapter Eleven analyses the outcomes for young people living in family group care compared to institutional and foster care.

Foster care arranged by state child welfare institutions

Foster care is care from families in their own home who have no kinship or guardianship relationship with the children. Internationally, foster care is usually a temporary placement, where either the state retains guardianship or the child's birth parents do not lose their rights and obligations as parents. Internationally, foster carers usually receive a payment for expenses or a salary to care for the children, and perform obligations for the placement. This is in contrast to adoptive parents, who are not usually treated differently to other birth parents. In China, children in the guardianship of child welfare institutions, which organize foster care, usually have no knowledge or contact information about parents or extended family members.

Development of foster care in China

In China, around 100,000 children per year are in the guardianship of state child welfare institutions. The figures differ slightly per year, but are generally on the rise. Welfare institutions face a practical problem about limited space in institutional care. Initially, to some extent, foster care was only tolerated because it relieved the financial pressure on institutions. Soon, the positive impact of foster care on children's development and growth was acknowledged by many government officials, but it did not gain extensive public recognition. From late 1990s, foster care, which had until then only operated in poorer areas to manage the high cost of institutional care, was replicated by Beijing and Shanghai following successful pilots. The *Interim Measures for the Management of Family Foster Care 2003* standardized foster care nationally. In 2014, the MCA finally formulated official management provisions for foster care.

The Standing Committee of the State Council passed the *Opinions on Strengthening Welfare Protection of Orphans 2010*, which recognized small group family care and foster care, but it did not position these forms of alternative care as preferred types of care. In 2010, social welfare institutions with foster care accounted for over 50% of all welfare institutions with children. Over 50% of orphans and children with disabilities in these institutions were raised in foster families, and foster care became one of the primary approaches to the care of orphans who were in the guardianship of these institutions (Shang and Fisher, 2014a).

Primary approaches to foster care

Over the last 20 years, foster care has become one of the main approaches to alternative care in China. Although institutional care continues to be the dominant type of care and policymakers continue to favour it or family care units over foster care, a gradual process of deinstitutionalization continues.

Three management types of foster care evolved: urban community-based foster care, urban discrete foster care and rural community-based foster care. Foster care in other areas adapted these types to meet their local needs and resources. The variation between the types can be explained by differences in policy objectives about social inclusion, the approach to managing risks and harm to the children, and managing costs within a limited budget.

Urban foster care is typical in Shanghai (Cui and Qin, 2000; Cui and Wu, 2000; Cui and Yang, 2002). The approach is social integration but it is difficult for the welfare institution to control risks as the children are dispersed in individual families. The participation of grassroots social organizations, such as neighbourhood organizations, contributes to monitoring the children's well-being, though this depends on the development of social organizations. The second type is urban community foster care, where groups of families living in the same neighbourhood each foster children, such as in Nanchang. Risks are easier to manage because the proximity of families makes frequent home visits and informal community monitoring feasible. The grouping of foster care families reduces the social integration, compared to the Shanghai model.

The third type is rural foster care, which originated in Datong. Children live in townships and are integrated into the local rural communities. Compared to urban foster care, the most distinctive feature is that children live in rural communities, where the service costs are much lower than in the city where the welfare institution is located. Rural foster care is better than institutional care for social connections during childhood. When the children grow up, they are entitled to shift back to the city because their residential registration is with the city institution. However, if they wish to take advantage of additional opportunities through urban migration, they face new social exclusions because they are disadvantaged by their relatively poor childhood environment and the lower educational level available in rural areas.

Among the three types, urban foster care offers the greatest opportunities for social inclusion. In this type, children live in regular urban families, attend local schools and receive health-care services at local hospitals. Their family and community environment is the same as other children in their community. It contrasts with institutional care, which separates children from the community and incurs a high financial cost. However, government control of the risks to children in foster care is more remote compared to institutional care.

None of the approaches or adaptations completely addresses the disability therapy needs of children with disabilities and high support needs. Some child welfare institutions introduced professional therapy in rural foster care and professional community-based foster care to respond to the increase in the proportion of children with disabilities requiring alternative care (Shang, 2012, 2013; Shang and Fisher, 2016).

Non-governmental child welfare

Some non-governmental organizations and community members also provide alternative care. Survey data from the MCA shows the positive contribution of the civil sector in accommodating children but also reveals challenges for the government in protecting the interests of children (MCA, 2013a). Wang (2016) also points to the contrasting approaches to care, as well as to questions about children's interests in different types of non-governmental alternative care, particularly if they also facilitate adoption. Chapter Ten examines the policies and experiences of children in non-governmental care.

Summary about alternative care

In summary, in addition to adoption, depending on the location, children subject to state guardianship might be in alternative care ranging from institutional care to foster care. Family-based care has not yet become a dominant arrangement in China. The impact of the different care types upon children's lives as they become young adults has not been examined fully despite the different impact of each type of alternative care on their future choices. This book uses the framework of social inclusion to examine the impact on transition to adulthood as a way to inform policy decisions about the policy preferences for these forms of alternative care.

THREE

Alternative care practices in child welfare institutions

This chapter introduces the alternative care policies in the research cities – Beijing, Taiyuan, Datong, Urumqi and Nanning. The institutions' policies and practices during the children's childhood and when they reach late teenage years affect the quality of the transition of young people out of care, such as whether they are required to leave, are supported to leave, have the capacity to leave and understand the benefits of leaving. The policies and practices affect the expectations and capacity of young people to achieve social inclusion in their young adulthood and to experience their rights to transition towards independent living in the same way as their peers in their communities, as well as support them to avoid the risks of social exclusion. The chapter is background to understanding the choices open to the young people who grew up in the guardianship of these institutions examined in later chapters.

Beijing and its districts' child welfare institutions

Beijing Municipality has multiple child welfare institutions because the city is so large, with over 20 million people. The approach to alternative care in Beijing is similar to other parts of the country, relying on adoption for a permanent family placement as the preferred approach. Otherwise, institutional care remains the dominant type. Two locations in Beijing, Daxing District and rural Yanqing County, have a 15-year history of foster care.

The information about the policy and its implementation in this chapter are from the city's policies about supporting young people in care and children with disabilities, as well as from interviews with young people who had left state care and were living independently. The Beijing Civil Affairs Bureau formulated the policy in 2009 which stipulated that young people in care must leave welfare institutions to live an independent life, as described in Chapter Four. Many young people do leave care, supported by the local governments where they initially became a state ward.

Beijing Child Welfare Institution

The Beijing Child Welfare Institution is the municipal-level welfare institution for children in state care, founded in 1984. It is located in Qinghe Town, Haidian District. Its main function is to receive children from districts and counties of the city. In the past, it looked after children aged under 14 years. When the number of children increased to unmanageable levels, its responsibility changed to caring for children aged under six years and some children with disabilities who need treatment until they are aged 14 years. It acts as the intake institution for the city when children first enter state care. When Beijing residents find abandoned babies, their local police station investigates the identity of the child. If the birth parents cannot be found, the child is sent to Heping Hospital, which carries out a physical examination and screening test and then sends the child to the Beijing Child Welfare Institution for a 40-day screening test. Children are then placed in different residential groups according to their needs.

When the children reach six years old, they are assessed for physical and intellectual development. If they are assessed as suitable to receive education and can independently care for themselves, they are sent to the Beijing Number 2 Child Welfare Institution, where they receive education within or outside of the institution. Children with higher support needs who are assessed as not suitable to receive education and therapy are sent to Beijing Number 2 Welfare Institution, where they receive daily care only.

At the time of the research in 2012, 430 children lived in the Beijing Child Welfare Institution. All of them had disabilities and 85% had high support needs but were assessed to be suitable to receive treatment. The institution is very large, with buildings for the residential care of 500 children, as well as other buildings for rehabilitation, health care, training, offices and other facilities. Cumulatively, over 700 children were placed in foster care by the institution. Four care types were in place at the institution when the research was conducted: institutional care, foster care, rest home care and international or domestic adoption.

Alternative care within the institution in Beijing

The welfare institution tries to arrange domestic or international adoption for children with no or mild disabilities so that they can live permanently in adoptive families as early as possible. Prior to placement for adoption, the welfare institution provides small group family care to help the children adapt to their future placement and to prepare them through family integration exercises.

Alternative care within the institution is the main form of care for all other children at the Beijing Child Welfare Institution. In each residential quarter, children live in large groups and receive integrated services provided by doctors, nurses, childcare workers, teachers, therapy staff, social workers, nutritionists and psychological therapists. Their tasks include daily care, monitoring growth, early childhood development training, formative education and special education.

All the children have disabilities and need special education and therapy services, according to their age. Children aged under three years live in the early development training centre, where they receive daily care and exercises in receiving food, cognitive development and fine motor and gross motor skills. Children aged three to six years live in a multifunctional education centre, where the education focuses on self-care and good habits, in addition to moral and cultural education designed according to the intellectual development level of the children. Children aged six years and above receive education at the institution in terms of literacy, physical movement, morality and mental health, in addition to daily care and basic education. Children with mild disabilities who are assessed as having sufficient intellectual capacity receive literacy education. Other children with more severe disabilities engage in special physical movement exercises. Children aged six years who are assessed as having sufficient capacity to learn and to live an independent life are transferred to the Beijing Number 2 Child Welfare Institution.

Adult institutional care

Some children with severe disabilities aged over 14 years are deemed inappropriate to continue residing in the child welfare institution or receive education and therapy. The Beijing Child Welfare Institution places these children in two adult institutions (mainly for adults with disabilities and older people), where the children receive daily care only, at Sunshine Seniors' Home in Pinggu District and Baikang Seniors' Home in Chaoyang District. This transfer of care responsibility eases the pressure on the limited places in the child welfare institution. It is unlikely that the children's rights and interests are protected by living in these adult institutional facilities.

Foster care in Beijing

Beijing developed its foster care project according to policies following the national *Interim Measures for the Management of Family Foster Care 2003*, which standardized foster care nationally. The Beijing Child Welfare Institution has 15 years' experience in Daxing District in the south and rural Yanqing County in the north-west, providing foster care for a small proportion of the children in Beijing state care. Children are eligible for foster care based on a therapy assessment by the welfare institution health professionals.

Some children living in foster care return to the institution for several reasons. First, some babies who are placed in foster care for one or two years become eligible for adoption and return to the institution in readiness for an adoption placement. Second, some foster children need medical support during their childhood and may be sent back to the institution for treatment. Third, when some children reach 14 years of age in their foster families and their disability outcomes are positive, they may be sent back to the Beijing Number 2 Child Welfare Institution for access to high-school education. Each of these practices are bureaucratically driven – when children reach 14 years old, responsibility for supporting them shifts to the Beijing Number 2 Child Welfare Institution, so the Beijing Child Welfare Institution no longer continues the previous arrangements. Children's rights and preferences are not considered during these transitions.

From 2011, Beijing increased the funding for child foster care. Foster children aged under 18 years received a monthly allowance of RMB1,600 to cover their basic living, health care, education, clothes and bedding. Foster care parents also receive RMB150 to support their care provision. The allowance granted to parents is too low to cover their time. The government does not provide an allowance for foster children aged more than 18 years, who do not receive education. This means that young people with higher disability support needs do not continue to live in foster care once they reach 18 years because their foster families can no longer afford to support them. Contrary to their preferences, and those of their foster families, they usually move to the adult welfare institution for care and support.

The management and monitoring of foster families has been a priority of the civil affairs departments. Before 2007, the Beijing Child Welfare Institution implemented direct management, sending two teams every week to the foster families to check on the situation of the children in care. This approach took a large amount of human and physical resources in travel and accommodation. From

2007, the welfare institution replaced its management approach with an agreement method, where it signed an agreement with the organizations recognized and registered by district and county civil affairs bureaus, entrusting the organizations to manage, monitor and support the foster families, for example, regarding the appropriate use of the allowances. At the time of the research, these organizations were the Lixian Town Foster Care Service Centre in Daxing District and the Yanqing Town Seniors' Home.

The welfare institution continues monthly ad hoc inspections of the management organizations and foster care, focusing particularly on the situation of the children in foster care, the daily records of foster families and the distribution of allowances to foster families, in order to safeguard the rights of children. Annually, the welfare institution carries out a comprehensive evaluation of the foster care management organizations, covering their finance, management and staffing, in order to determine whether to renew the agreement for the next year. The welfare institution also provides training to the foster care management organizations, which then provides secondary training to the foster families, in order to ensure proper care of the children in the families. Through the monthly ad hoc sampling inspection and the annual evaluation, the welfare institution tries to ensure the rights and interests of the children and improve the foster care.

Foster care in Daxing

The largest Beijing foster care programme is the rural community-based foster care in Daxing mentioned earlier (Wu et al, 2005; Shang, 2008b), with over 400 children in foster care living in Lixian Town, Daxing. Instead of establishing institutional care in Lixian, the local civil affairs department only has a foster care service centre, which is responsible for coordinating the foster care. The centre is a public institution that is entitled to state funding disbursements and public institution staffing. All children in state care identified in Daxing only stay temporarily in the centre when they are first found, where they receive a physical examination and assessment and are placed directly in a foster family. Although this is a usual procedure internationally, it is the only known place in China that uses this immediate family-based care process.

The background and organizational responsibilities are explained here to demonstrate the policy context in which the programme has emerged (see Table 3.1). This context affects the choices available to young people leaving care from the foster care programme, including their forced transfer to institutional care during childhood or when they reach adulthood, if they do not have the means to achieve financial independence.

Table 3.1: Organizational responsibility for Beijing foster care in Daxing District

Organization	Responsibility
Beijing Municipal Government	Regulations.
Financial Department	Funds for institutions, foster care programme and allowances to families and children until the child is aged 18 years.
Civil Affairs Bureau	Policy.
Beijing Child Welfare Institution	Guardianship of children found in four districts (8 districts, including Daxing, until 1997).
Foster Care Office	Technical support to and supervision of foster care programmes. International adoption.
Beijing Number 2 Child Welfare Institution	Institutional care for children 14 years and older attending local school, including children from foster care.
Beijing Social Welfare Institutions	Institutional disability care for children aged over 14 years and adults with high disability support needs, including children from foster care after 18 years, and aged care.
Daxing Local Government	Guardianship for children found in Daxing since 1997. Funds and operates the foster care programmes for Daxing children and Beijing Child Welfare Institution children transferred until the mid-2000s.
Foster Care Service Centre, Daxing	Coordinates the foster care programme and supervises foster families and children.
Hongxing Social Welfare Institution, Daxing	Adult care in Daxing. Children with very high disability support needs also lived there until a child welfare institution was recently built.

Note: Data from 2013.

Background to the foster care project in Daxing

In the past, when the Beijing Child Welfare Institution was the only child welfare institution in Beijing, it accepted all the children found in the eight urban districts of Beijing. However, given the increase in the number of children whose families could not be found, the Beijing Child Welfare Institution could no longer accept all the children from the eight districts. Instead, since 1997, the Beijing Municipal Government changed its policies several times to manage the increased need. It established the Beijing Number 2 Child Welfare Institution and required all 16 districts and counties (counties changed to districts after 2015) to be responsible for the care of any children found in their area. The children were cared for either in a district child welfare institution or in adult institutions until they built their own child welfare institutions. At the time of this research, the Beijing Child Welfare Institution now only accepts children from four urban districts.

One of the rural districts is Daxing. Children found in Daxing after 1997 are the responsibility of the local government of Daxing district (those who were found before 1997 lived in the Beijing Child Welfare Institution and continued to do so). The district developed a child foster care project in 1997 in response to the policy changes outlined earlier and with the support of the Beijing Child Welfare Institution.

The background to the foster care initiative was that it was seen as a way to manage the excess number of children requiring alternative care beyond the capacity of the institution. In the early 1980s, only 20 to 30 children were found each year in Beijing. At that time, most of the children had severe disabilities and the conditions in the Beijing Child Welfare Institution were so poor that many of them died. This meant that the number of young children at the institution remained basically unchanged each year. Following the late 1980s, the number of abandoned babies increased substantially, overwhelming the institution. The serious shortage of staff meant that toddlers had few opportunities for physical activities, which affected their physical growth. Under financial pressure, the institution decided to set up a dedicated establishment for alternative care in the suburbs, in Daxing. Initially, it only provided more institutional care, which replicated the same problems. In 1995, the institution in Daxing placed three children into families, two of whom had cerebral palsy and the third child was deaf. A month later, the staff were pleasantly surprised to see that the situation of the three children had improved significantly. The institution invited experts to assess the situation and concluded that foster care might be a good approach. As a result, in late 1996, a medium-scale trial was launched in Daxing.

In selecting Daxing as the pilot area, the Beijing Child Welfare Institution had several considerations. First, child welfare institutions are not government departments and the development of foster care had to have support from local government. Foster care had the potential to employ local residents, which would be a reason for local government to support it. Second, local people had to be charitable and open to caring for children in need. The welfare institution preferred Lixian Town, Daxing County, where both Hui and Han nationality people reside and the people in the community had a reputation for generosity.

Since the welfare institution took into account local interests, the local government of Daxing strongly supported the initiative and designated the deputy town chief to be responsible for foster care. At the beginning of the medium-scale trial, the staff of the institution had no idea whether the children would be accepted by the local residents, and the local residents had no idea whether they could appropriately bring up the children. Mrs Ma, the local director, visited the households to learn about their circumstances. The local residents selected some children with minor disabilities and tried providing foster care. When the children's conditions improved significantly within a month, they accepted the children. The institution was then confident to launch foster care at a larger scale.

A Foster Care Office of the Beijing Child Welfare Institution was set up to manage international adoption and foster care by providing technical support and a car to the Daxing programme. They established a management system to coordinate between the institution, the town government and the foster care management on-site team. In 1998, the Finance Department of the Beijing Municipal Government approved the institution to establish a foster care service centre on-site in Daxing and paid for its staff – a director, doctor, accountant, cashier and driver. They are responsible for monitoring and supporting the foster families, including the supervision of foster parents, the management of children's records and home visits to the foster families. The regulations described here were current at the time of the investigation.

The Beijing Child Welfare Institution defined very stringent eligibility criteria for foster parents. First, their income must be above the local average level in order to ensure that the state allowance for children in foster care is used for the child, not to support the family. Second, the foster parents must have their own children, be around 40 years old and have an education level of junior high school or above. The families must have two parents, preferably with three generations in one household. The families should have a sound relationship among family members and with neighbours, and no family member should have a criminal record. Eligible foster parents submit an application. If they pass the evaluation, they receive training provided by the welfare institution and sign a contract. Afterwards, one to three children are placed in the foster family.

The staff visit the foster families twice a month to observe the children, focusing on hygiene, feeding, therapy and education. A scoring system based on the quality of the foster care was established; the full mark for each month is 100 points and the annual total is 1,200 points. Points are deducted for non-compliance with the requirements, such as poor hygiene conditions, long fingernails and scars on the child's body. Foster care families are evaluated at the end of the year and receive a reward if they have a high score.

If the children in foster care have a mild illness, the families pay for the medical costs; if the illness is serious, the welfare institution pays. The children are enrolled in their local schools, and school fees are paid by the service centre. Most children attending school have average academic performance. The child welfare institution supports the local schools with multiple supports and resources.

In the early stage, the development of the foster care programme dealt with several transitional challenges. The first challenge was how to manage possible negative events that might risk a political reaction. The second challenge was concern about how to manage fewer funds in the welfare institution as the children and the funds were transferred to foster families. Institutional care costs were very high because of the many full-time staff members required. Finally, the most critical issue was that the Beijing Civil Affairs Bureau preferred institutional care to foster care.

As risk mitigation, the Beijing Civil Affairs Bureau also established the Beijing Number 2 Child Welfare Institution, which enrols children attending local regular high schools. It ordered the welfare institution to reclaim children residing in foster families for several years and transfer the children from regular schools to the welfare institution for schooling. When these children were forcibly taken back from the families, many children and parents were very upset. The children we interviewed also mentioned that they strongly objected when they were taken back from the foster families to the welfare institution, but the objection was ignored by the Civil Affairs Bureau. Children and families are not consulted in this practice about where the children would prefer to be placed.

An option to respond to child and family preferences would be to transform the foster care into adoption in order to enable the children to obtain a permanent home within the foster care family. Under the current policy, this is not viable for the families because they are not in a financial position to cover the costs of disability support for these children. As foster carers, they receive the orphan and foster carers' allowance, but if they adopted the children, they would no longer be eligible for financial support. Similarly, once the children turn 18 years old, even if they have severe disabilities, they are no longer eligible for the living allowance in foster care. The families said that if such financial support policies were changed, they would adopt the children who had grown up in their families. At the time of the research, the Civil Affairs Bureau reiterated its preference for institutional care instead, despite the higher cost.

Current foster care in Daxing

In the mid-2000s, the Beijing Child Welfare Institution started to reduce the scale of its foster care project and instead resumed relying on institutional care for newly accepted children. It also tried to shift children from foster care back into institutional care. Some children already in foster families continued staying in families. At the same time, Daxing started to develop its own foster care project independently of the Beijing Child Welfare Institution. In Daxing, over 400 children were receiving foster care at the time of the research, including about 250 children in the guardianship of the Beijing Child Welfare Institution and about 150 children in the guardianship of Daxing District government. Instead of caring for children in the local adult welfare institution, children found in Daxing are now placed directly with foster families after an initial health check. The policy seems to be working well.

The only child welfare government agency in Daxing is the foster care service centre of Lixian Town. The centre is a self-funded organization directly managed by the town government. The funds for operating the foster care project are disbursed by Daxing District government for children found in Daxing, as well as the governments from where the children were sent, such as the Beijing Child Welfare Institution. The town government pays the salaries of the staff members at the standard defined for public institutions, and it also accepts public donations. The numbers of staff in the centre also increased. It had over 10 staff during the research, responsible for the management of all children in foster care. Unlike foster care programmes in other parts of the country, the programme has developed entirely in response to local practices, and is funded and supported by the district government. The director of the foster care service centre also participated in training courses run by international non-governmental organizations (NGOs).

Daxing follows a similar practice to other districts of Beijing when a baby or child is found. Most children are aged less than one year old or more than three years old and are found by local residents or the police, and then placed with the street children protection agency. The public security department investigates and reports the new child to the district Civil Affairs Bureau, which issues a reference letter to the foster care service centre. The service centre organizes a physical examination from the health department and treats any illness found. The service centre then places the child in a foster family. Children with disabilities are not sent to foster families until their condition is stable.

The foster care service centre maintains a register of potential foster families. It evaluates and selects families based on the family structure, educational background of the parents, size of the housing, household income and their willingness to foster. The centre provides parents with at least four training sessions annually. Foster families are divided into family groups, consisting of several families and a director, in order to facilitate management and supervision. The project director is accountable for the safety of children in foster care and visits the households monthly. The district and city civil affairs departments conduct sampling checks irregularly.

The allowance for foster care has increased each year. At the time of the research, the allowance for each child in foster care was RMB150 monthly, and, on average, each household had two foster children. The monthly living allowance for each orphan was RMB1,600, which is distributed to the foster families to spend at their discretion, including minor medical costs. Hospital expenses for major illness and surgery are reimbursed by the civil affairs department at the district or county level of government on an application from the foster care service centre. The local government also covers health-care insurance for all children in foster care.

Most of the 150 children in foster care in Daxing District have high disability support needs and only a dozen children were attending school. The decision to attend school is made by the children and their foster carers. If they decide to attend school, the foster care service centre arranges enrolment at the local primary school. Children with disabilities who need therapy attend exercises at a therapy training classroom at the foster care service centre with their foster parents. The practice of leaving these decisions to the family reduces the capacity of children to live and work independently later in their lives. If they do not gain that capacity, they are likely to be forced to live in the adult institution.

Transition from foster care in Daxing

The registered permanent residence of children in foster care in Daxing is the non-agricultural resident collective household of

Daxing affiliated to Lixian police station. When they reach 18 years old, they are provided with job opportunities if they are capable of working. If they have severe disabilities and no means of economic independence, they are sent to Hongxing Social Welfare Institution, Daxing, a disability and aged care institution. Several children with severe disabilities who were aged over 18 years could not work but shared such strong emotional attachment with their foster parents that they would not separate from each other. They were allowed to stay with the foster families and their registered permanent residence remained the collective residence. This was possible because the Daxing Civil Affairs Bureau is responsible for both children and adults with disabilities in Daxing. It is generally a permanent arrangement under the existing policy.

In 2005, the Beijing Municipal Civil Affairs Bureau required all districts and counties to build child welfare institutions funded by district governments. Despite the Daxing District preference for foster care rather than institutional care, it also built a district-level child welfare institution. At the time of the research, it was nearly completed and was expected to be operational from 2014. The welfare institution is integrated with the Home for Disabled Veterans and the Seniors' Home, and is expected to accommodate 150 beds. It was not yet decided whether to transfer some of the children in foster care to the welfare institution. The decision was to be made by the civil affairs department of the district government; however, the policy of the municipal government will have significant influence on the local government's choices. Such a decision to move away from family-based foster care back to institutional care would be contrary to the positive experience in the area and international good practice (UNGACC, 2009). Losing the opportunity to form family attachments in a foster family would be likely to affect the children's childhood and lifetime trajectory.

Alternative care in the Beijing Number 2 Child Welfare Institution

The Beijing Number 2 Child Welfare Institution was established in 1999, and is situated in Shunyi District in the north-east of Beijing. It had 63 full-time and 50 part-time staff members. Children admitted to the institution include those taken back from foster families to receive education and those transferred from the Beijing Child Welfare Institution who are at least six years old without severe disabilities and can receive education. The Beijing Number 2 Child Welfare Institution plays a major role in providing education to children in state care. It also facilitates the transition of young adults who grow up in welfare institutions to leave and live independently in the community.

At the time of the research in 2012, 266 children were in the care of the Beijing Number 2 Child Welfare Institution, almost all of whom had mild or severe disabilities. More than half were boys (178 boys and 78 girls). The oldest was 29 years old and the youngest was six years old, though most were aged 14–29 years (150 children). They were attending school, working or unemployed. Most of the children lived primarily in the institution, except for some children who were working in other regions as migrant workers or attending schools and returned to the institution during weekends or holidays. Most of the school-aged children were receiving education within the institution (130 children), and the education options varied by age and disability.

Institution special education

The welfare institution established a special education school in the institution in 2010, with the approval of Shunyi District Education Bureau. Most of the children who attend the special school have severe disabilities (130 children). They are facilitated by teachers to do exercises that promote rehabilitation. The teachers have professional special education training, and the textbooks are the same as those used in other special education schools in a bid to allow the children to receive education comparable to that provided by other special schools, though not the same as mainstream schools. Due to limited resources, the welfare institution does not organize professional, systematic therapy. Children receiving special education in the institution wake up at 5:00, tidy up, enjoy free time and attend lessons at 8:00 after the teachers have sent off the children who attend other schools in the community. Similarly, the afternoon session begins and ends 30 minutes later and earlier than in regular schools because the teachers have to send off and pick up the children attending community schools after lunch.

Community schooling

The Beijing Number 2 Child Welfare Institution arranges for children who can attend school on their own to attend primary school, junior high school or senior high school close to the welfare institution. The welfare institution arranges the timetables of the children according to the local school requirements. In the summer and autumn, children attending schools out of the institution get up at 5:30 in the morning, set off to the school at around 7:10, return to the welfare institution for lunch and nap at 11:30, set off to the school again at 14:00, return to the welfare institution at around 17:00, and have supper at 18:00. The teachers arrange self-study in a classroom before supper. After supper, junior high students do another hour's self-study, while primary school students enjoy free time. At 21:00, primary and secondary school students go to sleep, while children of higher grades and unemployed older children go to sleep at 22:00. In the winter and spring, the timetable is the same except that they return to afternoon school earlier at 13:00. The institution covers the costs for education and provides monthly pocket money, according to their age. Some children reside in the schools from Monday to Friday and return to the welfare institution on weekends. The welfare institution pays for the education costs of these children too and pays a living allowance according to their age.

Transition out of care

Many children growing up in welfare institutions have limited capacity to compete for independence in the community, such as finding employment, housing and marriage. They have limited means to make a living by themselves. As a result, most young adults who have grown up in this way continue to rely on the welfare institution for basic needs, a place to live and income support.

In 2009, the Beijing Civil Affairs Bureau issued a policy called 'The Social Placement' for the placement of young people in care in the community, requiring governments at street (*jiedao*) and community (*shequ*) levels to assist young people who had grown up in institutional care and who have the ability to work to obtain jobs and registered local permanent residence. If they achieved this independence, the governments could revoke the guardianship obligation between the welfare institution and the young people (Beijing Civil Affairs Bureau, 2009).

In 2011, however, the implementation of this policy stalled without further notification. While the policy is still valid, the problems relating to its implementation are multiple. For example, housing costs greatly increased during this period and the labour market became tighter, which seriously affected the placement and employment of young people leaving care. Many young people in care remained unemployed and had to stay at the welfare institution because they had no other means of independence. Some young people who secured a job or married left the institution but returned once they lost their jobs.

When the social placement policy was being implemented between 2009 and 2011, some young people leaving care, mainly from the Beijing Number 2 Child Welfare Institution, did manage to be placed by street or community governments, and their registered permanent residences (*hukou*) were transferred to that location. When the implementation of the social placement policy stalled, some young people lost their registered permanent residential document. These young people had to return to the institution to regain registered permanent residence with the institution.

Many young people in the institution who have completed schooling are unemployed and stay at the welfare institution, watching TV or playing games. Sometimes, the institution organizes vocational training for unemployed young people in care, such as training on cooking and computer skills, but the fieldwork investigations found that the depth and intensity of the training sessions were limited, and the training outcomes were generally poor.

Summary of alternative care in Beijing

The institutional arrangements and facilities at the Beijing Child Welfare Institution are materially reasonable. However, the arrangements are focused on operational efficiency rather than the individualized best interests of the children: children are placed into different welfare institutions by age group, which interrupts their relationships and development during their childhood. Some children are taken back from foster care to institutional care irrespective of the preferences and attachments of the children and their foster families. The institutional arrangements are not conducive to a childhood with family-like emotional attachments to adults or social connections and family and child peer relationships. Neither do they assist children to develop the social expectations of other children in the community about the utility of education, social connections and future employment.

Taiyuan Child Welfare Institution, Shanxi

The Taiyuan Social Welfare Institution was founded in 1953, and the Child Welfare Institution, an affiliate institution, was established in 1992. They share the same management, staff, building and facilities. It is the only social welfare institution in Taiyuan and is responsible for accepting and caring for orphaned children and other urban residents who cannot live independently and do not have any employers or other people responsible for supporting them. Most people in their care are children, homeless people with severe disabilities and older people. At the time of the research, it had 76 full-time staff and served over 720 residents, including over 630 children, most of whom had disabilities. The institution has 260 beds. It has 16 divisions, including the general office and divisions for personnel, finance, administration, in-kind donation management, gardening, security, nutrition, medicine, foster care, adoption, children, adults and older people.

Foster care in Taiyuan

Foster care is the main form of alternative care for children in the Child Welfare Institution. It has three approaches to foster care: foster care contracted to NGOs, rural community-based foster care and urban foster care. Considering that the best interests of children are to live in a family, the welfare institution commissioned NGOs to provide foster care to 40 children, while retaining guardianship of the children with the institution. It regarded the NGOs as a better choice to provide the care because of its foster care experience and better funding.

The institution prioritizes rural community-based foster care for the other children. Foster care is primarily based in one village and extends to 11 adjacent villages. At the end of 2012, 346 children lived in rural foster care. With the process of urbanization and growth of the city, the rural areas near the downtown area have gradually become urban areas. This urban–rural integration also affects foster families. The lifestyle gap between rural foster families and urban residents has decreased. The third type is urban foster care. A small number of urban residents living in the city have also applied to the welfare institution to become foster parents. As a result, about 10% of children in state care live in urban foster care families.

The institution is also responsible for supervising and supporting the foster families. It has policies on the management of foster care that it implements in a standardized management system. The institution strives to achieve a professional foster care operation. The institution has rural and urban foster care offices responsible for managing the different concerns of each type of foster care. In the rural foster care, foster care management stations have also been established because the locations are spread. Altogether, a five-tier management system covers the institution, offices, stations, family groups and families. In addition, designated health clinics conduct health-care home visits. The foster care parents receive regular training, including at least three training workshops annually, covering knowledge about childcare, child rights protection, therapy for children with cerebral palsy and counselling for distress when a foster child is removed for international adoption.

History of foster care in Taiyuan

When the central government issued the *Interim Provisions on Family Foster Care 2003* to officially recognize and support foster care, the Taiyuan Child Welfare Institution set up a foster care department the same year. It developed the *Implementation Protocol of Taiyuan Child Welfare Institution for the Foster Care of Children*, covering the implementation of foster care, the responsibilities and obligations of families providing foster care, a management flowchart of foster care, and living expenses for children under foster care. The foster care project was launched in 2004.

Foster care began when institution staff took some children home and became foster care families themselves. The story passed to neighbours, who applied to the institution to become foster parents. The institution held a ceremony to sign foster care agreements with the first batch of foster parents in 2004. Media reports on the event attracted public attention and each day more than one hundred people made calls to apply to become foster parents. As a result, the number of foster families increased rapidly, mostly in the villages near the institution. The institution designated selected villages where foster families were concentrated as the primary foster care community in order to contain the costs of foster care and monitoring. This established rural community-based foster care.

The origins of urban foster care were different. Many of the urban foster care families had first informally cared for the children without going through any legal procedures. Their relationship was later formalized as foster care under the responsibility of the institution. This benefited families who were coping with many difficulties associated with the children's needs, such as medical costs, disability support, economic pressures, health conditions of old foster parents, registered permanent residence so the children could attend school and the parents ineligibility for formal adoption. The parents had struggled with problems such as the children being unable to attend high school because they had no registered permanent residence. The parents had to resort to the welfare institution for help. The institution supported the informal carers by granting the children the collective registered permanent residence of the institution, and providing them with an allowance for their living costs, health care and education. Converting the care to formal foster care effectively ensured that the children continued to grow up in the same stable family environment that they had known throughout their childhood. Their experience is explored in more detail in Chapter Ten. Policies and experiences of transitions out of care are not well developed in Taiyuan and are covered in other chapters.

Alternative care in Datong

The Datong Social Welfare Institution, Shanxi Province, was selected as an additional research site because it has a long history of mixed alternative care (Shang, 2003). The institution has organized rural foster care for more than 60 years. The institution was founded in 1949 and is a comprehensive welfare service, with the largest accommodation in Shanxi Province, accepting children and people with disabilities, with no income or who are homeless. The institution did not have sufficient funds to provide institutional care to all the children, so it found people to adopt or foster the children (Shang and Fisher, 2014a). By December 2007, the institution had cared for 832 children, including 480 children in foster care, 80 children in institutional care and others who had become adults and had the capacity to work and leave.

In the foster-family environment, the children are provided with comprehensive care from the foster family, supported by staff from the institution, including access to the health and disability facilities at the institution. In this way, they have the dual benefits of a family environment and free formal health and social support. Many state wards in Datong grew up in foster families from when they were babies. They have strong family ties with their foster families and many of them have successfully found jobs. These young people became economically independent from the institution and their foster family, and some now even provide for their foster parents like other adult children. This success is rare in other welfare institutions because many have only more recently begun foster care programmes and the children are not yet old enough to consider independence.

Urumqi Child Welfare Institution, Xinjiang

The Urumqi Child Welfare Institution was set up in 1947. It is the sole child welfare institution in the capital city of Xinjiang. In 2012, the institution was the guardian for 345 children, including 40 children without disabilities. It also provided disability therapy and special education support to 33 children who lived with their families, for which the institution charged a small amount of fees to the parents. As of 2012, the institution had 184 staff (23 with intermediate professional titles, 39 with junior professional titles, two with professional social worker certificates, six with professional childcare worker certificates and 12 unqualified childcare workers).

Like all child welfare institutions, the first preference is for children to be adopted, which is usually only open to children without disabilities in Urumqi. In 2012, 39 children were adopted, including 16 adopted domestically (41%) and 23 adopted internationally (59%). Four children returned to their birth families. All the children who were adopted or returned to their families had no or minor disabilities.

The approaches to care included: institutional care (182 children), mainly in 22 family care groups; foster care (154); and contracted foster care (nine) with charity organizations. Most children did not attend a local school. Instead, most of the children with disabilities attended the Special Educational Centre in the institution, which was also attended by 33 children from the community whose parents pay fees for the services – four children were in preschool, 15 in primary school, five in junior high school and one in senior high school. Only a few young adults were also in education – two were attending technical school or secondary vocational training school, three were attending colleges, and two were unemployed. The rest of the young adults remained in the institution waiting for further employment or adult care arrangements.

Transition out of care was undeveloped in the institution. The institution was responsible for 103 young people aged 16 years or above, including 15 who did not have disabilities; one of the young adults had gained employment, one was attending college, nine had been transferred to other institutions responsible for adult care and none of them lived independently.

Nanning Welfare Institution, Guangxi

Responsibilities of the institution

The Nanning Welfare Institution is affiliated to the Nanning Civil Affairs Bureau. It was established in 1951 and has 789 beds. It is an integrated welfare institution that accepts older people without family, people with disabilities and children in state care in Nanning City. It also provides services to the general public for a fee, including care for older people, therapy for children with disabilities and nursing and education for young children. Transition policies to leave care are not well developed in Nanning and are discussed in the other chapters.

At the time of the research in 2012, the institution had a general office and divisions for administration, finance, adoption management, health care and therapy, education, and social work (Chen, 2009). It is divided between care for adults and children. The child welfare section includes units for babies and for children, a rehabilitation exercise centre, and a kindergarten (Nanning City Social Welfare Institution, 2009). The responsibilities of the child welfare section are to arrange adoption, care and protection, nursing, health care, therapy, education, foster care, and parenting support.

Initially, the institution only provided institutional care to children with disabilities for their care, treatment and education. The care was individualized for their age-specific management, education and treatment based on a diagnosis and assessment of functions, intelligence and disabilities. Some children mainly received care; some received both care and education; and some mainly received functional therapy training. Some young people with disabilities received education and were organized to engage in labour activities and receive occupational skills training in order to enhance their self-care, labour-related skills and preparation for establishing their own small businesses.

From 2000, the child welfare section began to emphasize 'children-centred and love' as the criteria for quality care. It emphasized providing children with feeding and nursing services, in addition to teaching and therapy activities, in order to ensure the emotional and physical health of babies and young children (Nanning City Social Welfare Institution, 2000). Later, psychological communication was carried out with children by considering the characteristics of the children and activities related to sound, colours and sunshine and outdoor activities, considering the age and physical differences of the children (Nanning City Social Welfare Institution, 2004). As the sole state welfare institution in Nanning City, the welfare institution is responsible for 'health care, nursing, therapy and education' for all children in state care in the city. The changes in childcare approaches from 2000 gradually reinforced the interests of the children and enhanced service quality.

The institution expanded its partnerships with international organizations to develop its organizational capacity. It proactively seeks international partnerships and cooperation in foster care, disability therapy and training for care workers. The institution also turned towards serving families in the community, while also drawing in community resources, and shifted its focus towards special education. These collaborative and outreach service types were conducive to the development of the institution and, more broadly, to improving the child welfare system in Guangxi.

Foster care

The Nanning Child Welfare Institution started foster care in 1994, with financial support from international NGOs. As the government only provided financial support for institutional care, the institution did not have funding for foster care at that time. Through international partnerships, hundreds of children were placed in foster care in a family environment, mainly children with disabilities or chronic diseases. Many of the fostered children were then adopted internationally. The children developed relationships in their foster families and communities that would not otherwise have been available to them if they had grown up in the institution. The funding from international NGOs covered parts of the children's living costs, training carers and rehabilitation facilities. The costs of foster care grew rapidly and government funding gradually replaced the funding from international NGOs.

Number of children in state care or adopted

The primary task of the welfare institution is to adopt children without known family members. In the past three decades, the number of children admitted to or residing in the institution steadily rose, increasing from 39 in 1985 to 497 in 2009 (see Table 3.2 and Figure 3.1).

Table 3.2: Number of children living in the Nanning City Welfare Institution, 1985–2009

Year	Number of children	Year	Number of children
1985	39	2000	440
1987	54	2001	425
1989	70	2002	381
1991	63	2003	372
1992	90	2004	367
1993	102	2005	472
1994	164	2006	530
1995	136	2007	387
1996	585	2008	403
1997	649	2009	497
1999	599		

Note: Data in some years are missing.

Source: Summary performance reports of the Nanning City Social Welfare Institution.

Figure 3.1: Number of children living in the Nanning City Welfare Institution, 1985–2009

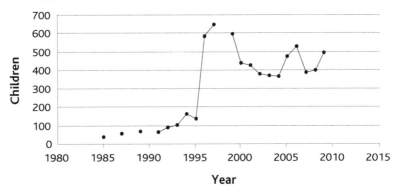

Note: Years with missing data are not joined to previous year.

Source: Summary performance reports of the Nanning City Social Welfare Institution.

Child adoption and permanent placement are the preferred placement approaches (see Table 3.3 and Figure 3.2). The institution follows the national adoption laws, regulations and policies, and proactively assists with domestic and international adoption, in order to ensure children's rights to live in a family. The reason for the 2007 peak is unknown to the researchers.

Table 3.3: Children placed by the Nanning City Social Welfare Institution for adoption, 2000–09

Year	Number of children placed for adoption	Children placed for adoption in China	Children placed for international adoption
2000	208	79	129
2001	244	88	156
2002	264	63	201
2003	129	30	99
2004	181	39	164
2005	192	76	116
2006	155	56	99
2007	197	109	88
2008	95	65	30
2009	49	17	32

Source: Summary performance reports of the Nanning City Social Welfare Institution.

Figure 3.2: Children placed by the Nanning City Social Welfare Institution for adoption, 2000–09

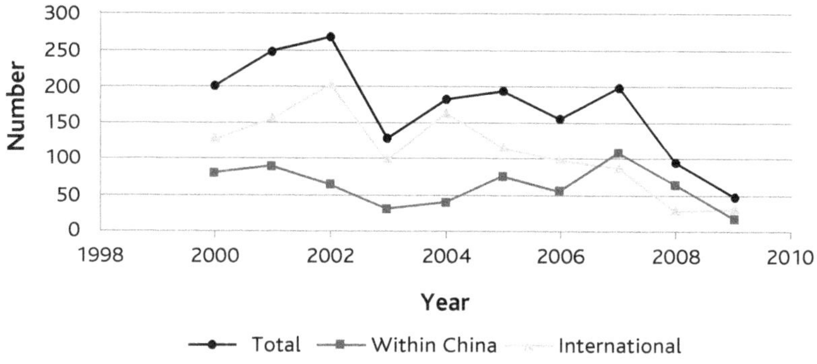

Source: Summary performance reports of the Nanning City Social Welfare Institution.

Development of community resource centres

An innovation of the institution was to establish community resource centres to provide services to children who remain with their families out of the institution. It also promotes cooperation in the community to facilitate children who live in the institution to attend schools and kindergartens in the community. These initiatives represent significant steps towards reform of the operation of child welfare institutions. It is consistent with new approaches promoted by the Ministry of Civil Affairs (MCA) since 2006 (information from interviews with MCA officials in 2006; see also MCA, 2006).

Specific examples of innovation include developing preschool education in the community for children with and without disabilities. In 2005, the institution established Ci Hai Kindergarten, located on-site, which is targeted at community participation and promotes integration between children living in the institution and community children. Its primary purpose is to provide quality preschool education to the children in state care, including integration with other children, their families and other community members, while also benefiting other children in the community. The kindergarten leverages the resources of the institution for the benefit of the children in state care and local community members. It seeks opportunities to develop new projects with this approach (Chen, 2009).

A second example of a community initiative from the institution is that it promotes special education targeted at the community. The institution established on-site the Nanning City Special School for Orphans and Children with Disabilities in 2005 for children with disabilities who are state wards or who live with their families in the community. The school is under the direction of the local education authority and enhances the facilities by pooling education resources from various parties. The school holds the same position as other special education schools recognized by the education authority. It has four classes and also provides occupational skills training, such as handcraft (Chen, 2009), but not the educational opportunities available in mainstream schools.

Summary of child welfare institution practices

The alternative care systems in the four research locations have progressed since the desperate times of *The dying rooms* documentary. The progress was initially in terms of the facilities and physical support of children in the guardianship of welfare institutions. The physical conditions for the children improved. However, as yet, there remains no policy or practice consensus on the best approaches for alternative care in terms of the best interests of the child. A variety of approaches and practices of care have emerged, including family-based foster care, which is increasingly recognized as one of the main forms of care, alongside the more traditional institutional care.

In Shanxi and Urumqi, foster care has become the preferred form of care for the welfare institutions. In Beijing, foster care is a form of alternative care that is still in development, with some trends towards re-institutionalization in some parts of the city. In the most deinstitutionalized area, Daxing, institutional care is only used for temporary care while new children are assessed before placement in a foster care family.

No policy or practice consensus has been reached about the vision for the development of the child welfare system, particularly the reform of the function and operation of welfare institutions, which differ from area to area. In Nanning, for example, the institution is repositioning to become a child welfare resource centre for the community and children who live with their families. In Beijing, however, institutional care arrangements that can damage children's development and relationships are still dominant care practices, such as: shifting children between child welfare institutions by age; cutting off links between children and the community that they formerly lived in; and forcibly sending children back to institutions from foster care. Beijing policy does not seem to have mechanisms to review, learn from and replicate good practices within the municipality, such as temporary institutional care for assessment before foster care in Daxing. Instead, these practices are threatened by the uncertainty of policy decisions by higher levels of government.

The likely implications of these alternative care conditions of younger children for their transition to adulthood are mixed. Some practices encourage social inclusion during childhood, such as foster care and changing the role of institutions to temporary care or residual community support. These practices enable younger children to develop family and social relationships that support their well-being during childhood and raise their social expectations about possibilities for their adult life. Other practices accentuate the exclusion of children and young people in state care, such as segregating children from possibilities of developing community relationships and severing relationships by forcibly removing children. Chapter Four more directly explores the formal policies and practices for transition to adulthood in these four sites in order to understand the possibilities for support towards independent living in the community.

FOUR

Leaving care policies

Chinese policies on support for children and young people in state care, including children with disabilities, initially focused on the immediate questions of survival and material well-being. As the reach of the Chinese welfare state expanded, expectations on the state changed to include achieving more than these basic needs. The expectations have grown to include supporting young people in state care and other orphaned children living in the community to achieve their full citizenship rights, including expectations to live independently, out of state care, in their adulthood. Equally, state practices that accentuate the multiple dimensions of social exclusion of children in state care are now subject to criticism. Both these pressures are motivated not only by the interests and well-being of children and young people, but also by the practical questions of minimizing the state's lifetime responsibility for children in state care and other orphaned children in the community.

In this context, this chapter examines the formal policies of the central government, and four locations – Beijing, Shanxi, Xinjiang and Nanning – as examples of the types of support offered to young people in state care as they reach adulthood. Except for Beijing, the policies also cover other children who are orphaned and cared for in their extended family, as well as other young people with disabilities living with their families. The gap between these formal policies and the experience of young people is analysed further in later chapters.

Overview of welfare transition policies

Welfare available to children in state care covers basic living protection, care and protection, education, health care, therapy, adult placement, and housing. The policies on basic living protection are generally implemented in most locations. In addition to children in state care, in some areas, orphaned children in the care of their extended family also receive a monthly living allowance to meet their basic living costs.

Most children in state care live in institutions or foster care. The Ministry of Civil Affairs (MCA) has stipulated provisions to categorize which children are eligible for adoption, the funds for child adoption, the obligations to be fulfilled in the period of adoption, the prerequisites for foster families and the roles and responsibilities of foster care service providers, as described in Chapter Three. Policies to formalize care and transitions for children and young people in non-government care are detailed in Chapter Ten. However, many other aspects of alternative care policy do not have detailed provisions for implementation. The implementation of the policies on foster care is also inconsistent, including children in foster care being sent back to institutions or even shifting back and forth between foster care and institutions.

Children with disabilities in state care receive additional services, including health care, therapy, special education and vocational training. The type of services, the quality and the government funding vary by area. In wealthier areas, the services available to children with disabilities in state care are even better than those provided to children with disabilities living with their families. At the extreme, this is one of the reasons some parents decide that it is in their children's interest to live in state care.

The shortcomings in the policies include that the support provided is largely confined to physical provision, while neglecting support for psychological, emotional and developmental conditions. The policies are often unstable, particularly the policies on foster care, which are important in planning for transitions to adulthood. Child welfare is primarily a local government responsibility and the policies differ by location.

Welfare policies for transition to adulthood

Welfare policies on orphans' transition to adulthood are primarily formulated at a local level. They typically cover lump-sum allowances, job arrangements and housing arrangements. Particularly in wealthier areas, the policies include support for costs of living, foster care and employment and housing placements for young people into adulthood.

The central government has not stipulated explicit provisions about when welfare support to young people in state care ends, which makes state child welfare institutions the only welfare institutions with responsibility to provide support from birth to death. The state care policies originate from the earlier communist planned economy era. Once children are registered as state wards, the state is forevermore responsible for preventing them from entering a position of unsustainable living. The policies about transition to adulthood are mainly oriented to placement out of state care (child adoption or adult job arrangements), and are inadequate in terms of supporting the orphans' economic and social independence. These policies result in many young people never having the opportunity for status as independent adults, potentially remaining the responsibility of child welfare institutions forever.

Policy solutions would be to define the conditions to achieve in order to end state care, the reorientation of services away from placement and towards pathways to support independent living, and a maximum eligibility age. This book explores the experience of institutions and the feasibility of attempting that change. In addition, as Chinese society is changing, gaps are growing between the welfare support in child welfare institutions and that available to children and young people in the wider community. Improvements to social welfare, particularly in housing security, are conducive to improving the transition of young adults in state care to independent living in the community.

All young people in state care hold the registered permanent residence of the city where they reside. They hold a collective registered urban *hukou* of the welfare institution, not individually registered. In China, registered permanent residence (*hukou*) has significant implications for urban life (Cui and Cohen, 2015). A resident must have a permanent address to register their *hukou*. Almost all public services targeted at residents are only accessible to residents with registered permanent residence. The collective registered permanent residence at the institution means that state wards who cannot transfer their registered permanent residence out of welfare institutions must permanently rely on welfare institutions to manage registered permanent residence, including their spouse and children, and cannot obtain an independent identity. In most areas, they can only obtain independence through home-ownership or their employer's registration. The MCA does not have any policy about obtaining independent registration. Among the locations researched for this book, only Beijing had formulated provisions regarding the registered permanent residence of young people leaving state care. Housing policy is discussed in detail in Chapter Nine.

Development of policies on leaving state care

The initial policies on leaving a state care placement primarily covered child adoption and adult job arrangements. The policy of prioritizing adoption enables the children to obtain permanent placement in a family early in their life and avoids reliance upon state care. This policy has been very successful. Prior to 1992, the majority of orphaned children were adopted within China. Welfare institutions in China only cared for several thousand new children annually, but the figure later increased to 20,000–30,000 (see Table 2.2 in Chapter Two).

In addition, during the planned economy period until the 1980s, the state arranged jobs for young people in state care who could independently work. Young people with disabilities were also provided with jobs at welfare factories and earned sufficient, independent income (Shang, 2008b). At that time, the income disparity in China was not large, and those who had a job were assured a sufficient source of income. The particular challenges of having lived in state care did not cause major impacts on their adult life.

Following the economic reform and opening up of the economy in the 1990s, Chinese society saw great changes (Blaxland et al, 2015). Prior to 2010, the state continued to implement the policies on young people in care of the planned economy era. Young people had access to job placements and were not subject to criteria for the termination of support from state welfare institutions once they entered adulthood.

The policies supporting the transition of young people in care to adulthood are based on the *Opinions of State Council General Office on Strengthening Welfare Protection of Orphans 2010*. This document provided the general provisions for state wards' basic living protection, education, health care, employment and housing, and included policies on the transition to adulthood. Except for the orphan basic living protection allowance, for which part of the funds are disbursed from central finances, the implementation of the rest of the policies relies on funding from local government finances, and the local governments formulate detailed policies for implementation.

From 2010, the state began to distribute a monthly basic living allowance of RMB600 per month (£66) to children and young adults in alternative care who were living in the community in order to address their economic needs. Introducing this policy required a new conceptualization about ongoing responsibilities to young adults, including who was eligible, in what circumstances and for how long. A maximum age was defined for eligibility to receive support as a young person in state care living in the community or the welfare institution. According to the policy, after receiving a lump-sum six-month basic living protection allowance, young people in alternative care living in the community who were already 18 years old would no longer be provided with a basic living protection allowance if they did not attend school. If they were attending school, the local civil affairs department would continue to distribute the monthly allowance until they completed their education. In many areas, before terminating the monthly orphan basic living protection allowance, the local government provides them with a lump-sum allowance of varied amounts to support their transition to independent living.

The policy about the availability of an orphan basic living allowance also applies to young adults still living at the child welfare institution, though, in practice, the institutions continue to provide care rather than terminate support when the young people no longer meet the age, education and employment criteria. Welfare institutions continue to provide comprehensive welfare support, including accommodation, therapy and physical support, in addition to the cash allowance. The policy does not explicitly state whether physical support would be terminated when young people in state care reach 18 years old. In practice, the welfare institutions do not stop providing support to the large number of young people in care who have not been supported to live an independent life out of the institutions.

In such a policy context, the paths for young people in state care are that responsibility for young people aged 18 years and over with high disability support needs and without support to work is transferred to social welfare institutions that care for adults. The policy is not explicit about discontinuing support to other young adults aged 18 years and over who have been supported to develop the capacity to work. In general, child welfare institutions are responsible for every aspect of the lives of children and young people in their care, with or without disabilities, including their living conditions, well-being, education and health care. When they become young adults but without access to employment and housing, the institutions continue to provide them with free accommodation, and some also distribute the living allowance (Yu, 2013).

In some areas, welfare institutions do not continue to distribute the living allowance to young people in state care. They are expected to work in the community and gradually give up their reliance upon the institution. For reasons explored in this book, few young people in care achieve economic independence through paid employment, and many of them choose to stay at the institution, relying on state support. This residual arrangement affects the support offered to young people and the capacity of young people growing up in state care to consider possibilities for an independent life.

The central government policies described earlier are the principles by which local governments are expected to formulate their operational policies. Local governments follow the MCA lead according to their willingness to prioritize the policy change and their financial resources to implement them. The implementation of these policies varies across

China. Four locations are analysed to explore the variation according to available funding and policy approaches to the independence of children and young people in state care, as well as, in some cases, other orphans and children with disabilities in these locations.

Beijing

The Beijing government formulated the earliest policies on the transition of young people in care (Beijing Civil Affairs Bureau, 2009). The policies of Beijing cover basic living protection, employment, housing and residence registration. Unlike the other areas, it only applies to young people in state care, not other orphaned children or other children with disabilities.

Basic living income protection and employment

Once children in state care in Beijing reach adulthood, those who can live independently and secure paid employment have access to placement support arranged by the district or county government that sent the orphaned child to the welfare institution. The young person is entitled to a lump-sum allowance of RMB150,000 (£16,500), paid to the government responsible for the placement from the finance departments of the city and the district or county, which is to be used to support the housing, employment and temporary living costs for the young person to move into the community. Child welfare institutions continue to provide for young people who attend school until they graduate, when they become eligible for this type of placement (Wang, 2009).

When young people leaving state care seek employment, they are eligible for several types of employment support. The first is that young people with disabilities in care can be included in the local service system to assist people with disabilities into employment. Other young people without disabilities can be provided with job vacancy information by job vacancy information service agencies designated by the district or county labour and social security department. In addition, public entities and businesses that employ young people leaving care are acknowledged by the Disabled Persons' Federation (DPF) as fulfilling their quota obligation to employ people with disabilities. Young adults leaving care eligible for enrolment into the defence forces can enrol as preferred candidates (Wang, 2009).

Housing and registered permanent residence

The second types of support for young people leaving care are about housing and registered residence. Each young person is provided with an allowance of RMB150,000 to support their house rental in order to reside in rented house in the community. Beijing was the only city to have provisions about the registered permanent residence of young people leaving state care. The first path to leave collective registered permanent residence is if their employer is entitled to host registered permanent residence, then the young person can use this method to gain independent residency. If the employer does not have that entitlement, the young person's registered permanent residence can be transformed into collective registered permanent residence for orphans reintegrating into the community, which is a new category specifically set up for the policy by local districts and counties. The practice began in 2009 in some districts and counties of Beijing (Wang, 2009).

In other areas that have not implemented this policy, owning a house is the only condition possible as a prerequisite for residential registration independent of the institution. In these areas, young people who cannot purchase a house continue to hold collective registered permanent residence based at welfare institutions. These young people can leave state care, in terms of living independently, but they cannot secure independent registered permanent residence.

Shanxi Province

The second example of an area that has policies about transitions out of state care is Shanxi Province and its capital, Taiyuan City. It has formulated policies for young people leaving state care, other orphaned children and children with disabilities about basic living, health care, education, occupational skills training, employment services and housing security (The General Office of Shanxi Provincial People's Government, 2011). The government required that the 14 relevant departments and organizations establish a working mechanism to support young people leaving state care based on government leadership. It is steered by the Civil Affairs Department with multi-sectoral collaboration and social participation from Civil Affairs, Finance, Development and Reform, Education, Public Security, Justice, Social Security, Housing and Urban Construction, Institutional Staffing, Population and Family Planning, Youth League, the Women's Federation, and the AIDS Prevention Association.

Basic living protection and health care

All children who are orphaned (both parents die or one parent dies and the other parent cannot be found) are eligible for the basic living protection, whether they live in kinship care or state care. Eligibility for monthly allowances depends on which type of alternative care the child or young person lives in. If they are raised in kinship care in their extended family, they receive a monthly allowance of RMB600 for basic living protection. If they are in state care, they receive a monthly allowance of RMB1,000. Young people leaving state care receive a lump-sum allowance to support at least six months' living when they reach 18 years old. If they continue to attend full-time education after 18 years or older, they continue to receive a monthly allowance for basic living protection until they complete their education (The General Office of Shanxi Provincial People's Government, 2011).

All children and young people in state care are included in urban resident basic health insurance, rural cooperative medical care and urban and rural health care relief. The local government pays the insurance fees from the urban and rural health care relief funds. From 2013, the over 500 orphans and children with disabilities in the Taiyuan City Welfare Institution were incorporated into Taiyuan urban resident basic health insurance, for which each person must pay RMB48 per year and, in return, receive reimbursement of a percentage of their hospitalization and health-care costs. The basic health insurance fee of RMB48 per year is waived for children in state care with severe disabilities (The General Office of Shanxi Provincial People's Government, 2011).

Education, training and employment

Children in state care receive free education. Eligible children with disabilities in state care attend regular schools. Others with vision, hearing, speech or learning disabilities attend special education schools or classes. In recent years, all school-age children in the Taiyuan Child Welfare Institution who were deemed capable of learning attended schools.

Once young people in state care reach 18 years old, they are eligible for occupational skills training and employment services in Shanxi. Employment support includes a vocational training allowance and a variety of vocational training targeted at the young people. Young people with the ability to work are offered preferential access to positions in public agencies or are supported to start their own businesses with concessions, such as tax exemption or reduction and micro-loans (The General Office of Shanxi Provincial People's Government, 2011).

Like all provinces, in 1992, Shanxi Province formulated a policy that all employers must employ people with disabilities or pay a levy to the Disabled Persons' Employment Security Fund, managed by the DPF. All government agencies, organizations, businesses, public institutions and rural or urban collective economic organizations within Shanxi Province must employ people with disabilities to a minimum of 1.5% of their total staff, similar to the rest of the country. It is not well implemented, either employing people with disabilities or paying the levy.

Housing security

Young people leaving state care have preferential access to local low rental housing and other affordable housing provided by the local government or are eligible for a rental allowance. The welfare institutions submit the application for housing support on their behalf (The General Office of Shanxi Provincial People's Government, 2011). Again, it is not well implemented. None of the young people in the research had received the low rental housing allowance, as detailed in Chapter Nine.

Xinjiang Uyghur Autonomous Region

The third area researched about policies on transitions out of care is Xinjiang Uyghur Autonomous Region and its capital, Urumqi City. Like Shanxi, Xinjiang established a multi-sectoral leadership group for social security for children and young people in state care. The group formulated policies to provide them with support, which cover basic living protection, health care and therapy, education, housing security, employment security, and registered permanent residence. The policies have limited provisions for promoting social participation, which indicates the limited awareness of policymakers on the rights of children to participation. The policies are similar to those in Shanxi.

Basic living protection, health care and therapy

The monthly basic living allowance is the same as Shanxi – RMB600 for orphans living in their extended family and RMB1,000 for children in state care. The cost of the allowance is covered by the Chinese central government finance subsidy, with the addition of the municipal finance contribution to the living costs of children living in the welfare institutions. The county or district government finances the basic living costs of orphans raised in their extended family. Children aged less than 18 years are eligible for the basic living protection allowance and young people who continue to attend education retain the allowance. If the young person in state care does not have the ability to work or other means of income, including no extended family, they can continue to receive a basic living protection allowance (Urumqi Civil Affairs Bureau, 2012).

Young people in state care rely on the health–care insurance system for the general public as there are no specific provisions for orphans. Orphans are incorporated into the health–care insurance system within the scope of urban resident basic health insurance or new rural cooperative medical care. The local government pays orphans' insurance fees with medical relief funds. If the insurances offered by urban resident basic health insurance or new rural or pastoral cooperative medical care do not completely cover the health expenses incurred, the costs are also paid with the medical relief fund. All orphans with disabilities are incorporated into the national, regional or charity health–care and therapy projects. The health departments are required to provide support and guidance to the hospitals, clinics and health centres of child welfare institutions, and encourage and support the health facilities to exempt orphans' medical costs.

In terms of medical costs, young people with disabilities also heavily rely on general health insurance welfare. All those who are on medical insurance will enjoy the benefits stipulated by the relevant provisions, and those who are not on medical insurance have to pay for the expenses. If they definitely cannot afford the costs, the district or county governments, civil affairs departments and DPF provide an allowance. The civil affairs departments also provide allowances to young people leaving care who are unable to work, have no other source of income and have no other legal carers (Urumqi City Coordinating Committee for Persons with Disabilities, 2002).

Education, training and employment

The Xinjiang government supports school-age children with disabilities residing in child welfare institutions to obtain compulsory education (Xinjiang People's Government General Office, 2011). In practice, except for the special education schools operated by welfare institutions, there are no general special education schools in Urumqi City.

The right of orphans without a disability or with a minor disability to compulsory education is generally protected by policies. Orphans attending public kindergartens are exempt from school fees. Public kindergartens are not allowed to refuse to admit orphans raised by extended families. Orphans attending primary or secondary schools (including secondary vocational schools) are exempt from fees for textbooks, exercise books, school uniforms and tuition and miscellaneous fees, and are provided with student grants; boarding orphans are exempted from fees for meals and lodging (Urumqi Civil Affairs Bureau, 2012).

Young people in state care who attend municipal higher vocational schools or regular higher education institutions are entitled to free education. The tuition fee is paid by the district or county finance departments if the orphans are raised by their extended family or paid by the welfare institution if the orphans are raised in state care. During the schooling period, they are provided with the maximum student grant of RMB4,000 per year (Urumqi Civil Affairs Bureau, 2012). While they attend school, the civil affairs department in the location of their permanent residence continues to provide them with the basic living protection allowance.

Young people leaving care are also entitled to employment support. The public career service, agencies of human resources and social security departments provide them with career support services. Young people who seek a job themselves or start their own businesses can apply for guaranteed micro-loans. If they start their own private business, they are exempt from administrative service fees, including fees for management, registration and certification, and their taxation is also reduced or exempted. If they are able to work but remain unemployed, they are supported to obtain public benefit positions (Urumqi Civil Affairs Bureau, 2012).

The Xinjiang government has also formulated provisions on the compulsory employment of people with disabilities and preferential treatment for their employment and business creation. These employment policies are also applicable to young people in care and children with disabilities (Urumqi City Coordinating Committee for Persons with Disabilities, 2002).

Housing security

The Urumqi policy is that young adults leaving care with the capacity to live an independent life are provided with appropriate housing security according to their economic capacity (Urumqi Civil Affairs Bureau, 2012). Similar to other cities in China, housing security in Urumqi includes public rental housing, low rental housing and affordable housing. State-subsidized housing policies are primarily targeted at low-income groups, without considering the special group of young people leaving care or with disabilities. Their eligibility to apply for rented houses or to purchase houses is the same as other people eligible to state-subsidized housing security, with the same criteria, in the absence of a targeted welfare policy provision.

Guangxi Zhuang Autonomous Region

Nanning City in Guangxi Zhuang Autonomous Region is the final city in the research about policies on transitions from care. It has similar policies for young people to cover basic living protection, education, health care, employment and housing. Basic living protection does not apply to orphans who are legally adopted or young people leaving care who reach 18 years old, are able to work and do not continue schooling. Only young adult orphans who continue in education are still entitled to welfare security, including free education support (Nanning City People's Government General Office, 2013).

The Nanning government policy supports the employment of young adults leaving care. Young adult orphans with the ability to work and who are eligible for employment assistance are prioritized as key beneficiaries, receiving free career services and allowances for vocational training and social security. Those who have difficulty finding employment are referred to public benefit positions established by the government. Those who start their own businesses are entitled to taxation exemptions. Young adult orphans with disabilities are referred by the DPF to job positions (Nanning City People's Government General Office, 2013).

In terms of housing security and services, the orphans are prioritized as a key target group for policy and financial support. Young people with capacity for independent living can apply to housing security departments for housing support. The city finances provide funds for housing until their income level reaches the average annual salary of the city's urban employees (Nanning City People's Government General Office, 2013).

Policy directions to support independence in other cities

The transition to adulthood of young people in care is a policy challenge for the governments of most areas of China. In addition to the research areas included in this book, other cities are also pioneering the exploration into policy solutions to address the challenge. The wealthy cities of Shanghai, Qingdao, Guangdong and other areas have formulated detailed policies to explore changes in policy directions. They are attempting to support young people in care to obtain jobs through government leadership, collaboration and social relief and support.

Qingdao in Shandong Province issued the *Opinions on Placement of Adult Orphans 2005*, which stipulated that young people in state care who are 18 years old with the ability to work and who have received professional or technical skills training are to be provided with job placement and vocational training by the district government (Ran, 2005). The four urban districts of the city are responsible for the placement of a defined number of adult orphans, allocating them appropriate job positions. In addition, the district governments are responsible for: purchasing and providing affordable housing from social public benefit funds for each of the young people to be placed; transferring their registered permanent residence out of the state child welfare institutions; and providing them with daily necessities and essential equipment to establish their independent life.

In Qingdao, the social welfare institutions are required to continue providing for young people in care with disabilities who are 18 years old without the ability to work. This last condition does not address the deeper question of education, training and therapy for children with disabilities in state care so that they can also aspire to independence and fulfil their rights to live in the community and contribute through meaningful work or other community participation when they reach adulthood.

Nanjing in Jiangsu Province has the *Interim Provisions of Nanjing on Management of Older Orphans in State Child Welfare Institutions 2008*, which aims to assist young adults leaving care to become motivated to earn their living if the governments provide them with affordable housing. In Nanjing, young adults in state care upon the age of 18 years are no longer eligible for welfare support from the state child welfare institution. They can continue to live in an apartment at the state child welfare institution for three years. During this period, if their monthly income is lower than the minimum living protection for urban residents, the institution provides them with additional support. If their monthly income is higher than the minimum living protection for urban residents, the institution does not provide them with additional support. At the end of the three years, they must leave the institution to live independently and their *hukou* is transferred out of the institution to wherever they shift to in the city. Young people with disabilities without the capacity to work are transferred to an adult welfare institution (Nanjing Ribao, 2008).

Summary of policies about transition from care and other orphaned children

Central, provincial and city administrative authorities have issued policies on the basic living protection for young people leaving state care and other orphaned children, covering the support for their transition to adulthood. These policies take account of various aspects of their social and economic well-being, including a basic living allowance, a transition allowance when they leave care, health insurance coverage, access to employment advice and referral, and preferential access to housing. The policies supporting young people to attain education and employment are the most positive. In some policy areas, particularly health care and housing, the implementation of such policies relies on general social welfare provision in the location. Where the general social services are well developed, the policies to support transition to adulthood are more likely to be implemented. Elsewhere, the policies remain aspirational only.

At the central government level, no policies directly address the transition to adulthood of young people and children with disabilities in state care. Very few provinces have made local policies about this support need. Addressing their needs remains at the discretion of local administrators. The shortfalls in the current policies include defining the age or conditions when the state ceases provision for young people in care. In this absence, young adults and children with disabilities sometimes permanently rely on state care. The welfare institution has no incentive or mandate to plan for and support the young person to achieve independence.

Second, support for young people leaving care who have just begun their independent living is inadequate, particularly with regard to housing. It is very difficult for young people leaving care to secure independent housing in the market and the policies for welfare-based housing are underdeveloped in most locations. Some young people resort to continuing to live in the welfare institution because they have no other social housing or affordable options, which is not conducive to their independent adult life. The current registered permanent residence system in China is heavily dependent on housing ownership. Young adults leaving care without independent housing generally have no independent registered permanent residence, and can only retain their collective registered permanent residence attached to the welfare institutions.

In summary, the lack of formal central policies and, in most areas, the lack of local policies to support young people to leave state care threatens their social inclusion in their young adulthood. The likelihood that they experience their rights to transition towards independent living in the same way as their peers in their communities depends on the local discretion of the welfare institution and other local government agencies. Where local policies have been formulated, they emphasize basic income support, education and employment, which, if implemented, at least address their basic living needs.

None of the locations dealt with social participation more generally, or the additional support needs of young adults with disabilities apart from their physical needs. The poor development of a social housing market means that many housing policies for young people leaving care remained unimplemented. It is unlikely in these circumstances that young people in state care, especially those with higher disability support needs, can gain the independence that they might otherwise seek. The next chapters examine these gaps further by analysing the experiences of young people as they attempted to gain independence and social inclusion equivalent to their peers.

FIVE

Social inclusion impact of a childhood in state care

The love and care that children receive in their families or alternative care are among the most important factors influencing the quality of the childhood experience. Young people in alternative care in China grow up in institutions, foster care or family group care arranged by state child welfare institutions, non-governmental organizations or kinship or non-kinship families. The alternative care experiences of these children affect the quality of their childhood and, later, their transition to adulthood.

This chapter introduces the young people in care who participated in the in-depth interviews (see Table 5.1). They were asked about their most unforgettable childhood experiences. It was a way to understand whether they thought that they had received the support they needed to feel socially included or excluded during their childhood and the likely impact on their transition to adulthood. They spoke of positive experiences about affection and love from families and community members, and negative experiences about violence in state care, both physical and emotional. Most of the children only spoke about positive and negative experiences since they had entered state care. Some children could only remember their lives since entering state care because they were babies when they were found. Other children did not have positive memories that they could recall or could only remember negative experiences from before they entered state care.

The descriptions in this chapter are a precursor to the subsequent chapters, which explore the impact of these childhood experiences on the transition of the young people to adulthood. The names used in the chapters are all aliases.

Table 5.1: Young people in the childhood research sample

Alias	Sex	Age	Disability	Education	Employed or studying	Housing	Married	Alternative care	Place
Bing	M	28	No	Technical secondary	Employed	Family unit welfare institution	Yes	Institution	Taiyuan
Zhong	M	26	Yes	Technical secondary	Employed	Private rental	No	Foster	Beijing
Bao	M	23	Yes	Technical college	Employed part-time	Dormitory welfare institution	No	Foster	Beijing
Hen	M	23	Yes	Technical secondary	Student	Dormitory school	No	Mixed	Beijing
Luo	M	23	No	Technical secondary	Employed[a]	Private rental	No	Mixed	Beijing
Bo	M	22	No	Technical secondary	Unemployed	Dormitory welfare institution	No	Mixed	Taiyuan
Zeng	F	22	Yes	University	Student	Dormitory school[b]	No	Institution	Urumqi
Miao	F	21	No	Technical college	Student	Foster family	No	Mixed	Taiyuan
Li	M	21	Yes	Technical college	Employed at welfare institution	Family group care	No	Family group care	Urumqi
Jian	M	19	No	Junior middle	Student	Dormitory welfare institution	No	Institution	Taiyuan
Zhang	M	16	No	Technical secondary	Student	Family group care	No	Family group care	Urumqi

Notes: M = male; F = female. [a] Waiting for a government-arranged job. [b] Family group care before university.

Positive experiences in childhood

The focus that young people spoke about when they reflected on their most positive life experiences during childhood was their feelings of affection, personal attention and love from others, whether from their foster family, carers in the institution or other people in the community. This response would not be surprising from most young adults, but was particularly poignant from these young people in alternative care because they had all experienced the most terrible loss of their parents, extended family and the associated family affection. The researchers observed the young people's craving for family or other loving affection as more intense than other children.

Family relationships

The alternative care arrangements of most children in state care in China are usually stable and seldom change, except to shift between institutional and foster care. If children are in foster care, they usually remain with the one family. This stability in the foster care relationship can be a positive experience. The young people who had lived in foster care referred to the love they received from their foster family as the most positive experiences in their childhood. Luo was a young man aged 23 years who spoke movingly about the love he felt in his foster family. He had initially lived in the institution and then moved to foster care. His most unforgettable experience was when he sprained his ankle as a child and a foster-family member picked him up from school on a snowy day, in what might be a seemingly small incident for other children. After life in the institution, this event impressed him deeply and gave him a positive outlook about receiving love in his foster family. He said:

> "One day it was snowing and the snow was very thick. I couldn't ride my bike at that time, so I was just sitting on my bike. My [foster] parents sent me to the school on my bike. When the school was over, other children were picked up by their parents, and I thought my [foster] parents definitely wouldn't pick me up this time. I walked out, and immediately saw my parent standing on the snowy ground."

Relationships in institutional care

Other young people referred to the affection they received from staff in the institution or school that demonstrated emotional attachment, beyond just physical care. Li was a 21-year-old young man whose deepest positive impression was about his birthday celebration arranged by a teacher at his school. He said:

> "My birthday is October 1st [Chinese National Day]. The school had a sports meeting at the end of September. Our class cleaned the designated area, and our head teacher, who was also my Chinese language teacher, specifically asked me to take out the last garbage. When I came back to the class, my classmates together sang happy birthday to me. This moved me deeply."

While they were talking about their most unforgettable experiences, the young people often mentioned the people they most admired during their childhood. The young people who had grown up in foster families generally did not name their foster parents or siblings as the people who made the deepest impression. Instead, they usually mentioned teachers, welfare institution directors or caring people in the community. For example, Zhong, a young man aged 26 years who had left foster care and the institution, spoke about his teacher. Zhong admired his teacher's persistence, passion and care for the children in the child welfare institution.

Many of the young people in one welfare institution mentioned the institution directors, who showed affection, respect and a deep commitment to the children and helped them overcome difficulties. Bo was a 22-year-old young man who had lived with an informal foster family but now lived in the institution. He said that the director "offered meticulous care to me". Bing was the 28-year-old man, introduced in Chapter One, who lived in a family unit at the institution at the time of the research. He demonstrated the respect that they had for the director: "'We regard him as our biological father. He always takes great effort to benefit us, trying to ensure appropriate clothing, lodging and food for us".

Bao, a 23-year-old man who had grown up in foster care, said that he was deeply impressed by the former director of his welfare institution (who had been promoted to a higher position for his outstanding performance) because he always put the interests and preferences of children first and treated them as his family members. Hen, a young man also aged 23 years who was in foster and institutional care in the same city, agreed, saying that the former director "Put high value on education and cared very much about us". Hen contrasted the attitude of the former director with the new one:

> "[The new director] always puts security first, that is, everything is just fine if there is no serious security problem with us. He does not care much about us. When a child is ill and complaining of stomach ache, the teacher just asks the child to drink warm water. Some children dare not complain of illness, and often the teacher will send them to hospital only when their pain becomes very serious. I'm not really happy about the welfare institution in all aspects now."

Community involvement in the institution

The young people who had lived in the welfare institution spoke about positive experiences with people in the institution and in the community who were caring towards them. A young man, Zhang, aged 16 years, who still lived in the institution at the time of the research, said: "The Christmas party of 2012 [last year] was a very impressive event for me. Many children nearby participated". He did not describe the party in detail, but emphasized his pleasure that the children in the local community had participated. He spoke of the community event as a fabulous scene that deeply impressed the children in the institution. His story implied that he felt that the staff at the institution had been thoughtful to arrange it and that the community members and their children had been considerate to attend. He enjoyed the social connections it afforded the children living in the institution.

Hen, who was older, at 23 years, had participated in many connections between the institution and community, which he saw as positive. He was disappointed that they had stopped:

> "The previous director of my welfare institution had connections with [a multinational company]. At that time, the company often visited us, making donations to us and taking us out to resorts, such as parks and zoos or out for other activities. But now, with the new director, there are no longer any activities, and there are very few companies or others making donations."

Zhang also referred to celebrating Spring Festival in the homes of caring people in the community. Spring Festival is traditionally an important family gathering. Many children in the institutions referred to this activity as a positive experience. In Taiyuan, another child referred to an older woman who invited the children to celebrate the Spring Festival at her home each year. Zhang described how his invitation to Spring Festival came from someone who had cared for him in the institution. He interpreted the invitation as reinforcing her continued affection for him. This probably struck him as a contrast to his experience before entering the institution. He said:

> "A caring woman gave me the deepest impression, because she provided meticulous care to me shortly after I arrived at the welfare institution in 2008, as if I were her own child. Last year I celebrated the Spring Festival at her home."

Jian had also been able to take advantage of the practical support that the institution had been able to arrange by linking up with community resources and volunteers to contribute to the children's development. Jian was still a student, aged 19 years, living in the institution. He said:

> "There is a kind volunteer who has given me a lot of help. I am very grateful to that lady, who is really helpful. She works at the Provincial People's Congress. She also helps other children. She helps me in my learning and many other areas. I feel sorry to have bothered her so much."

Significant life changes

Some of the young people noted events that were the most positive childhood memory for them because they contrasted starkly with the difficult times that they had had before. Zeng was a 22-year-old young woman who had experienced ongoing serious domestic violence throughout her early childhood in her birth family. She had witnessed serious family violence, which ended in a house fire that killed her parents and damaged her face. She then lived for some time in an adult welfare institution, but, of course, it was not an appropriate home for a child. In fact, she was thoroughly relieved to leave the institution. She said that her most positive experience was being placed in family group care at the child welfare institution:

> "The most unforgettable experience for me was May 28th when I entered the child institution. Two days later, we had the Children's Day [an official national celebration in China]. I felt as if I just jumped out of an abyss into heaven."

She revelled in her new life in the child welfare institution in contrast to living in the adult facility. Interestingly, her comparison did not explicitly extend to her previous experience living with her abusive family. The new opportunities in the child institution were the first time she had experienced age-appropriate care. She explained that after transferring to the child institution, "for Children's Day, we visited many interesting places which I'd never been to. For example, having a buffet at a restaurant and swimming. I felt I was in a completely different world. So I was most deeply impressed".

Personalized support

Other young people spoke positively of times when the institution considered their individual needs over considerations for the overall management of the institution. For example, Li, the 21 year old introduced earlier as impressed by his teacher's classroom birthday greetings, also experienced mental health problems from the pressure of managing the chronic illness hepatitis B, which was believed to be incurable. He was very sensitive to being discriminated against. He spoke about his most positive childhood experience as being when the institution decided to try a new expensive treatment to help stabilize his illness. He said:

> "I heard that a new drug had become available that was very expensive. At that time, I thought the institution would definitely not care about the drug, as there was no effective cure for my disease. But I remembered our teachers and the director showed strong concerns about my illness condition. I felt deeply moved. I felt loved and cared for after all."

Negative experiences in childhood

The young people also spoke about the negative experiences during their childhood, which mostly related to violence, forced loss of relationships and discrimination.

Emotional support

The practices of welfare institutions during these young people's childhoods did not intentionally deprive the children and young people of their names and personal belongings, but some practices still restricted their identity and privacy. Examples were procedures during reception, including practices that cut them off from non-kin social relationships, as well as 'information collection' that was so detailed that it infringed privacy. These applied to all children entering institutional care.

Some young people also commented that the institutions also needed to improve their social, psychological and emotional support. Bao and Luo, the young men who had grown up in foster care after an initial stay in institutional care, felt that the institutional care was insufficiently focused on the emotional needs of the children. Bao said that welfare institutions had "good enough facilities", but he increasingly felt that "The welfare institution is no more than a place to live in". Luo was more cynical about the lack of emotional support in institutional care, adding that "The teachers were just like machines – they just pass to us the instructions that their bosses have passed to them".

Violence and abuse

Many of the young people had experienced violence living in an institution. The researcher at a focus group of young people living in an institution summarized the discussion about their negative experiences. While talking about whether they had experienced physical violence from the welfare institution staff, all the children became agitated and said that they were beaten or scolded by staff. They said that when they refused to help the workers with the chores, they were beaten and ordered to stand on their knees outside or run outside in the rain as a punishment because, officially, physical punishment is prohibited.

A young woman said that, once, she would not help a worker do chores, and just stayed on bed, ignoring her demands. The woman kept urging her and she quarrelled with the woman. Finally, the worker kicked her hard. She said the kick made her feel great pain. When the teacher at the institution heard the story, she sent her to be checked by the doctor. The young people said that the violence took place when they were young and no longer happened when they grew up because when they were bigger, they could fight back.

Luo, the 23-year-old man introduced earlier who had positive experiences in foster care, had also lived in the institution when he was very young. His said that his worst experience was regularly being denied breakfast as punishment:

> "When I was young, I used to be denied breakfast if I wet the bed. Somehow, I kept wetting the bed and the teachers refused to give me food. But older children offered me some food, and, at that time, I liked to play with them."

Such maltreatment affected their emotional development, as observed by the researchers, including strongly self-protective behaviour, violence and abusive name calling towards each other and the workers. For example, Zhong, the 26-year-old man mentioned earlier, spoke about being physically punished in childhood, which led to him to beat other children:

> "The staff disciplined us strictly … sometimes improperly. They might beat or physically punish children. Some children even had broken bones or other physical injuries.… Shortly after we arrived at the welfare institution, they disciplined us in a harsh way in order to effectively control us. The physical punishment was severe, and the impact on children was negative. For example, children were denied dinner or were beaten or scolded.… So we were both bullied by older children and disciplined by the women staff, facing dual pressures. In a word, we were not very happy there."

Zhong said that he used to beat younger children, replicating his own experience as a younger child. However, he specifically mentioned that after being positively influenced by a teacher, he stopped beating younger children:

> "We had a teacher … who bought educational books, particularly books written by American or UK education experts. I read some of the books, and stopped the habit of beating other children. Instead, I began to oppose beating children. I no longer believed beating was an effective way of disciplining them."

Young people who grew up in informal non-kinship care families also experienced violence in their families. They described how some parents physically punished their children as a way to educate them.

The young people reiterated their affectionate relationship with these parents because they understood the violence as from the love they felt from the parents and the parents' concerns for their children's futures. One young woman, Miao, who was 21 years old and had grown up in an informal non-kinship family, said:

> "I once failed the examination. My teacher made a phone call to my [foster] mother and told her about my examination result. My mother waited for me at the door, holding a rolling pin. I dared not enter the home. My mother wished me to become talented, but I wasn't good enough. Finally, I asked my older sister to enter our home together with me."

Dislocated relationships

Formal foster families managed by welfare institutions are prohibited from physically punishing children; otherwise, they become disqualified from caring for a foster child. No young people who had grown up in foster care mentioned physical punishment in their foster family. Instead, the worst experiences of young people who had lived in foster families were associated with lost affectionate relationships with the families, particularly when they were forcibly removed from the family with whom they were emotionally close. Some children were transferred back to the welfare institutions from the foster families due to the Beijing policy changes described in Chapter Three. They said that this was their worst childhood experience.

One example was Hen, the 23 year old who had moved between institutional care, foster care and back to institutional care. At the age of 14 years, Hen was transferred back to the welfare institution from the foster family where he had lived since he was four years old. Initially, Hen was not accustomed to the welfare institution environment. Everything in the institution was unfamiliar and he felt the loss of his foster family. He vividly described the contrast:

> "Previously, all my family members sat around table, having dinner. But now [at the institution], a group of children sit in row, having a restricted dinner and stopping even if we do not feel full. At the beginning, I felt very homesick, but I never told the other children about my bad feelings. My parents visited me several times, but the stipulation of the institution prohibited frequent visiting. One year, they

picked me up to celebrate the Spring Festival at home....
All in all, everything started over. I felt like a chess piece
placed by others at will."

This feeling of loss when relationships were broken by administrative
decisions was also shared by young people who had grown up in family
groups within institutions. In one institution, all the young people in
care participating in the research grew up in family group care and
treated each other as siblings within the family group. Li, the 21 year
old referred to earlier who had treatment for hepatitis, recounted that
when a younger child he looked after at the welfare institution was
adopted internationally, Li never saw the child again. He said that he
would always feel pain from this loss:

> "In my childhood, some older children were charged to
> look after younger children. I looked after a child much
> younger than me. He made a strong impression on me.
> But he was taken out of the country.... He was basically
> brought up by me, and I was responsible for his clothing
> and dinner. So I felt heartbroken when he was taken away."

Discrimination

Within some formal foster families arranged by welfare institutions,
some young people felt that the parents treated their birth children
better than them, which made them feel unhappy. Hen, the 23-year-
old young man introduced earlier, felt this inequity, but, despite
this, he said that he still felt deep affection towards his foster family
and missed the family very much after he was forced to leave and
return to the institution. This tension and acceptance of a less-than-
ideal relationship might be explained by the lack of similar familial
relationships in their lives.

Other young people who grew up in an institution felt discriminated
against and stigmatized by other people in the community because
they lived in state care. Bing, the 28-year-old married man mentioned
earlier, explained:

> "When I attended school [in the community], teachers
> and classmates discriminated against me because I have no
> family. I was looked down upon by all the people. I even
> wanted to die in the past and felt everything in the world
> was meaningless, particularly because some students are

accompanied by their parents and they enjoy love and care from families. I felt even worse seeing that."

Summary of experiences of support during childhood

This chapter has focused on the young people's memories of the good and bad parts of their childhood to understand how their experience of state care contributed to their social inclusion during their childhood. It introduced some of the young people who reappear in the later chapters because this examination of childhood experiences is important for understanding the context and likely impact on their adulthood, their transition, their expectations and their aspirations for independence from state care or not.

When asked about their memories of their childhood, most of the young people only referred to the time in state care, either because they were too young when they entered care to have earlier memories or because the time in state care was the most formative for them. They referred to positive experiences that reinforced their motivation for greater participation in the community with other children and young people, such as kind acts from adults in the institution and in the community, and opportunities to play, celebrate and learn with other children. The care shown by people in the community to the children, particularly exhibited in repeated, direct interactions, such as New Year parties and invitations to join families in the community for significant celebrations, left the children with good memories of the willingness of community members to consider them as part of their community. If they lived in foster care or family-based care, they recounted close family relationships that included love and affection and reinforced their sense of belonging within the family.

Institutional care does not offer family relationships and only limited community integration with other children who are not in state care. However, the young people referred to positive relationships within that constraint, such as sibling-type relationships if they grew up in family group care in the institution and attended a local school. If they suffered discrimination in these settings, not all these experiences were positive. The young people referred to some positive relationships with teachers and institution directors when they felt respected and benefitted from the commitment of the person looking after their well-being.

While they referred to the stigma of being in state care, particularly if they were living in an institution, very few of them referred to the disadvantage of their disabilities. Perhaps this is because they were socially isolated in general, the institution staff did not discriminate against them on the basis of their disability and the costs of disability therapy and medical support were covered by the institution. Some of them referred to how their early experiences negatively affected their later years, for example, violence from peers and workers in the institutions. Sadly, the loss of positive early experiences, such as being forced to leave foster care, meant that the negative contrast of shifting to institutional care was even harsher.

Violence, maltreatment and social discrimination towards children in care lead to unforgettable harm and pain, affecting their emotional development and behaviour. The most prevalent negative experiences were associated with memories about violence in the institutions from workers and older children, despite the official view that 'institutional care is safer for children'. It implies that the violence experienced by children in institutions is hidden from people outside the institutions. In addition, the young people referred to administrative violence, such as forcing children who were living in foster families to return to institutions, ignoring the preferences of the children and families. These administrative traumas were heightened by the practice of discouraging continued contact between the child and their former foster family. Similar emotional damage was experienced when children were separated from their peers by adoption, without mechanisms to continue the sibling-like relationships that they had established in the institution or foster care.

In contrast, the young people who had grown up in foster care did not refer to physical violence in their families, which indicates that the monitoring of foster care standards that prohibit physical punishment might be reasonably successful. Vigilance to maintain the implementation of these standards would continue to contrast it with both institutional care in China and poor-quality foster care in many other countries. The next chapters explore the experience of these young people when they consider their future beyond state care.

SIX

Self-identity of young people leaving state care

The remaining chapters address four aspects of the transition to adulthood of young people leaving care: establishing self-identity; employment and economic independence; independent housing; and social participation, friends, family and social networking. Each chapter examines the experience of the young people in their transition to adulthood and leaving care against the child rights and social inclusion framework. Does the welfare institution support them during their childhood and teenage years to achieve social inclusion in their young adulthood and do they experience their rights to transition towards independent living in the same way as their peers in their communities? This chapter explores the self-identity, with reference to social inclusion, of the young people in care in their transition to adulthood and the possibility of independent living. It focuses on how the various aspects of social inclusion during childhood and young adult years might affect their identity.

Formation of identity

In addition to the usual dynamic identity formation of teenagers, young people leaving care also negotiate the shedding of an identity as someone in the care of the state and the acquiring of an identity as an independent young adult. These processes have important policy implications because they imply that transition to independence of children in state care requires a care approach and environment that are supportive to positive identity formation during childhood and adolescence (Anghel, 2011).

Identity crisis is a concept proposed by American psychologist Erikson (1968). In its simplest description, identity is the perception about who the self is, how the person fits in their community, what they will become in the future and how they become the person that they want to be. During teenage years, children's rapid physiological and emotional growth repositions them in relation to the adults in their lives as they explore new ways of expressing their independence. Their sense of identity changes in relation to these adults, their peers and other people around them. Is this the same for young people leaving care in China?

Erikson argues that the dynamic changes during teenage years can also affect adulthood if questions of identity are threatened. If they fail to reach satisfaction in their identity, they may continue to experience role confusion, affecting their future life. He argues that this time is critical to young people because it is a time of transition away from childhood to young adulthood and future responsibilities. During childhood, they become aware of who they are, what they can do and the various roles that they can play. In teenage years, they are at a point when they can reflect on the knowledge and experiences about themselves and the community that they have accumulated so far, and begin to make decisions about their approach to their life possibilities. These reflections, decisions and approaches contribute to their sense of identity as a young adult.

Rather than relying on Erikson's predictions about crisis or the linear development of identity, the chapter uses his framework to understand the dynamism of identity in the context of state care. Wang and Viney (1997) also applied Erikson's framework to understand identity in children in China, but from a developmental approach rather than to understand the impact of the structural context on children.

More recent literature has built on Erikson's framework to focus on identity status (about current conceptions) or narrative identity (about understanding the past). McLean and Pasupathi (2012) propose a return to Erikson by incorporating these two theoretical approaches to understand how identity exploration is carried out through narrative processing. This chapter applies this narrative approach to Erikson's framework by analysing young people's stories to the researchers about their past and current experiences. In this way, their narratives reveal their feelings about their identity during this time of transition.

Young people living in state care face additional challenges while they grapple with their changing sense of identity. This chapter examines this question in relation to social inclusion because it offers a way of understanding these additional challenges. Erikson's argument is that childhood experiences affect their process of identity formation. Young people in care are likely to have experienced many challenges, related to the loss of their birth parents, their disability, their isolation if they live in institutional care, stigma and social attitudes towards their status, and other differences experienced or perceived. The chapter applies Erikson's questions to understand how the young people understand these challenges and the impact on their identity formation: 'Who am I?'; 'What position shall I occupy in the community?'; 'What kind of

Table 6.1: Young people in the identity research sample

Alias	Sex	Age	Disability	Education	Employed or studying	Housing	Married	Alternative care	Place
Mao	M	40	Yes	Primary	Unemployed	Dormitory welfare institution	No	Institution	Taiyuan
Jing	F	38	Yes	Junior middle	Employed at massage clinic	Family unit welfare institution	Yes	Institution	Taiyuan
Mei	F	34	Yes	Junior middle	Employed at child welfare institution	Family unit welfare institution	Yes	Institution	Taiyuan
Bing	M	28	No	Technical secondary	Employed	Family unit welfare institution	Yes	Institution	Taiyuan
Liao	M	26	No	Technical secondary	Unemployed	Dormitory welfare institution	No	Institution	Taiyuan
Jin	M	26	Yes	Technical college	Employed at massage clinic	Dormitory welfare institution	No	Institution	Taiyuan
Xue	F	29	Yes	Technical secondary	Student	Dormitory welfare institution	No	Institution	Taiyuan
Xi	F	24	Yes	Technical college	Employed at child welfare institution	Dormitory welfare institution	No	Mixed	Taiyuan
Xin	M	23	No	Technical secondary	Employed[a]	Dormitory welfare institution	No	Mixed	Beijing
Luo	M	23	No	Technical secondary	Employed[a]	Private rental	No	Mixed	Beijing
Bo	M	22	No	Technical secondary	Unemployed	Dormitory welfare institution	No	Mixed	Taiyuan
Miao	F	21	No	Technical college	Student	Foster family	No	Mixed	Taiyuan
Guan	M	21	No	Technical secondary	Employed	Private rental	No	Mixed	Beijing
Ning	F	20	No	Technical college	Student	Dormitory school	No	Mixed	Taiyuan
Jian	M	19	No	Junior middle	Student	Dormitory welfare institution	No	Institution	Taiyuan
Jiang	M	19	No	Technical secondary	Unpaid intern	Foster family	No	Foster	Taiyuan
Miu	F	16	No	Technical secondary	Student	Dormitory school	No	Mixed	Taiyuan

Notes: Data from 2013 in Beijing. M = male; F = female. [a] Waiting for a government-arranged job.

person do I want to become in the future?'; and 'How can I become the person that I want to be?'.

The case examples are a subset of 14 of the young people participating in the research (see Appendix 1), including seven young women and six young people with disabilities (see Table 6.1). Two of them lived in foster families and two boarded at school. The rest of them had grown up and still lived in the institution. Two of the women were married.

Who am I?

The first part of Erikson's framework for understanding identity seeking in teenage years is 'Who am I?'. Children growing up in stable family environments are likely to experience various early life relationships that help them discover consistent, positive responses to this question. In contrast, the multiple significant events and relationship changes in the childhood of most children in care could be expected to affect their teenage identity processes.

Self-knowledge about being abandoned as a baby

Many children growing up in welfare institutions have memories or stories about being abandoned or losing their parents or carers. Their experiences of loss and lack of emotional connection, in the absence of alternative stable parental love, particularly for children living in an institution, could be expected to challenge their sense of self during their teenage years.

Some young people in state care were abandoned by their family to the state welfare institutions when they were very young. Others were raised by community members in a family environment before they sent the children to the welfare institution. The reasons for becoming state wards ranged from difficult but instrumental decisions about access to necessary medical and disability interventions, to poverty and family planning restrictions. Irrespective of the reason, knowing that they were abandoned by their families seriously affected the emotional well-being of many of the young people. They spoke about how the thought that 'nobody wants me' was the deepest pain in their heart.

Not all the young people described their feelings about when they initially knew that they were abandoned by their family. Many children were placed in the institution when they were very young. Unless the alternative care that the children received was in a foster family, they remained in the institution at least until their adulthood.

They only had a vague perception of 'being abandoned' and weaker emotional reactions compared to children who had ever lived in a family environment. In the interviews with these young people, most of them simply mentioned the fact of abandonment, without giving the narration with strong feelings. For example, two young adult women who still lived in the institution said:

> "My name is [Xue]. I'm 29 years old. I was abandoned at an early age due to spina bifida. Then, I have stayed in the welfare institution for nearly 30 years."

> "I was sent to the welfare institution even before my umbilical cord came off." (Jing)

Other children receiving financial support from the child welfare institution were raised by community members and spent all or part of their childhood in families, discussed in detail in Chapter Ten. During their childhood, due to school enrolment or other reasons, the community families needed to register the children for permanent residence and approached the welfare institution for this purpose. These children had a stronger emotional reaction to the loss of their birth family. Some of these children described their feelings about initially being told about their early family experience as deeply disturbing. Even when they had later experienced strong alternative family connections to the informal foster care families, the fact of their abandonment remained distressing. For instance, Xi, who was aged 24 years and now lived in an institution, described how:

> "One day in 1988, I was born to this beautiful world. Due to congenital disability in both hands, I was abandoned by my cruel-hearted parents. I was then picked up by a woman collecting recycled materials for her livelihood, and raised by her until I was 12 years of age. Without her, I would definitely have died in the cold winter."

Similarly, Miao was raised by her foster 'grandmother' when her parents abandoned her. When her foster grandmother died, she entered state care and was placed in foster care. She was aged 21 and still living in foster care at the time of the interview, in which she said:

> "Since I could remember, I had lived with my grandmother. In my view, she was always warm, kind and easy-going....

After my grandmother passed away, I often recalled my nice memories of the times together with my grandmother. I think although my grandmother is no longer in this world, the cherished memories created between us will always be kept in my heart.... I came to know about my background when I was 12 years of age. My heart was then overshadowed by endless introversion and inferiority, and I became uncommunicative and did not like to spend time with other children."

The child welfare institution that had guardianship for Miao has well-developed practices to support continuity for children found in the community. It facilitates arrangements for the children to stay with their informal foster family and provides the foster family with financial and other support. Only if the informal foster family could definitely not continue to care for the children, such as in Xi's case introduced earlier, do the children shift to institutional care. These arrangements allow the children to grow up in a household in the community with known relationships.

However, when some children moved between different forms of care, they described the emotional damage that the shift had done to them. Unlike the two young women, Xi and Miao, earlier in this section, Bo, a young man aged 22 years without disabilities, felt disadvantaged compared to children growing up at the welfare institution since they were very young. At the time of the research, he was aged 22 years, living back in the institution, unemployed and unhappy to be living there. He said: "No, and I think I might have been mentally hurt more seriously. The experience of receiving foster care first, and being sent to the welfare institution, and then back to foster care is particularly terrible".

Bo's history was that he was found when he was very young. The woman who found and looked after him as his informal foster 'grandmother', died when he was eight years old. The nurse of his grandmother then became his informal foster mother until he was 13 years old. He believed that his foster grandmother and foster parents treated him as their own child. When his foster father became unemployed, they had no way to support him, so they sent him to the welfare institution. As is the practice at Taiyuan described earlier, the institution sent him back to his foster parents with financial support. When his foster parents left Taiyuan, he moved back to the institution because he was already more than 18 years old and could receive housing and other benefits. He maintains regular contact with his foster family.

Naming children in state care

Some historical practices of welfare institutions inadvertently had negative effects on the development of the identities of the children in their care. For example, the family name of most of the children was unknown, so they were given a nationalistic family surname, such as Dang, Fu or Guo, when they entered state care. Dang means Party, as in the Chinese Community Party, implying that they were children of the Party; Fu means welfare; and Guo means country. The practice of renaming them Dang or similar names was intended as an honour, but the effect was to label the children as orphans without family, attracting stigma. In addition, they were also often only called by a nickname rather than their real given first name or they were only named with a number as their given name. These practices started to end in the 1980s in the better institutions.

The young people in the research recounted how during their teenage years, the surname Dang was a source of shame because it indicated that they were raised in an institution rather than a family, and they tried to evade the surname by claiming it is a different 'Dang' surname. In contrast to children growing up in their family environment, they viewed their surname as a source of shame. For example, Jin, a young man aged 26 years who grew up at the welfare institution and still lived there, said:

> "While speaking to my clients [at the massage clinic], they might ask me 'Doesn't the surname of "Dang" suggest children raised at the child welfare institution?" But I do not want them to know I was an orphan, and I just say that there is a traditional Chinese family name 'Dang', because I do not want them to view me as pitiful."

Most children raised in foster families have a different surname from their foster parents, which draws other people's attention to their status as an orphan. For example, Bo shifted between informal foster care, institutional care and back. He said that when he lived with the family, having a different surname was a problem for him at school because of the stigma of being an orphan. He still keeps his orphan status secret, which is easier because his surname is not Dang. He described how difficult the name problem had been in the community:

> "My surname was different from that of my foster parents, so I was viewed by some people as an abandoned child ever since I attended primary school. But my surname is not Dang, so out of the school, people do not know that I was raised at a welfare institution. Only my best friends know that; my average friends do not know that, let alone strangers."

Some young people who grew up in an institution said that the institution staff did not show them respect – the staff called them by nicknames related to their physical disabilities, rather than their given name, which was stigmatizing. Jing, the 38-year-old woman introduced earlier, described her reaction to the institution staff using these nicknames:

> "I did not care about that when I was not attending school, but after I started school, it affected my self-confidence. When I was back at the welfare institution, I told them not to call me by the nickname. They said they had always called me that, so why had I never reacted negatively until now? I said I had begun to attend school and had grown up. Later, they gradually became used to calling me by my real name."

Jing attended a school for children who are blind, where the teachers paid attention to not using discriminatory names and language. She had low vision rather than complete blindness, and had done well at school, gaining a job and marrying, though she continued to live in a family unit at the institution.

My position in the community?

Erikson's second question about identity processes during young adulthood is: 'What position do I occupy in the community?'. The type of alternative care that the children lived in and their exposure to social discrimination during their childhood and teenage years affected their expectations about their social relationships, their place in their community and where and who their community is. The young people discussed the effect of stigma on the way they thought of themselves, in relation to the people they knew, their communities and the way members of the community treated them. At worst, they described stories of thoughtless and explicit discrimination.

Family relationships

Most children who grew up in foster families reflected on the strong care and emotional bonds with their foster parents and extended family. Children who had grown up in institutional care did not have the opportunity for family relationships. With a strong sense of belonging, Ying, introduced in Chapter One, said of her foster mother: 'My mother now regards us as her own children". Talking about leaving home for school, she said:

> "I didn't want to leave but then I changed my mind, thinking that it was not bad to go out to see the world. In addition, for whatever difficulties I would have out there, the home would always be my harbour where I could get my broken heart together. Now, when I am in the community and see the competition around me, I feel more of the warmth of my family home."

Many foster families continued to have close bonds with the young people after the formal foster relationship had finished. These young people had continuous relationships with their foster families, which had reciprocal emotional and material benefits. Asked whether he comes back to visit his foster family now that he has grown up, Luo said: "Sure I often come back, at New Year and other festivals or whenever I want, like going back to my own home". Even though he lived and worked independently at age 23 years, his foster family supported him, as would be expected by other young people his age. Luo said: "I earn my own living, but I can ask my mother for more money when I need it".

The different feelings between the young people about their relationships with their foster families depended on many factors. They included how old they were when they entered foster care, how many times they had changed alternative care before foster care, the foster care style of their foster parents and whether the foster-family dynamic was compatible with the child's personality. Some children and young people were integrated into their foster families and were treated as if they were any other child in the family. However, some young people were not comfortable with their foster-family life. Some of them who lived with other children of the foster family felt that the foster children were sometimes unfairly treated. Guan was aged 21 years and had grown up in institutional care and later in foster care. He was one of the few young people who had left his foster care family and was living in private rental housing. He said of his foster-family home:

> "I don't think that is my home because I don't have a feeling of family there. They foster us just for the state subsidies, and we went there just because the welfare institution asked us to experience the life there."

Social relationships

The young people's relationships in their social networks reflected whether they had grown up in institutional or foster care and where they had attended school and work. Like other young people, their connections included friends, schoolmates and workmates. In addition, they had connections to peers and staff at the welfare institutions or foster-family members.

Friendship circles included schoolmates, workmates and peers at the institutions. These peer relationships were particularly important for the young people in institutional care because they filled many of the functions of other intimate and family relationships. Some young people had acquired their jobs through recommendations by their friends, discussed more in Chapter Eight. Not all the young people in the larger study had attended school, particularly if they had disabilities, and many of them did not have employment in the community. These young people had almost no opportunities to make friends outside the institution.

Most of the young people who had made friends at school during their childhood or work when they left school said that they had not encountered overt discrimination. Others experienced discrimination about their disability, being a state ward and living in the institution. Now that they were older, some young people avoided further discrimination by not telling other people, especially workmates, about their state ward status until they were established friends. For example, Xin, who was aged 23 years old and did not have disabilities, described how he explains his family experience to his workmates: "I don't tell any other person about my story until we are intimate to a certain degree". He had grown up in institutional and foster care and still lived in the institution dormitory because his job did not provide housing and he could not afford to live elsewhere.

Almost all the young people in the case studies were unmarried. Three of the oldest who had grown up in institutional care remained living there with their spouses: Bing, aged 28 years, was the only man;

and Jing and Mei, 38- and 34-year-old women. Three other women were also married and had grown up in foster care or a mix of care. Mo was aged 28 and had grown up in foster care, but now lived in a family unit at the institution with her husband. Hai, aged 29, and Min, aged 21, both lived in private rental with their husbands. They all had disabilities except Bing and Min. Their stories are told in later chapters.

Most of the unmarried young people in the research were probably too young to draw firm conclusions about future marriage. Some staff from the welfare institutions observed that it was difficult for state wards, especially for young men, to find love and marriage due to their low socio-economic status, lack of employment and housing, and discrimination, discussed more in later chapters.

The major difference between the social networks of the young people was whether they had any experience of foster care or other community living during their childhood. Those who had foster care experience had additional ties with their foster families and other people in the local community of the foster family. Some of the young people who had foster families had also lived in institutional care, so they also had ties in the institution. If they had left institutional care when they were very young, these ties were distant or only functional. The young people who had only lived in institutional care did not have ties with families in the community.

Stigma about disability, orphans and state wards

Some of the young people recognized how their social position was marginalized through their childhood experiences and discrimination. Many of them had a clear understanding of their current social position from having grown up in state care. For example, Long was a young man aged 35 years old and living in the institution. His parents had died when he was aged six years old. He wrote:

> "We are marginalized and different from normal people. Except the limited support from the government, we have to earn what we need by ourselves, such as income, networking and relationships. What I need most at present is a preferential low-cost rental flat or a cheap non-commercial apartment for low-income families."

Some of the earlier examples also demonstrate the stigma that some of the young people received about their disabilities, losing their birth family or being raised in state care. This was particularly the case during their childhood with social interactions in the community, such as attending school and playing with other children. In addition, once they reached their teenage years, these negative childhood experiences contributed to low self-esteem in their current identity formation. They described wanting to reject their situation, including where they lived, their disabilities and how other people treated them. They were susceptible to feeling inferior and discriminated against. Sometimes, the circumstances were discriminatory; in other situations, the young people wanted to change their conditions. For example, some of the young people with disabilities were very sensitive to their physical impairments. Jing, the young woman who had married and was working, described her reaction when she was a child to the discrimination about her disabilities and as a state ward:

> "I have albinism. I had my hair dyed when I was 26 years old. Before that, I always attracted people's curious eyes. If they only stared at me without saying anything, I still felt OK; but if they made verbal comments, I would feel very bad. I was reclusive before I was 25 years old and stayed in the room by myself most of the time. When some adults visited the welfare institution to offer care and assistance, other children would go out to meet them and receive snacks or something interesting, but I would stay in the room alone, with my back facing the window. The visitors would look into the room. Maybe they thought an old woman lived in the room."

She also described that now she was older (38 years), she was more comfortable with her situation and more confident about social interaction. She gave an example of confidence in her work at a massage clinic, which is common professional training and employment for people with vision impairments. She explained:

> "When I grew up, I worked at a massage clinic. A man had met me at the welfare institution when I was young. While receiving the massage service, he met me again, and asked whether my surname is Dang. I said yes. He said he used to see me at the welfare institution. He talked to me for a while, and said that I had looked very introverted and reclusive at the welfare institution, but that now I had changed completely."

Some of the discrimination was from the lack of protection and the position of pity that the children were placed in by the institution in order to gain support for the work of the institution. Often, when community members came to the institution, their words, actions and inactions ignored the emotional interests and choices of the children. Xi, a young woman, had physical impairments in her hands and was now working in the institution. She described the stigma that they felt about themselves and the discomfort she endured from interactions with visitors to the welfare institution and local community members when she was a child:

> "The visitors looked at us with a strange facial expression, as if we were elephants or monkeys at the zoo. People living nearby also knew that we lived at the welfare institution. We were born with a label of the institution, as if the words 'welfare institution' were printed on our faces. We felt uncomfortable at hearing people mentioning the institution."

Qian (2014) similarly refers to this as the violence of philanthropy, where children are positioned for the benefit of visitors and donors. One young man, Jin, now 26 and working but still living at the institution, said that the lack of control over participating in the visitors' activities continued even into his young adulthood:

> "Some activities organized by the welfare institution are just superficial and purely utilitarian. Many media are invited and we have to cooperate in having photos taken of us. They are not caring for us from the heart. We have our own privacy. Such activities demonstrate a miserable life for children in the welfare institution. In fact, we have satisfactory living conditions. Outsiders generally view us through coloured spectacles. We feel uncomfortable and are reluctant to meet them."

In contrast, some trustworthy community members showed repeated, reliable care for the children. These people were liked and remembered by the children, contributing a positive impact on their sense of identity and possibility in their lives. Jing, a 38-year-old woman, referred to one regular visitor with the respectful, affectionate term 'Grandma'. Jing said of her:

"Grandma Jia is an opera performer and very kind to us. Since 2004, we have a get-together at her home three times every year, respectively on May 3rd, October 3rd and the third day of Chinese New Year [traditional family celebration days]. Each time, she offers a big meal, sings songs together with us and talks with us. We are all very happy at her home. Grandma Jia never looks down upon us and we enjoy the feeling of equality."

Expectations for social connections, education and employment

Having grown up feeling marginalized and discriminated against, many of the young people felt that their social position was compromised and that this affected their ability to build rapport with others. Xi, the 24-year-old young woman working in the institution, said:

"I feel inferior communicating with strangers. I'm afraid that they will mention my hand disability and that I grew up in the welfare institution.... Some people want to help me find a husband, but I worry that other people will dislike me because I was in the welfare institution and my disability."

They also distrusted some people in the community and felt unvalued by them because of the repeated poor experiences during their childhood. They gave the example of visitors to the welfare institution failing to follow up on their commitments to the children. Xi said:

"Outsiders are always busily taking photos. We don't like it. Some college students visiting the welfare institution promised to come soon, but failed to keep their word. For example, some children talked very happily with a girl for the whole morning. By the end, the girl told the children that she would come soon, but never came back. All children liked her and hoped to meet her again. She did not keep her word and the children felt hurt. In fact, many visitors made such promises, but failed to keep their promises. Many children [living in the institution] face many psychological problems after attending school."

Some orphans had extreme reactions to the discrimination they faced, such as refusal to attend school and unwillingness to work. If staff in the welfare institution did not protect the children, at worst, they dropped out of school. Some of the children refused to attend school due to discrimination, leading to lifelong regret. One such young man was Bing. He had since found a job and married, though he still lived in the institution. Reflecting on the discrimination in his school, he said:

> "I remembered in the second semester of Grade 7 [at a school in the community], my younger sister [another child in the institution] was bullied by other students [who lived with their families]. I went to help her and fought with these students. A teacher criticized me. I kept silent at the beginning. Later, another teacher came and also criticized me. I countered: 'Do orphans deserve to be bullied?'. The teachers said 'Yes'. After that, I gradually started to refuse to attend school and finally dropped out of school."

The impact of discrimination and low confidence had a detrimental effect on some young people's work opportunities. Xi was the young woman working in the rehabilitation department of the institution because she had not been able to tolerate the discrimination in the open labour market. She said of her previous jobs in the community:

> "After I started to work, I was discriminated against by others and had to avoid their eyes. I was unhappy and had a deep feeling of inferiority. Due to psychological pressure, I finally came back to the welfare institution and now work as a temporary worker."

Social discrimination from various sources, especially in schools, has a tremendous negative impact on the state wards. Some consequences will lead to lifelong regret for children, such as their refusal to continue to attend school, and weaken their trust in the community. They needed support in the welfare institution to prevent and address the psychological problems facing the children. The lack of such services influenced the development of the children.

What kind of person do I want to become in the future?

Erikson's third identity question is: 'What kind of person do I want to become in the future?'. Social exclusion and discrimination during childhood can have a negative impact on the way in which young people consider the various aspects of this question, including knowing that they can have life goals, identifying what their goals might be and having the capacity and support to pursue them (Shang et al, 2011). The young people in the research were bewildered about what a life goal was and answered the question with the encompassing response that their life goal was to be "living like normal people". Normal, in this context, represented to them the flip side of the stigma described earlier: to live independently with their own home, job and family.

Historically, most welfare institutions did not support the children to think about or plan for their life goals or to develop ambitions. They did not provide the children with guidance about how to develop life goals. In retrospect, this rather artificial process would have been necessary because without family members or living in a community, they were isolated from the usual family and community role models from whom they would develop such aspirations. As a consequence, many of the young people had not thought about their life goals. Jing, the 38-year-old woman, said that when she was ready to leave school, "The teacher asked me what my aspiration was. I was confused and said I did not know what an aspiration is". Similarly, Jin, the 26 year old who works in a massage clinic, recounted his confusion when he was asked a similar question while he was still at school:

> "I like singing and want to be a musician. However, when the teacher asked me what my ideal was, I said I want to be a writer. In fact, I did not know what a writer was and thought that a writer was a singer. I was embarrassed after the teacher explained what a writer is."

A few young people in care were fostered informally or formally and grew up in families. Compared to the young people who had grown up in institutional care, they had higher expectations for their future, including creating their own businesses. Jiang was aged 19 years and lived in a foster family. He already had a range of employment experiences and had ambitions for how to gain economic security for himself and his foster family. He said:

> "I did many different jobs, such as selling TVs, drinks and shampoos. I want to first find a stable job and then open my own store. In this way, I can make great improvements to my family and my life."

Despite her initial bewilderment about what having ambitions meant, now that Jing was 38 years old, married and had experience working in a massage clinic, she was starting to consider opening her own massage clinic in several years. Most of the young people identified their ideal as 'living like normal people'. One young man, Mao, described his ideal as follows:

> "I'm in my late 30s and still worry about marriage and my knowledge gap. Orphans like me hope to live a normal life, enjoy normal marriage and have adequate social relations. We want to enrich ourselves and keep up with the community. I also dream to attend classes, enjoy smiles from students and teachers and witness the access of special children to comprehensive education. Thus, I'm eager to return to school with those just like me and realize our dreams."

Xue was aged nearly 30 years and was a student who still lived in the institution at the time of the research. Her ambitions were general, based on having learned craft skills, but she did not refer to particular jobs or a path towards employment. She said:

> "I never went to school due to my disability [spina bifida], but I try my best to read and I know many words and have learnt a lot. Under the guidance of teachers and other people in the welfare institution, I have mastered skills for knitting woollen garments and underpants and making crafts. I have come to like cross-stitch embroidery gradually and now it is my strong point. I hope to have a stable job and enrich my life!"

Jin was working in a massage clinic and said that compared to children who had grown up in a family, he had limited capacity to find a good job so that he could form meaningful relationships. He said that:

> "I hope to earn my own living in the future. I lost my parents at an early age, so some things may be different for me from normal families. It is easy for people with a family to get married, but marriage is a luxurious dream for people like us. The chances are very few and we have to make all efforts by ourselves. First of all, it is essential to have a stable job. Then, I can leverage what I have learnt

to help other people reduce pain [as a massage therapist], become a productive member in the community and realize my own values."

All the young people hoped to return to the mainstream community and live a normal life like other young people. Those who had lived in families, through foster care or informal care arrangements, had more ambitious life goals and higher expectations for their future. The older young adults who had grown up in institutional care and had successfully secured employment, such as Jing and Jin, also seemed to gain these more ambitious goals as they grew older and attained more work and social experience.

How can I become the person that I want to be?

The final question in identity formation is: 'How can I become the person that I want to be?'. The findings show that the social exclusion of the young people during their childhood was reflected in their shortage of human, social and economic capital when they reached the point when they were making plans about how to enter the community in the ways they wished. Although most young people in state care, particularly those in institutional care, had only basic life goals to live like normal people, in practice, they had few resources to draw on to achieve this. In addition, they were trying to enter the community at a time when China is undergoing social and economic change, removing the previous structures that might have supported their reintegration.

Education and interpersonal skills

The young people's shortage of human capital was reflected in the low level of education that most of them had received and achieved, as well as the limited disability support and disability-inclusive education available to many of them during their childhood. The exceptions were young people who had grown up in the community through informal foster care arrangements and whose foster families had contacted the welfare institution once they reached school age to obtain permanent residence registration to access schooling. These children were generally healthy and only had mild disabilities. They were brought up by their informal foster parents as their own children, with the usual expectations about gaining educational qualifications.

Like most urban children, they had received higher education at technical colleges and universities.

In contrast, most children in the welfare institution had more severe disabilities and very limited access to education. Without an inclusive childhood, including access to education and social connections with peers without disabilities who grew up in families, it was very difficult for these young people to even articulate and realize the most basic goal of leaving the welfare institution and living a similar life to their peers in the community.

When they attempted to find paid employment, they began to recognize the importance of educational attainment and their missed social and educational opportunities relative to other children. Mao was aged 40 years, left school after primary school, was unemployed, had a physical disability, lived in the institution and was unmarried. He lamented the segregated care, lack of education and social isolation experienced by him and his peers during their childhood in institutional care. He blamed that segregation on his lack of capacity to achieve his goals during his adulthood:

> "Children with normal intelligence should receive normal education. It is very important for children to know more about the community. Orphans can live a normal life if they possess necessary skills. Otherwise, they can only stand in the way of social progress without an adequate educational background and skill mix."

As well as formal education and job-related skills, many young people who grew up in institutional care without an experience of family life had limited interpersonal communication skills. Again, they began to recognize and regret such deprivation when they sought independence as young adults. Jing, the 38-year-old woman, had entered the institution as a newborn baby and spent her entire childhood there. Now she had her own children, she described the contrast with her own childhood experience:

> "When I was young, workers in the welfare institution were temporarily recruited from neighbouring villages and did not go through formal examinations. Temporary workers were poor-quality, posing a negative influence on children. They said rude words and so did the children. When I was at the primary school, teachers had a bad impression of me. They thought I was very uncivilized and always called

me names. Now, I have learnt a lot about interpersonal communication, but I still need further improvement."

Jing concluded that staff in the welfare institution did not care for the children in the same way as parents would, both in emotional development and teaching them socially acceptable behaviour. She said:

> "At that time, some nursery staff were willing to stay with children for a long time, but they did not know how to encourage children emotionally. Good children are always a result of being encouraged and praised. However, only very few nursery staff and teachers were familiar with encouraging children and increasing their self-confidence.... Parents will remind children not to say rude words all the time. In the welfare institution, children will also be reminded, but not every time. Consequently, I looked like a naughty boy in my childhood and was criticized by other people."

Social isolation

The second aspect of barriers to attaining their future goals is social isolation during childhood. Most children growing up in institutional care, especially historically, were socially isolated, with a single social network restricted to within the institution. Not only did they lack family connections, but they also lacked social connections with other children and wider community interactions. They seldom had opportunities for incidental interaction with community members, such as walking in the street or shopping, let alone organized social settings, such as schools and sports and social clubs. Some institutions now offer some children who live in institutional care greater opportunities for this type of interaction, for example, if the children with mild disabilities attend a local school. The stigma and discrimination about their disability, having been orphaned and being state wards described earlier does not necessarily mean that these are wholly positive experiences.

Life within the welfare institution is in the context of restricted living space and limited scope for interpersonal interaction. Communication is mainly with peers, staff and visitors. Relationships with peers in the institution can be frequent, deep and direct, as well as a source of emotional and practical support and solidarity within the group of children living together. Equally, the intense interaction can be negative, including violence from staff or peers, as described in Chapter Five.

The strength of the mutual support and solidarity formed during childhood can be a protective mechanism for children in institutional care. Jing, the 38-year-old woman who had grown up in the institution, said: "Children in the welfare institution develop solidarity. If one child is bullied, other children will help the child strike back". They were referring to protecting each other within the institution and in the community. In institutions where the children attended a local community school, their mutual support extended to the school playground. Mei, who had grown up in the institution as a child with disabilities and now worked there, described this solidarity in her own childhood and in that of the children she now cares for: "In school, children from the welfare institution tend to play with each other". Mei explained that as young adults, they continued this tight pattern of friendship with the people they knew from the institution: "We generally organize our own activities, such as going to KTV [karaoke] halls and parks, and seldom have contact with others. This is because many of our peers have disabilities and are looked down upon by others".

These young people shared common life experiences and emotional attachment, but also shared stigma, discrimination and limited experience of forming relationships with other children or young people. Jing also drew conclusions about the impact of her isolated childhood on her self-confidence and capacity to interact with peers as a young adult. She said:

> "I also feel confused in communication with others during work. I have never had many friends, perhaps because I was self-reclusive since I was very young. I did not know whether others were kind to me or not. Even if others held a bad attitude towards me once, I would have a horrible feeling about myself. This feeling still affects my family now."

The economic situation of many of the young people also accentuated their social difference in their young adulthood. Few of them had stable jobs and adequate economic resources, which further inhibited their possibilities for participating in other social activities with young people who had wider resources. In contrast, the young people in care who had grown up in a formal or informal foster family had a larger social network. Jiang, the 19 year-old man who was raised in a foster family, was more active in job hunting, for example. He had the understanding from his family contacts about how to use social relations to help him find a job. He explained his strategies to look for work:

"I went to [the city] human resource department, labour market and work units of friends. I worked as a salesman. I like such jobs. I hope to obtain support from the welfare institution [to find a permanent job], and I will try my best too."

The limited social networks of and lack of family support for the young people who grew up in institutional care restricted their opportunities to gain external support during their young adult years when they were seeking greater independence, including economic security and social mobility. In China, many young people receive economic support from their parents to attain their independence in employment and housing (Bian, 1997). In rural areas, economic support mainly consists of the tradition of building a new house for marriage. In urban areas, economic support often includes providing a deposit for the marriage apartment and a contribution to the costs of settlement. None of this economic capital is usually available to young people in state care, as explored further in later chapters.

High-risk labour market

The third barrier to attaining their future goals for independence from the institution was the changing labour market. Most of the young people who grew up in institutional care did not have stable jobs. Institutions refer young adults in their care to the city government for employment support, which usually means finding a position in a government or state organization. The lack of national policy requiring city governments to provide support inhibits the effectiveness of these referrals. As described previously, many of these young people are poorly prepared for a tight labour market because their segregated childhoods mean that they have limited human, social and economic capital compared to other young job seekers. It is little wonder that city governments are reluctant to take on job support when institutional care has so poorly prepared them for the job market.

In one of the research sites, the welfare institution had referred 28 young people in two years to the city government for employment support, but no progress had been achieved. The institution blamed the failure of effective support on the lack of national policy, which meant that the institution could not force the city government to provide adequate support. At the time of the research, only one young man from this institution, Bing, had been employed by an agency under the Department of Civil Affairs after he left the army. All the other young adults at that institution had to try to find jobs themselves. With the same selection criteria and risks as other job hunters, they faced discrimination and exclusion from the labour market due to their disadvantaged childhoods.

Consequently, it was difficult for the young people to find any employment, let alone their desired positions. Sadly, their naivety and visible vulnerability meant that they often encountered dishonest employers and agents who cheated them during the process of job hunting. Without awareness about how to protect their rights and without access to social resources and support, they had no recourse during these scams.

For example, Jin, the young man who was now employed in a massage clinic and still lived in the institution, mentioned his bad experiences: "I did several jobs, but was fired after a short period of time and was not paid for my work". Jin was introverted, not good at direct communication and spoke very slowly with a lisp. Other young people mentioned how Jin had found several jobs but was cheated every time.

In Jin's institution, except for two young people with vision impairment who worked in the massage clinics, none of the other interviewees had stable jobs, except as temporary workers in the welfare institution. They all lived and ate in the institution, and received a low salary or allowance. If they left the institution, they would face many challenges without the necessary skills or stable jobs.

The shortage of human, social and economic capital, in combination with a changing labour market, were major barriers for young people in planning to achieve their life goals, and caused despondency in the development of identity of many of the young people about how they would become 'like other people'.

Positive identities

Many of the stories about identity from the young people so far in this chapter have been negative, illustrating the challenges to identity formation. The research also found examples of socially inclusive aspects of childhood that contributed to the positive development of identity. These children benefited from more inclusive environments relative to the other children living in institutional care, which were in special education schools and informal foster families. Within these more favourable environments, they built self-confidence and developed a more positive self-identity through hard study and work.

A caveat to these examples is that these environments were relatively inclusive compared to segregation within the institution. It is not to idealize or claim that their childhoods were inclusive. As the case studies reveal, the capacity of the young people to articulate and attain their goals and identity were delayed relative to what might be expected from other young people who grew up in a family, but they also demonstrate young people's possibilities, even when their childhoods are disadvantaged with notable social exclusion. Eventually, they were able to envision and enact the dimensions of their developing identity that supported a more confident, independent life.

Positive contribution of socially inclusive employment

Introduced earlier in this chapter, Jing was relatively successful compared to the other young people. At the time of the research, she was aged 38 years, was married with two children, working in a massage clinic and lived in a family unit at the welfare institution. In contrast, she described herself as very reclusive before she was 25 years old. Her turning point was the opportunity to participate in massage training specially designed for people with vision impairment. She described the training as the start of opening her heart. At that time, massage was a low-grade job, but over time, it has become standardized and the income has increased.

Joining the massage industry was a chance for Jing to gain confidence and realize her potential. Following three months of training, she started in a position. The job opened a new world to her and enabled her to gain new insights into herself and broaden her social experience. Although the income was not high, the institution provided free housing, a small monthly subsidy and arranged a job for her husband. In this way, she described herself as having had a successful transition to adulthood. She met her future husband through an introduction in her job, had her own family and two children, and had bought an investment apartment. She planned to move to the apartment if the housing in the institution was no longer available to her family. Jing described her own transformation as follows:

"I have poor eyesight. After graduating from the junior high school, I did not enter senior high school due to unsatisfactory academic performance and had to work in the canteen of the welfare institution. At that time, three candidates would be sent to [the city] to receive the training on massage, and I was selected. In fact, people who did massage were discriminated against by many people because it was associated with the sex industry, but I had no other job opportunities and had to receive the training. In the temporary training agency, I studied for three months and then started to do a massage job. Since 1997, I have felt more confident and also communicated with clients during the process of massage.

In the training agency, I built my ability, found a job, defined my position in the community and built my self-confidence. I was employed by another participant in the training workshop. He encouraged me to get to work and then settle down. He also introduced my current husband to me."

Having found a new self-confidence, she said that she could reflect on and have a new understanding of her previous experience in the welfare institution. She thought that her endurance through her disadvantaged childhood had given her the stamina to develop all her strengths and opportunities to achieve her life goals through hard work. She explained:

"I never complain about my hard work and have had nearly no rest since I started to work. Having lived in the welfare institution from an early age, I can endure hardship. In fact, I was a relative healthy child in the welfare institution. Although my eyesight is poor, my arms and legs are healthy. I helped empty the trash, carry water and do other small jobs, and increased my living capacity. Some other children in the welfare institution have fewer disabilities than me, but they cannot endure hardship and finally return to the welfare institution after a short engagement in various jobs. During my stay in the welfare institution, teachers were very kind to me, although they did not give me emotional encouragement."

Jing had found new meaning from her job and had plans to build on her experience within her profession:

> "Although my initial dream was to become a PE teacher, I had to give up this dream and do the job of massage in order to survive. Anyway, I feel very happy now and recognize my own value when I witness health improvement in my clients."

She said that she also felt respected by her clients and colleagues, which helped strengthen her confidence and satisfaction in her job and in her life more generally. She said of her colleagues:

> "There is no discrimination in the workplace. Other members with full sight or younger than me call me 'older sister'. I have done the job of massage for more than 10 years. They like to consult me in case of any problem. I'm happy to help them."

She said that her reflection on her own life is now without any grief or hesitation. She was also strict with her children and asked them to study hard and receive better education. She hoped that her children could have the chance to live a more active life than she had, with more choices. Her philosophy in parenting was to encourage her children by contrasting her own deprived childhood with the possibilities available to them, both in their current educational achievements and the implications for their future goals. For example, she said: "I try not to impose corporal punishment [on my daughter]. I just educate her or tell her my own story and let her understand that good academic performance is fundamental to achieving life goals".

The second case study is Jin, the other young man who also trained as a massage therapist and worked in a massage clinic. He lived in the institution and, at 26 years old, was unmarried. He had a strong sense of his achievements and self-identity. Jin had a clear understanding of his situation and his future goals. He said of himself: "I'm bright and cheerful in disposition, full of enthusiasm in life and hopeful about the future".

He had grown up in the institution but had the advantage of attending a school for children with vision impairment for several years. The school has a respectful attitude to the children. He said that he was very happy in the school, made many friends, found his first love and learned basic living skills. After graduating from the special school, he attended a technical college for three years and gained a medical qualification. Massage is labour-intensive work but has many employment opportunities. For a child growing up in institutional care, Jin's schooling and vocational training experiences were strong starting points for an independent adulthood. They exposed him to other children and adults and useful job skills for a job with many prospects.

Confidence from foster care and continued education

The third case study is Ning, a 20-year-old student who lived in the school dormitory while she was at technical college. She was an example of the different trajectory of children who grew up in a family environment. She had completely different life experiences and social networks compared to the children who grew up in institutional care. Ning had been fostered by an associate professor in a university. She grew up in her foster family with the love and care from her parents and two older brothers. She has an open personality and describes herself as follows: "I have grown up healthily and happily over the past twenty years".

When she had become a state ward as a baby, she was given the surname Dang, but she had not lived in the institution. She did not reject her surname Dang. She was applying to join the Communist Party and was highly satisfied with the support that she and her foster family had received from the government and the welfare institution. She described her satisfaction:

> "Nowadays, I have enough food and clothing thanks to strong support from the government and the welfare institution. I have enjoyed many preferential treatments not accessible to others. I feel very happy with the love and care from the government and the welfare institution."

As well as her foster family love and relationships, she also had a different social network from children growing up in the institution. Ning described her college life:

> "My life in the college is colourful. I study hard in order to have success at school. There are many interesting societies, activities and people in the college. As a [Communist Party] League member, I have grown from an ordinary organizer

to the Student Union minister. Now, I want to apply to join the Communist Party."

Conclusion about the identity of young people leaving state care

Young people in state care in their transition from childhood to adulthood are likely to struggle more with their identity formation compared to other children. They are likely to face many additional disadvantages and forms of social exclusion, including disability, knowledge about having been abandoned by their families and stigma as a state ward.

Many of the young people in care in this study were susceptible to feeling grief and inferiority in establishing their identity due to the knowledge that they were abandoned by their parents at an early age. Few of them knew the details of how that came about, including the difficulties that their parents may have faced or the choices that their parents had to make so that their children could access life-saving medical attention. While they were growing up in an institution, they may have been labelled with derogatory nicknames and experienced disrespect from staff, teachers, other adults and children, which shattered their confidence and their development of identity about the question of 'Who am I?'.

The young people spoke about the limited exposure within the institution to opportunities to think and dream about who they were and who they might wish to become. This lack of modelling about opportunities or guided reflection, and the layers of social discrimination and disrespectful actions that led to distrust, affected their process of understanding the second identity question of 'What position shall I occupy in the community?'. Some children and young people responded negatively to these painful situations, such as refusing to attend school or work and returning to the welfare institution. They did not have the confidence or skills to address such challenges, and had not had sufficient support to live independently.

In answering the third identity question of 'What kind of person do I want to become in the future?', most of the young people simply said that they hoped to live like normal people. Such a basic life goal was a common call from the young people living in the institution. A few of them expressed stronger personal life goals, such as entering a government job, running their own business or becoming a singer or kindergarten teacher. Few of them had the human, social or economic capital to know how to pursue those goals. The current policies do not support institutions to assist them to develop such goals or to insist that other parts of the government support those social and economic endeavours.

The young people who were most confident about their futures were those who had grown up in a family environment, either in formal or informal foster care, and had additional training support to introduce them to job opportunities. These young people had social role models from families, friends and other adults about what independent adult life could look like and what application was needed to achieve it. Most of these children had been in foster care since they were babies, so they had continuity through relationships, possessions and care, which is important for a sense of self (Ward, 2011).

In contrast, the young people in the institutions only had vague notions about what 'living like normal people' meant. Their goals for a job, house, marriage and children were empty of specifics of how to move towards them. Partly, this was because their social circles were so narrow that they did not personally know people with that type of life, and also because their childhood in the institution had not given them sufficient educational and social support to acquire the social skills to participate and compete in the wider community.

Growing up in an institution, no matter how benign or charitable the intentions of the director and staff, did not give the young people opportunities to form family-like relationships and other social relationships with reliable adults or other children in the community. This meant that they did not have the social relationships or social skills from which to observe and learn about what it might mean to be an independent adult. They had no emotional ties to adults or young people from whom they could model why education and social relationships might be important for the future, or what employment or a career path might look like. In fact, in addition to the disadvantage of their disability and lack of extended family, they experienced further discrimination from the stigma of being a state ward living in institutional care. In contrast, the children who had grown up in a foster family or boarded at a school in the community had those role models and social networks, which were sufficient for a more confident transition when they became young adults.

The young people's experiences have implications for policies about alternative care and the practices of welfare institutions. Choices about the type of alternative care, particularly between institutional and family-like care, not only affect the daily experiences of children as they are growing up, but also affect their choices in young adulthood. Diverse social connections, emotional attachments to reliable adults and engaging social networks with a variety of adults in the community who demonstrate the rewards of education and hard work are not experiences that are available to children in institutional care, no matter how well structured that care is. In contrast, young people described unsafe, violent relationships.

Expecting young people without these childhood experiences to be ready for a competitive job market is unrealistic in practice, even when supported by policy. Many of these children have disabilities and do not have the educational or disability support to be job-ready. At the least, these children, who have been disadvantaged by socially segregated childhoods, need intensive educational and job support when they reach adulthood, organized by agencies responsible for education, employment or disability. Hopefully, future generations of children without family will grow up in family-like environments rather than isolated in institutional care so that they are not so socially excluded by the time they reach young adulthood.

This chapter has deepened the stories about some of the young people in relation to their own sense of their identity and their dreams for the future. Chapter Seven looks more specifically at their economic independence and security in order to further understand how their expectations are fulfilled or otherwise.

SEVEN

Economic security of young people leaving care

This chapter examines the economic security of young people with and without disabilities leaving state care as they reach adulthood. Chapter Four outlined the policies about transition to adulthood, which highlighted the policy gaps, including the age and conditions when the state might cease support to young people in state care. This chapter continues that analysis to examine the effect of the scarce policies, including the impact on the economic independence of the young people. It uses examples of the experiences of the young people in the research to examine the various paths towards economic independence or the reasons that these paths might be blocked. Some of these reasons were due to the exclusionary childhood experiences in state care. Other reasons were due to the inadequate responses to their needs and preferences in this transition stage of their young adult lives, which had the effect of continuing to exclude them from the economic and social opportunities expected of other young people. In the worst cases, irrespective of their personal capacity, it would seem unlikely that some of these young people will ever leave state care, suspending them in the status of never becoming independent adults.

This part of the research examined whether socio-economic outcomes were different for young people who had foster care or institutional care. It applies the social inclusion framework to examine how the form of state care affected the facilitators of social inclusion in their transition to adulthood and the impact of the facilitators on their economic outcomes. The facilitators considered were social contact and the use of education, health and disability support services. The outcomes are educational achievement, economic security and activity, housing, and social networks. The chapter focuses on how the children and young people in state care seek an economically independent life when they have grown up into adulthood: how do they live their life? Can they earn their own living?

The chapter is based on qualitative analysis of the field investigation in the four research areas described in Chapter One. These areas are capital cities in economically developed or moderately developed regions. The 54 young people were aged 16–38 years (see Appendix

1). They included young people who the institutions viewed as successful because they were physically healthy or had mild disabilities and they had tertiary education and had found jobs. It also included young people who had some capacity to work but had not found a job and continued to rely on the institution. The institutions considered that they all had at least partial capacity to work, to live independently in the community and to secure economic independence.

Policy context for economic independence

An important aspect of the transition to adulthood of young people from state care is establishing an economic foundation for independent living so that they have a source of income. Consistent with the social inclusion framework in this book, the level of income would be expected to be a relative measure for an average person in the local area to cover daily living expenses, including rented or purchased housing, social connections, marriage, and provision for the family and children.

State welfare institutions are the one of the few agencies in China that still provide welfare support from the cradle to the grave to disadvantaged citizens, and the support is far greater than to children without parents who are not in state care. As described in Chapter Four, the state has not explicitly stipulated the age or conditions by which young people in state care are no longer the responsibility of the state. The policies are generally oriented to new placement in adult state care rather than preparing and supporting economic independence. Many young people in care remain in state care for a long time or forever.

During the planned economy until the 1990s, the state would not allow children or adults in state care to fall into unsustainable living, which meant that the policies were only to rearrange state responsibility for young adults who had grown up in state care, without any policies to plan and implement discharge from state care. The state arranged jobs for young people who grew up in state care and who could independently work. Young people with disabilities in state care could also be placed in a welfare factory job and obtain a reasonable income to live independently (Shang, 2008a).

The reform and opening up that started in the 1980s brought great changes to employment and state support. Prior to 2010, state policies on job placement from the planned economy era continued. However, the introduction of the orphan basic living allowance in 2010, described in Chapter Four (p 55) (RMB600 per month), required dynamic management and exit mechanisms. The policy was not explicit about discontinuing support to young people with the capacity to work. In some areas, the institutions discontinued the living allowance to these young people in order to force them to cease relying on the institutions. Even then, many young people in care did not achieve economic independence and chose to stay in the institutions, continuing with state welfare protection.

In Beijing, for example, by 2009, the 15 child welfare institutions were responsible for over 1,310 state wards. Over 100 young adults aged 18 or more with capacity to work continued to live in the institutions. Some were already 50 years old. At the Chengdu Number 2 Welfare Institution in Sichuan, there were 49 adult orphans whose registered permanent residence was still the state child welfare institution. The institutions continued responsibility for all their welfare needs, including housing, income, education, health care and a monthly living allowance of RMB560. The continuous accumulation of young adults not exiting state care tripled the number of children and young people in state care within 10 years (Yu, 2013). Similar situations were seen in other areas. The transition of young people out of state care became a major social policy issue that perplexed the civil affairs authorities (Wang, 2009; Wen, 2009; Yu, 2013).

From the interests of the young people, such 'protective' policy ultimately affects their potential to integrate into the community as independent adults. The state policy for supporting the transition of young people in care to adulthood was described as rearrangements. It did not explicitly stipulate when or under which circumstances the young people in care were ineligible for state support and when they must earn their own living. It did not include supporting policy or the policy was not feasible to support employment and housing during the transition of young people in care to adulthood. As many young people remained in the welfare institutions, which exerted pressure on the financial viability of the institutions, some regions began to formulate transition policies, as described in Chapter Four. The four major challenges, each interrelated, were about how to stop reliance on welfare provision from the welfare institution, employment, housing and individually registered permanent residence, as introduced in Chapter Four. This chapter examines the economic experience of the young people in this situation.

Becoming adults – three forms of income support

The 54 young people in the research had capacity to work (see Table 7.1). Their employment status was full-time jobs, odd jobs, unemployment or in education.

Table 7.1: Employment status of young people in care

	Full-time job	Odd job	Total
State child welfare institution	4	2	6
Outside the welfare institution	9	6	15
Total employed	13	8	21
Unemployed	12	–	12
Training or education	21	–	21
Total	46	8	54

Note: Data for 2013.

The source of income of these young people leaving care was employment, state cash allowance or state welfare support. The cash allowance was very low, primarily consisting of the orphan allowance and urban resident minimum living protection, and was inadequate to support independent living. Most of them continued to live in the institution instead. Since most young people leaving care do not have an independent registered residence, they would not have been able to obtain the minimum living protection allowance independently without a referral from the institution. Most of the young people leaving care continued to rely on the welfare support from the state child welfare institution because it covered all their necessities, including food, housing, health care and a small allowance for clothing and pocket money.

Some of the young people had obtained some level of economic independence, ranging from full-time work through part-time work to occasional work. Other young people gained economic independence by continuing to live with their foster family or marrying someone with sufficient economic security to move out of state care. In general, whether the young person had disabilities affected their transition. Most of the ones who had achieved independence or were striving for that goal were young people with no or mild disabilities. An exception were young people with vision impairments because of the structured vocational training and employment paths in jobs with adequate income in the service industries set up by the Disabled Persons' Federation (DPF).

In addition, whether children with or without disabilities had grown up in foster care also generally enhanced the likelihood of them achieving independence, though there were some exceptions to this. Long-term foster care meant that they had a family and social network, interpersonal communication skills, and an aspiration for independent living that were not available to most of the young people from institutional care. The lives of the young people who achieved these means of independence are described here.

Economic independence through paid employment

Only a few young people, primarily those with tertiary education, had gained economic independence by finding a good job or starting their own business. Although the number was small, their success had inspired others. Most of these young people worked in a welfare institution or civil affairs department and were employed as formal staff members of public institutions. Other young people who had mostly lived in foster care had found jobs through army veterans' support or vocational training arrangements, such as support from the DPF.

In Beijing, which offered active support and required young people to leave care, some young people had found jobs in the community. All the young people in Beijing in the research had graduated from at least secondary technical school. When they completed their vocational training, the schools recommended a job to them or they could also choose to find other jobs. The rent allowance provided by the government allowed them to leave the welfare institution and find other housing in the community, as discussed in Chapters Four and Nine.

Young people in independent employment generally had a better education background, mostly attended college and had at least received vocational training at secondary technical schools. However, the jobs or businesses were generally low-paid and often insufficient to support independent living, so many of them continued to rely on the welfare institution to meet their other needs, particularly housing. Table 7.2 summarizes the cases of the employed young people further described in this chapter.

Table 7.2: Employed young people cases

Alias	Jing	Luo	Hu	Li	Ning
Sex	F	M	M	M	F
Age	38	23	24	21	20
Disability	Yes	No	No	Yes	No
Education	Junior middle	Technical secondary	Technical college	Technical college	Technical college
Employed or studying	Employed at massage clinic	Employed[a]	Employed	Employed at the institution	Student
Housing	Family unit welfare institution	Private rental	Dormitories at work and welfare institution	Dormitory welfare institution	Dormitory school
Married	Yes	No	No	No	No
Alternative care	Institution	Mixed	Institution	Institution	Mixed
Place	Taiyuan	Beijing	Nanning	Urumqi	Taiyuan

Notes: M = male; F = female. [a] Waiting for a government-arranged job.

Jing was the 38-year-old married woman introduced in Chapter Six, whose employment success depended on the vocational training and job placement arranged by the DPF. She described how that support and training had been vital to acquiring a useful skill, which had led to social and economic independence. She said:

> "A classmate at the training told me that the training was organized by DPF. Afraid of being despised [because of the stigma about massage and sex work], I originally didn't want to attend the massage training class at the city's school for children with vision impairment. A former classmate of mine was doing the massage job after receiving the training, and he advised me to do the same, arguing that there were no other jobs available for people like us. And I considered that the cost for the DPF training class was low (I paid about RMB400). So I applied for it to the welfare institution, and the institution approved it. I was still single at that time and belonged to the welfare institution, and so they would provide help when I needed it."

Luo was the 23-year-old man living in Beijing, introduced in Chapter Five, who had the positive continuing relationship with his foster family. When he was very young, he lived in the institution and later shifted to the family. He attended his local primary school and then junior high school. When he finished school, the institution transferred him back to institutional care so that he could attend technical secondary school. He found a part-time job in a hotel while he was in school. After he finished the technical school, the institution arranged a job for him but he was unsatisfied with it. Instead, he found a new job through the Internet and accepted training in logistics. He planned to enter higher education as his next step. At the time of the research, he had just graduated from the technical school. He and a friend from the institution rented an apartment together. His income from his small business selling toys was meeting his basic living costs while he waited for a government-arranged job. He said that if the government-arranged job did not satisfy him, he would find a job himself. His registered residence was still hosted collectively by the institution.

Luo said that he believes that many of his peers who had only grown up in institutional care were not clear about community-held social aspirations, expectations and behaviours because they had not been exposed to them. For example, he said that although the children living in the institution studied at a local school, they only attended a separate class, which cut them off from connections with other students. The school did not give the class of children from the welfare institution equal educational resources. Only if they reached secondary school were the children from the institution allowed to communicate with students from families in the community. This meant that during their school years, they did not learn about the usual aspirations for education, training and employment, and so were disadvantaged when they were expected to leave the institution and enter the labour market.

Hu was a 24-year-old man who entered state care when he was four years old and had grown up in institutional care. He graduated in architecture from a technical college two years before the research and was working on a building site as a civil engineer. The fees for college and living expenses were paid by the institution. His monthly salary was very low, at RMB1,000 (less than half the average wage for Nanning), though his work provided housing and meals. He usually lived at the building site but returned to the dormitory unit at the institution on holidays and weekends.

Hu was the most successful case among the Nanning research participants. Other young people still studying, such as Yong, who is introduced later, considered him a role model. Hu had found his job without relying on the institution. He said that he was not confident about finding a girlfriend as he grew up in state care and did not own a house or assets. He was strongly concerned that the government should improve policies to support low rental housing and to encourage young people leaving care to start small businesses.

The third young man was Li, who was aged 21 years, referred to in Chapter Five as having positive and negative experiences. He entered the institution at the age of four or five years, probably because he has hepatitis. He lived in the institution except for one year in foster care. He attended a technical college, where he studied civil administration. He had a full-time job at the state child welfare institution, where he cared for children, contributing to their education and lessons. His housing at the institution was rent-free and the institution paid him a very low after-tax monthly income of RMB1,600. The institution considered that Li was one of the successful cases as he held a college degree and a full-time position in a reliable job in the institution. He said that his remaining problem was having no means to afford housing at the market price in the community, which also precluded him from finding a wife.

As compared to those who lived in welfare institutions, the children in foster care had additional ties with their foster families, which can be of great benefit to finding a job. Ning, for example, had a part-time job in her foster brother's company and wished to continue working in the company when she finishes education. Her situation was unusual because her foster parents were urban citizens. Most foster parents are rural villagers with limited social capital. While rural foster care provides family supports and potential opportunities for future employment, most of the foster parents typically earn their living as farmers or migrant workers and have limited ways to help their foster children to find jobs.

Employed temporarily at the state child welfare institution

The second set of young people was those who primarily relied on the welfare institution for their livelihood, and supplemented their welfare through odd jobs. They tended to be physically healthy, with no or mild disabilities, and were considered as able to work. They had grown up in the institution so they had not received a good-quality education and their education level was low. With only limited social connections, they were disadvantaged in the job market and could only find low-paid physical work. It would be difficult for them to achieve economic independence.

Most of them did not work, except temporarily at the institution. The reasons that they said they could not secure a job and had stopped work or trying to find a job varied, including: limited understanding of the community; being cheated at work; failure to be paid for their work; the work was too hard; or the work was for such a low income. If they had found employment, they had sometimes quit the job after a short time and returned to the institution for housing and support.

When the institution gave them the opportunity, they engaged in odd jobs at the institution, such as cleaning, caring for children and therapy exercises. Their income was minimal but they said that they were not concerned about their survival because the housing and support was free and they earned occasional money from odd jobs. Four young women with disabilities, Xi, Mei, Hong and Ming, were examples of young people in this situation (see Table 7.3).

Table 7.3: Young people occasionally employed at the state child welfare institution

Alias	Xi	Mei	Hong	Ming
Sex	F	F	F	F
Age	24	34	37	30
Disability	Yes	Yes	Yes	Yes
Education	Technical college	Junior middle	No schooling	Junior primary
Housing	Dormitory welfare institution	Family unit welfare institution	Dormitory welfare institution	Dormitory welfare institution
Married	No	Yes	No	No
Place	Taiyuan	Taiyuan	Nanning	Nanning
Alternative care	Mixed	Institution	Foster	Foster

Notes: F = female.

The young woman introduced in Chapter Six, Xi, was 24 years old. She had been fostered by a woman in the community and sent to the institution at the age of 12 years when her foster mother became chronically ill and could no longer afford the living costs for Xi and three brothers. When Xi grew up, she worked in the community part-time, but she returned to the institution because she could not adapt to the situation and felt discriminated against due to limited function in her hands. She did odd jobs in the rehabilitation department in the institution.

Mei was aged 34 years. She was taken to the institution when she was very young due to her disability. She graduated from junior high school, but due to her speech impediment, she had never shifted outside the institution for work. After she married in the institution at the age of 20 years, the institution arranged odd jobs for her, caring for children or older people, so that she could earn a small income. Her housing and food support were through the institution and she could afford to care for her own children and family. Since Mei's husband did not hold a local residency card, the officials of the state child welfare institution allocated a dedicated apartment for the couple to reside in, and also arranged a temporary job within the institution for her husband.

The final two cases were Hong and Ming, aged 38 and 31 years, respectively, both women with disabilities. They grew up in the institution from when they were very young and lived in the young people's apartment building at the institution. Hong never attended school. Ming attended school for one year only and dropped out as she found it difficult to learn and keep up with the other students. At the time, the institution was not responsible for picking up children in state care from school and it was very difficult for her to get to and from school due to her disability, so she had to abandon schooling. Both Hong and Ming worked in the institution, being responsible for washing and folding children's diapers. They received only token monthly salaries (of RMB100–200), with free food and lodging. They worked 6.5 hours per day, and their job was not busy or tiring. They both believed that they were competent at their job.

The full research sample included many similar cases in the institutions. Many young people in care could not obtain a job outside the institution. The institution gave them free food and housing and would consider them first for any odd jobs. Such jobs did not offer a high income but their living costs were low.

Unemployed and relying on state child welfare institutions

The third group was some of the young people with disabilities, such as Ping, Yao and Jie, who had some ability to work but were incapable of independently finding a job in the community and continued to rely on the welfare institution for their living, probably for their whole lifetime (see Table 7.4).

Table 7.4: Young people unemployed or occasional jobs at the state child welfare institution

Alias	Ping	Yao	Jie
Sex	M	M	M
Age	27	20	16
Disability	Yes	Yes	Yes
Education[a]	None	None	None
Employed or studying	Employed at state child welfare institution	Unemployed	Employed at state child welfare institution
Housing	Dormitory welfare institution	Dormitory welfare institution	Dormitory welfare institution
Married	No	No	No
Place	Nanning	Nanning	Nanning
Alternative care	Institution	Institution	Institution

Notes: M = male. [a] They had not received formal schooling because they had learning disabilities.

Ping, Yao and Jie were young men aged 16–27 years. They all had intellectual and physical disabilities and had lived in the institution since they were very young. Yao used a wheelchair, Ping had mobility and communication impairments from polio and Jie had moderate learning disabilities. All of them lived in the young people's apartment building at the state child welfare institution. They all relied totally on the institution for their basic living. The institution allocated nominal jobs to Yao and Ping, such as washing clothes, mopping the floor and house cleaning for 6.5 hours per day. The monthly salary was RMB100 only, but was due to increase to RMB200 in the near future. It was only a token wage to give them a sense of accomplishment and avoid a lack of activity in their day. The salary was not distributed to them personally, but kept by the monitor. Ping said that he would buy an electric fan once he got the money as his bed in his apartment was so high that the floor fan did not reach it and the bed was too hot. Jie said that he felt bored without a job and he admired his peers who had jobs. He expressed a strong wish to work. Young people at the institution without regular jobs like him awoke at 7 o'clock in the morning, had breakfast and watched TV or sat outside.

Table 7.5: Young people leaving state care through continued foster care or marriage cases

Alias	Sex	Age	Disability	Education	Employed or studying	Housing	Married	Place	Alternative care
Remain in foster family									
Shu	M	19	Yes	Primary	Employed part-time	Foster family	No	Datong	Foster
Jiang	M	19	No	Technical secondary	Unpaid intern	Foster family	No	Taiyuan	Foster
Marriage									
Hai	F	29	Yes	Master's degree	Employed	Private rental	Yes	Datong	Foster
Min	F	21	No	Technical secondary	Homemaker	Private rental	Yes	Taiyuan	Mixed

Notes: M = male; F = female.

Other options for economic security in order to leave state care

In addition to the three modes of economic security described earlier, some young people achieved independence through two other situations: continued foster care and marriage (see Table 7.5).

Some young people with disabilities who grew up in foster families continued to live with them. Such cases were identified in Datong, where the welfare institution was responsible for children and adults and was the first institution in China to run a foster care programme (see Chapter Three). The young people were either in paid employment or, when their orphan allowance stopped because they were too old or had left school, they lived on the minimum living protection allowance. Among these young people who remained in their foster families were those with severe disabilities who would be likely to live permanently in foster families and who received minimum living protection from the state.

Young people with the ability to work were entitled to the minimum living protection allowance and stay in foster families while they looked for a job and secured a source of income for independent living. They continued to benefit from their family support and share the common experiences and examples of their peers in the community. Jiang, the ambitious 19 year old introduced in Chapter Six (p 100), who had done lots of odd jobs, and Shu, whose story is told in Chapter Eight, were examples of young people who had grown up in foster care and were inspired to find work and remain independent.

The final means of livelihood for young women leaving care was to marry a husband, leave state care and obtain economic support and a normal family life. Young men rarely had such opportunities and none were found in the research. The cases of women in this research who managed to achieve this way of leaving care, Hai and Min, both had some experience of foster care or living in a family, suggesting perhaps that these childhood experiences gave them wider social experiences to enable this outcome. Min was a young woman aged 21 years who had grown up in a mix of family and institutional care. At the time of the interview, she lived in a private rental with her husband and daughter and was a homemaker. She did not have disabilities and had graduated from technical secondary school. Hai's case is discussed further in Chapter Eight and Min's in Chapter Ten.

Social protection or social exclusion?

All the young people had economic security, either through their own means or through continued support from the institution. This section summarizes the positive and negative implications for economic independence of the lifetime care responsibility taken by the institution, including the permanent safety net, low-income work and marriage.

Welfare institutions' permanent safety net

None of the young people in state care were left bereft of income support and a place to live – once in state care, it remained the state's responsibility to continue to support them until they chose to leave. In adulthood, most of them continued to rely on state welfare provision, particularly living in the institution, even if they had paid work. Since the economic reforms of the 1990s, few groups in Chinese society continue to benefit from social welfare throughout their lifetime. The state welfare institutions provide the most complete package of welfare benefits only to groups of people in the most serious difficulty, without any other sources of social support. Along with the improvements to the state's financial situation and the increase in the funding for welfare institutions, the level of welfare benefits is continuously rising.

In contrast, if the young people in care found a job after becoming adults, they and their *hukou* were transferred out of the welfare institution and they would no longer benefit from the various welfare supports of the welfare institution. If they became completely detached from the welfare institution and worked in the community in unstable or low-income jobs, they could be left in insecure situations without an assured source of income if they became unemployed. Instead, if they did not move out of the welfare institution, they could continue to enjoy the benefits forever. Between economic independence and the continued safety net, many young people in care chose the latter, despite the compromises that implied for their independence.

The choice of continuing with the institution's safety net was also a potential poverty trap. Security of the known but very low government welfare reduced the motivation of some of the young people to find work or be able to take advantage of the other social opportunities in the community. The lack of support during a childhood in institutional care to plan for independence inhibited their capacity to strive for this aspiration. Some of the young people with disabilities had neither received support during their childhood to develop their capacity to anticipate a working life, nor received the disability-specific support as young adults to enable their capacity to enter the labour market.

Low income inhibiting independence

The welfare institutions' safety net was not a poverty trap for all young people in care. Some young people obtained further qualifications or a college degree and found good jobs. They had strong intentions to change their life situation and obtain economic independence, such as the cases discussed earlier and in Chapter Six. However, even many of these young people with jobs struggled to achieve independence from institutional care because they did not have the economic or social means to obtain independent housing. Even though they had secure jobs and independent income, their income level was comparatively low and inadequate for housing costs.

Hu, the young man introduced earlier who worked at the building site on low wages and returned to the institution on the weekends, was a typical case of what was seen as a successful transition to adulthood at the child welfare institution. However, the job he had was so low-paid that he did not have economic independence. Some of the children and young people in state care at the same institution in Nanning said to the researchers that they viewed him as a positive role model. For instance, Yong was an 18-year-old student attending technical college. He lived in a dormitory at his college and had grown up in foster and institutional care. Yong viewed Hu as a successful figure and he hoped to follow Hu's path. He had even chosen to major in the same subject at college so that he might have that opportunity.

However, the income of these employed young people was not sufficient to secure the economic foundation for independent living, even if they were in white-collar jobs, except in Beijing. Only the young people in Beijing could live independently because they received an allowance for housing provided by the government or rented apartments out of the welfare institutions. Even so, one young person in Beijing left several jobs because the jobs did not include free lodging and he had no other way to manage his expenses.

The young people leaving care differed from most of their peers because they did not have family support to help them secure housing in the initial phase of their transition to adulthood. Income at entry-level full-time work was inadequate to support their independent adult life. The rising cost of housing in recent decades has been an urgent concern for most young people in China. Most of them cannot afford housing on their own and many rely on their parents to solve this problem. Young people in state care do not have this option to rely on family. When the Beijing government recognized this problem by providing a housing allowance, many young people chose to leave the institutions. Housing is discussed more in Chapter Nine.

Few of the young people who had grown up in welfare institutions had attended college and found full-time jobs. Those with low education levels had to compete in the labour market with migrant workers. The welfare benefits in the welfare institutions were equivalent to or better than the benefits that they could obtain from such low-paid work. Many chose to abandon work opportunities rather than risk the possibility of losing the state welfare safety net forever.

In short, the vision of many of the young people in care was basic – a place to live and the ability to earn sufficient income for themselves – yet their income was inadequate for these basic demands. They were not in a position to detach themselves from the security of the welfare institutions, nor able to secure independent *hukou* or establish families.

Marriage or poverty trap

Many of the young people strongly demanded that the local government implement policies for low rental housing allowances for state wards. In most areas, a precondition for obtaining low rental housing is a marriage certificate. In a circular policy trap, though, most young men in care could not marry because they had no housing and were not eligible for low rental housing until they married. The only young people in the research who had successfully applied for low rental housing were married and were women, like Hai and Min introduced earlier.

The limited choice of insecure work or secure institutional care affected the marriage choices of young women in care because once they married, their registered residence would be transferred out of the welfare institution and they would become ineligible for the associated welfare institution benefits. Many of them choose to stay at the welfare institution instead of marrying to avoid the risks of instability in married life. For example, the young women who still lived in the institution, Hong and Ming, had chosen not to marry, even when other people recommended suitable male friends to them. Hong said:

> "How would we dare marry? It would be fine if the life after marriage was satisfactory; but if it is not, we would

even have no place to live as our registered residence would have been transferred out of the welfare institution. Besides, how can we raise our children [since we have disabilities]? So, we would rather avoid marriage."

In summary, the welfare institution policies were intended to protect the security of the young people living in the institutions by providing a place to live and basic means to live there. This approach also had the perverse effect of denying them the means and motivation to become independent adults. In the absence of support to secure their independence, they chose not to work in low-paid jobs in the community, but, rather, depended on the protection offered in the welfare institution so that they avoided the risks of an unstable independent life.

Most of the young people who remained living in the institutions lived a very thrifty, simple life, without the opportunity to save money. Although the institution was their safety net, it was not a path to economic independence. Most of them did not have the means to find housing, marry and establish a family. They could not afford the costs associated with living as an adult in the community, including socializing with friends, marriage and supporting a family of their own.

In contrast, the young people who had grown up in foster care had much less concern about the economic risks of living in the community. They generally held ambitions and were successful in obtaining support from their foster parents, siblings and relatives to find jobs and marriage partners.

Conclusion about economic security

This research about the economic security of young people with or without disabilities leaving state care found that in most parts of China, the policy is vague about the age, conditions and support for young people to leave the protection of the welfare institutions. Instead of planning for and supporting their economic independence, the current policies focus on rearranging continued state protection for these young people. Many of the young people do not transition to independent living, remaining dependent on the institution, irrespective of their capacity. If policy was clearer about when support to state wards ceases, then the policy goals could change from rearranging permanent support, to support for transition with the aim of independent living.

Some locations have new policy directions to support transition, as summarized in this chapter and with more detail in Chapter Four. The cases here have shown that these first policies are a start but unlikely to be sufficient alone. Many of the young people who grew up in institutional care are not yet prepared to take the risk of detaching from the security of the welfare institutions and live independently. They have relied on that security for their entire lives and do not have alternative security from an extended family network. Young people who grew up in foster care have that alternative experience; therefore, extending that security to all state wards by living in the community in a family environment during childhood could presumably reduce their fear of the risks of independence in adult life. Future policy directions will need to consider these fundamentals about the implications of different forms of alternative care during childhood if the state is to be successful in supporting and motivating state wards to leave state protection when they reach adulthood.

The research found that, even in the best cases, the young adults with good full-time jobs struggled to establish a secure economic base for independent living because they lacked the social connections for affordable housing. In most cases, they relied on the institution to address their housing needs, but without independent housing, they could not obtain independent registered permanent residence to finally leave the responsibility of the welfare institution. Without appropriate policy support, most of the children growing up in welfare institutions remained dependent on state welfare. In some places, the dependence was compounded when the young people married and their children continued living with them in the institution, also relying on state welfare provision.

In most of China, the problem of ignoring the transition needs of young adults in state care is prevalent and is a current unsustainable policy conundrum for local civil affairs departments. Governments responsible for children in care need to consider how to plan for a positive transition to independence. As these young people have had little or no experience of social inclusion during their childhood, it is not sufficient to merely focus on the immediate problems of how to encourage young people to leave care, find a place to live and gain paid work. It is the responsibility of the state to redress the disadvantages of current generations of children and young people who grew up isolated in institutional care. In the short term, they need additional transition support to establish the social networks that segregated care prevented them from developing during their childhood. They need housing, employment and income support to avoid poverty, gain economic security and form the social and intimate relationships otherwise closed to them. With this suite of costly, yet time-limited, support, they might yet be able to attain independence, as demonstrated in the cases in Beijing.

Avoiding the preventable layering of social exclusion from childhood experiences in segregated care is a state responsibility for the new generations of children entering state care. Focusing on today's young children entering care is an opportunity to plan policy more strategically in order to avoid transition problems. Policy change could start from reconsidering the forms of alternative care and building on the positive experiences of family-based care. Young children growing up in family-based alternative care have the family and community connections necessary for economic security in the community.

Only with this twofold approach could the state expect to set conditions for ending responsibility for state wards without risking further social exclusion: first, where it addresses the transition support needs of the current children and young people who have endured state practices that accentuated their social exclusion; and, second, where it embraces alternative care practices that enable children in state care to grow up in a family environment where the conditions for social inclusion are more likely to prevail during their childhood, which are a precondition for transition to independent adulthood. Children and young people with disabilities in state care require and are entitled to additional support in both these approaches in childhood and young adulthood if they are to fulfil their rights to independence.

If the state were committed to resourcing this twofold approach, it might be justified in explicitly defining the maximum eligibility age or conditions for ending state care for young people who are state wards. The gradual improvement of general social welfare provision to all Chinese people may also reduce the difficulties facing these young people in state care and help them in their transition to adulthood. Chapter Eight develops this conclusion further by examining the link between social networks and the employment of young people who grew up in foster care.

EIGHT

Social networks and the employment of young people leaving care

Most young people in Chinese state care became state wards as very young children and have disabilities. When they reach adulthood, many of them remain unemployed. Before the economic transitions in the 1980s, the government provided most of these young people with jobs when they became young adults, or they gained employment in welfare enterprises with tax concessions to employ people with disabilities. After the economic transition, many welfare factories reduced their employees or closed down, and state directives for job placement were dismantled.

Many young adults now struggle to find or keep jobs. They then depend on support from the welfare institutions, which prolongs the social isolation they experienced as children in institutional care. Welfare institutions must continue to provide support throughout the lives of the young people in state care, which is financially unsustainable and precludes social inclusion, as revealed in Chapter Seven. It could be expected that the young people who developed greater social networks during their childhood would have improved employment options. Insights from the experiences of the young people who grew up in foster care, rather than institutional care, is a way to examine that question.

Job placement for young adult orphans has become a challenge for child welfare institutions and a bottleneck for the support of new children entering state care. Without a solution, the young adults may have to rely on government support without opportunities to fulfil the usual expectations of adulthood and social inclusion. This chapter analyses the job placement cases of young adults who grew up in foster care in Datong. The chapter applies social network theory to analyse data from the case studies about how young adults used their social connections in their job search. It explores whether the young adults used strong or weak ties to find jobs, and identifies the support that was available to them to overcome the disadvantages in the job market arising from their childhood as state wards, their having disabilities and their growing up in poor rural areas.

The chapter explains the type of social network theory about strong and weak ties used to analyse their experiences. It draws conclusions about the social networks available to them as children who grew up in foster care and the implications of alternative care during childhood and employment support when young people in state care are preparing for transition to adulthood and independence.

Social network framework

Social network theory is a useful framework for analysing the job searching of young adults because it considers the interrelationships between the social networks of the person and of the people they interact with, their communities and wider society. This section introduces the apparently contradictory weak and strong tie theories of social networks as they have been applied to job searching internationally and in China.

Weak tie social network theory

A social network is a relatively stable system between actors formed through social interaction, or a social structure (Wellman, 1988). A social network is an interdependent network of ties in which members share different portions of resources. In this way, it incorporates both individual agency and structural constraints upon people in the social network (Ruan, 1993). This chapter analyses the perspective of the individual in the social network because the unit of analysis is the young adult orphan, though it also has implications for the whole social network. One way of analysing individuals in a social network is to investigate the network of interpersonal ties that influence individual behaviours by looking at the types of ties between people.

Granovetter (1974) introduced the concept of the strength of ties, and the strength of weak ties hypothesis. He noticed that people may find more suitable jobs through weak ties than through strong ties because more job information is available through weak ties since they connect to people who have different information sources and social backgrounds. They can be used as bridges to cross social boundaries and to get information and other resources. Strong ties have a lower probability of fresh job information because only similar information is available since they connect to people who have similar information sources and social backgrounds.

Key to his hypothesis is the view of weak ties as information bridges. Granovetter defines strong and weak ties through interaction frequency, emotional intensity, intimacy and reciprocal services between people. He regards friendship as a strong tie and acquaintanceship as a weak tie. The strength of weak ties hypothesis influenced social network research and many studies on job searching within the labour market. Most recently, for example, studies show that relying on social networks is most likely to be successful when the introducer is higher in status or senior to the person and is familiar with their strengths (Trimble O'Connor 2013).

Strong tie social network theory in China

Social network or social capital theories sit well in the Chinese context because of the predominance of *guanxi* (interrelationship) in discussions about social relationships (Bian, 1994). Bian (1997) and others modified social network theory when they introduced the contrary concept of the strength of strong ties hypothesis in the Chinese employment context. Research in Tianjin, China, in 1988 found that in the job placement system of the Chinese planned economy, more people gained jobs through strong ties than through weak ties. The ties between people are used for accessing information about decision-makers and influencing them about job placement. The ties are less likely to be used for collecting information about jobs. This is because even if job information is available, job searchers may not get the job without the influence of decision-makers who have strong ties. Maximum job-search support is available when intermediaries have strong ties to both the job searchers and the decision-makers. In this way, strong ties, instead of weak ones, work as bridges between people who are not connected to each other (Bian, 1997).

Researchers have applied social network theory to job seekers in China (eg Gui et al, 2002, 2003; Zhao, 2002, 2003; Zhang et al, 2004; Tang, 2007; Chen, 2012). Most findings show the same characteristics: that in China's institutional and cultural background, the social network significantly influences job search and placement, and job searchers particularly rely on the strength of strong ties in their social network. Others have found similar reliance on strong ties in other transition countries (Kogan et al, 2013).

The theory continues to be applied in China to analyse the employment behaviours of different social groups (such as redundant middle-aged women) and to analyse the relationship between employment behaviours and Chinese cultural traditions (Cai, 2003; Gui et al, 2003; Sun and Bian, 2011; Su and Meng, 2013). That research found that the reliance on strong ties, based on *guanxi*, may lead to market fragmentation, state intervention and rent-seeking activities (Lin and Si, 2010). This disadvantages state wards if they have fewer social ties than other people. Research has also found that new generations are forming weak ties, which may be influenced by their educational attainment, income level and occupation (Liu et al, 2012).

The framework follows Bian's social network study, dividing social relations into three types: family relationships (strong ties); friendship (strong ties), including friends, neighbours, workmates and fellow villagers; and acquaintanceship (weak ties), including direct and indirect ties that are not relatives or friends. It distinguishes the strength of the ties in the case studies by applying the criteria of strong ties and weak ties, with the types of ties and emotional intensity as the main indicators.

The framework also takes account of the particularity of orphans growing up in foster care. For orphans, strong ties include close relations with institution staff, including their responsibility to find them a job, administrative responsibility and power and organizational connections.

This chapter analyses the strength of both the strong and weak ties in the job-search experience of young adults in order to understand which ties were available to them and which were useful in finding jobs. It also examines whether young adults' reliance on the strength of certain ties had a direct or indirect effect on difficulties in finding jobs.

Case study of young people leaving foster care

The Datong Social Welfare Institution, Shanxi Province, was selected as the research site because it has a long history of mixed alternative care (Shang, 2003). The institution has organized rural foster care for more than 60 years. Many orphans in Datong have lived in foster families, and have successfully found jobs. They have become independent from the institution and their foster family, and some now even provide for their foster parents like other adult children. This success is rare in other welfare institutions, some of which have only more recently begun foster care programmes.

Analysing the experience of young adults who have lived in foster care enables examination of their household ties, which are one of the important strong ties in a social network. Some young adults in Datong foster care lived with their foster families for more than 10 years and their social networks were well developed. In contrast, young adults in institutional care do not have household ties, so strong tie analysis is not possible. The city of Datong is in the north of Shanxi Province.

At the end of 2007, Datong had a population of 3,159,600 and a gross domestic product (GDP) per capita of about RMB16,000 (RMB10 = £1). The Datong Social Welfare Institution, founded in 1949, is a comprehensive welfare service with the largest accommodation in Shanxi Province, accepting children without families and people with disabilities, with no income and who are homeless.

The institution did not have sufficient funds to provide institutional care to all the orphans, so it found people to adopt or foster the children (Shang, 2003). By December 2007, the institution had cared for 832 children, including 480 children in foster care, 80 children in institutional care and others who had become adults and had the capacity to work and leave.

In the foster family environment, the orphans are provided with comprehensive care from the foster family, supported by staff from the institution, including access to the health and disability facilities at the institution. In this way, they have the dual benefits of a family environment and free formal health and social support.

The data collection in 2009 included a document review and qualitative interviews to inform the five case studies. Documents collected and reviewed included local policies regarding children in care, annual reports, archives and publications produced by the institution. The purpose was to understand the differences and constraints on policy, practice and aspirations. A case-study method was chosen to generate in-depth information about the orphan in the context of support from their family, community and institution. All recruitment was hands-off – the institution approached the young people and asked if they would like to participate in the interview. Participation was voluntary, with the right to say no or withdraw. They were reimbursed for their expenses.

A sample of five young people was selected from the people recruited (see Table 8.1). They met the sampling criteria and were a sufficient number to cover the variation in their circumstances, including: employment status – employed and looking for a job; health and disability status; path of employment – self-found job and employed at the institution; level of education – technical school, technical college, bachelor's and master's; types of job – physical and skilled; and gender.

In addition, the researchers interviewed two managers and three support staff at the institution, who had experience with supporting young adults. Topics included employment outcomes, support, job paths and government cooperation. Foster parents of two of the orphans were also interviewed.

Table 8.1: Young people leaving foster care cases

Alias	Sex	Age	Disability	Education	Employed or studying	Housing	Married
Kang	M	25	Yes	Higher secondary	Employed	Own subsidized house from welfare institution	No
Shu	M	19	Yes	Primary	Employed part-time	Foster family	No
Mo	F	28	Yes	Higher education	Employed	Family unit welfare institution	Yes
Fang	M	20	Yes	Technical secondary	Intern	Dormitory employer	No
Hai	F	29	Yes	Master's degree	Employed	Private rental	Yes

Notes: Data for 2009 from Datong. M = male; F = female.

The research team included Dr Shang and postgraduate students from Beijing Normal University. They conducted interviews for one to two hours at a place chosen by the young person. The interviews were semi-structured, with open questions to encourage the young people to elaborate on their experiences. Topics included: demographics; housing; job-search path, status, job type, satisfaction, pay, training and discrimination; childhood; future expectations, work, marriage and family; and support from family, the institution and the government. The researchers contacted some interviewees for second interviews to fill missing data in 2012.

The main limitation of the analysis is that all the interviewed children had, at most, mild disabilities, so they may encounter fewer difficulties seeking employment than if they had more severe disabilities. Datong, however, has the longest history of foster care in China, so the cases of the interviewed young people are the best available. The employment policy for state wards with or without disabilities in Datong has not changed since 2009.

The young people's experiences of the strength of strong and weak ties are presented about each function of a social network in job search for young adults. The case-study summary in Table 8.2 includes the young people's characteristics, their schooling, the strong and weak ties available to each person, the ties used to find a job, and their current employment. In all cases, strong ties included the foster parents, foster siblings and the welfare institution.

Table 8.2: Ties used by young adult orphans to find employment

Alias	Kang	Shu	Mo	Fang	Hai
Marital status	Single	Single	Married	Single	Married
Schooling	High	Primary	University	Tertiary	University
Housing	Foster home	Migrant worker	Institution-provided	Work-provided	Rented home
Ties available					
Foster parents	Strong	Strong	Strong	Strong	Strong
Foster siblings	Strong	Strong	Strong	Strong	Strong
Welfare institution	Strong	Strong	Strong	Strong	Strong
Young peers in village	Weak	Weak	–	–	
Teachers, schoolmates	Weak	Weak	Weak	Weak	–
Job websites	–	–	Weak	–	–
Other orphans from the institution	–	–	–	Weak	Weak
Hospital contact from another orphan	–	–	–	Weak	–
University teacher	–	–	–	–	Weak
Main ties used to find a job	Strong ties	Strong ties	Weak ties first, then strong ties, foster parents intermediaries	Multiple weak ties	Weak ties
Employment	Car driver	Migrant worker	Teacher	Dentist	University teacher

Notes: Data for 2009.

Foster parents as strong ties in job search

The foster care family was the most important strong tie for all the cases, consistent with a social network analysis of young adults from intact families. The foster family was important in job searches for some orphans but not others.

Family strong ties for job search and support

The first two cases, Kang and Shu, lived with the same foster family. Their foster mother, who was a rural villager, participated in the interview. Kang was in his late 20s and had high school education. His foster mother and the welfare institution tried to support him to get a university place because his school grades were good when he was young, but his final results were poor. After high school, the welfare institution found him a job, which he did not like and he quit. Later, he got his driver's licence with the help of his foster mother's son, who paid more than RMB2,000. He works as a driver in a primary industry job. When there is not much work, he helps his foster parents with farm work.

The second case is Shu, a foster brother in the same family. He was younger than Kang and had primary school education. After he left school, he stayed unemployed in his foster family for years, but the institution helped him find work in a food shop. He was later injured and lost his job. When he was ready to work again, his foster mother was worried about his safety so she asked a family member to take him to a city for work and look after him.

The foster mother said she pays part of the travel costs for the children to find work and she does her best to help the children when they have difficulties. She said she cannot provide as much help for the young adults. Both the young men received employment help from the strong ties of the foster family – Kang was supported to get his driver's licence with the help of the foster mother's son, and Shu worked under the care of the foster mother's relative and with travel costs paid by the foster mother.

These orphans, who had low education and skills, relied on the strength of strong ties from their foster family. They worked in physical labour because of their low education and skills and the limited capability of their rural foster families.

Family strong ties as an intermediary to welfare institution strong ties

Kang's and Shu's cases also illustrate the foster families acting as an intermediary to the welfare institution strong ties. The foster parents helped their foster children find jobs through the institution. Other foster parents said that they did the same thing. Foster families believed that the welfare institution should be responsible for job placement since they are state wards and registered urban residents, which should give them additional privileges in the difficult job market. For example, Kang and Shu's foster mother repeatedly mentioned that they should be able to rely on the welfare institution for their employment, and she expects them to be provided with stable jobs and their own housing.

However, the attitude of some foster parents to the strong tie job support role of the welfare institution also seemed to negatively affect some young adults' approach to work. A welfare institution director blamed misinformation and overindulgence by foster parents as the reason why the young adults expect the institution to continue to take primary responsibility, even after living in the village during their childhood.

Welfare institution strong ties in job introduction and employment

The second strong tie for young adults is the welfare institution. Welfare institutions are the legal guardians for orphans, undertaking responsibility for their welfare during their childhood. In Datong, they contract this responsibility to rural foster families to provide the support. When a young adult orphan finds a job and is no longer dependent on the welfare institution, the formal responsibility ceases.

The case studies showed that in Datong, the institution took a far greater role than the statutory duties of guardian and provider, taking on the responsibility to find jobs and contribute to their well-being after they leave the family home or when asked by the young adult or foster family. The staff find jobs through the strong ties of the welfare institution and even of personal connections. The director was an intermediary for the first job for both Kang and Shu, discussed earlier. These two cases, however, indicate that a job placement may not be sustainable if it is found without considering the suitability of the job for the person and without job support to maintain the job.

Most young adults maintain contact with the welfare institution. They said that the welfare institution was the greatest contributor to their development and employment. When they had any difficulty, they still turned to the welfare institution first. Mo's case illustrates the use of the strong ties with the welfare institution after unsuccessfully attempting to rely on weak ties first. Mo was in her late 20s and has a university qualification. As a child, she had a physical disability that was fixed with surgery arranged by the institution. She has a university degree in English-language teaching. She worked in the foster care division of the welfare institution, responsible for education and language translation. After graduation from technical college, she unsuccessfully tried to find a job herself. At first, she thought that she should not rely on the welfare institution any more since they had already raised her.

Initially, she got job information mainly from her teachers, schoolmates and job fairs. She was a probationary teacher at a private English training class and a local high school, but was not made permanent. She attributed her failure to being too nervous and a lack of preparation for the job interview. When her foster mother visited the institution, she heard that they needed someone to replace a support worker on leave. She recommended Mo to the director, who agreed. Her first job was a temporary support worker at the welfare institution and she was later made permanent. The management transferred her from the support worker position to the foster care division. The request from the director for the special position on permanent staff was approved by the institution management, the city director of civil affairs, then the mayor.

She gained her BA degree in English by continuing her education in her spare time (with tuition paid by the welfare institution). She also received professional training paid for by the welfare institution. She regarded her employment at the institution as a successful, fortuitous process since she had intended to find a job herself without relying on the welfare institution, but the vacant position was a good opportunity for her and she was grateful for the stability.

Mo tried to rely on weak ties but failed until she got a good job when she turned to strong ties with the welfare institution through her mother as an intermediary. This is consistent with the strength of strong ties and intermediary hypothesis. Initially, the welfare institution offered her a casual job because of its ties to her as her official guardian. When they wanted to formalize her position, they acted as intermediary to the agencies with authority to approve it, which would have been impossible for Mo to do herself.

The case demonstrates not only the guardianship and foster care management role of the institution, but also a strong tie that some young adults expect to rely on for job placement. This was beyond the institution's duty to foster children. The director was personally involved in the request for the permanent position, using his personal strong ties to solve problems. The need for such senior intermediary intervention highlights a vulnerability for orphans who do not have this strong support from senior managers in the institution. Not all heads of welfare institutions have strong social ties and personal power, and not all mayors respond to special requests from welfare institutions.

Acquaintance weak ties in job search

The fourth case, Fang, had a mixed experience with weak ties, but was eventually successful when using stronger weak ties through an acquaintance. Fang was aged 20 years. Surgery arranged by the institution to repair a cleft lip and palate had left him with unclear speech. He grew up in a rural foster family. He majored in oral health care at a technical high school. At the time of the interview, he was about to graduate and was in an internship at a private dental clinic, where he would continue to work after graduation.

Fang did well in his professional training, but encountered difficulties when he tried to arrange an internship and job. First, he got job information through his school teachers and classmates. He was unsuccessful finding an internship at a major hospital because of the fees and because they did not want to accommodate his communication support needs. Finally, an acquaintance who was a schoolmate and an orphan from the welfare institution, and who had internship experience at the dental clinic, introduced him to the clinic.

He wanted to eventually open his own dental clinic by gaining an associate degree while working part-time but thought that it was too difficult to realise all this alone, and his rural foster family could not help. He planned to ask the welfare institution for help in the future if he had problems that he could not solve, or he could work at the institution. Most young adults would only be able to start a business with government support, which would require relevant departments to introduce concessions, such as loans and reducing business administration and taxation. Only the institution could be an intermediary to manage these ties with government departments.

In Fang's case, his first job searches failed through weak ties and then succeeded through stronger weak ties through an acquaintance. He attributed his success in finding the internship and job to the connections to acquaintances through the welfare institution because his rural foster family had no relevant connections. When his weak ties failed, he used his other weak ties to solve the problem – asking the acquaintance to introduce him. He planned to use his strong ties with the welfare institution for help when he established his own business in the future. Whether the institution had the resources to fill this intermediary role was another question.

Both Mo and Fang first tried to find a job on the basis of their education and skills, using indirect weak ties, but returned to direct strong and weak ties to solve their lack of competitiveness in the open market.

Building new weak ties

While most young adults got their jobs through strong ties, especially through their foster family or the welfare institution, some of them did so entirely through weak ties. The final case was Hai, who was in her late 20s. She had a master's degree and worked as a teaching assistant at a university. She was abandoned as a new baby because she had a physical disability. The institution sent her to a foster family immediately. Her foster family was poor and the living allowance was a reason why the family accepted her.

When she passed her university entrance examination, she worried about the tuition fees, so she chose a local university. The university waived her fees and provided a national scholarship, making it possible to complete her Bachelor of Arts. The university decided to sponsor her graduate education at another local university and signed an employment agreement with her to work as a teacher after her graduate education. Her goal was to gain a PhD through on-the-job education.

She attributed her successful job placement to the combination of her hard work, academic performance and support from the university. One teacher was moved by her experience and capability and helped her gain employment through connections from the teacher's husband, who worked in the personnel department of the university.

She emphasized that information about opportunities was important. Her foster family could not advise her because they were poor farmers, so she had to make decisions herself, but without information, not all of her decisions were correct. She suggested that the welfare institution or relevant departments should provide more information and opportunities to young adults so they could find suitable job positions.

This case demonstrates the utility of the weak ties hypothesis for job searching. For Hai, the university was a weak tie, though the local connection between the institution and university may have helped. She relied on a weak tie with a university teacher to act as an intermediary to other parts of the university.

Her experience is consistent with social resources theory, which states that weak ties are powerful in circumstances where they can help people move from their original social circles and make contact with people who hold more social resources (Lin et al, 1981). Hai had strong ties with her foster family and the welfare institution that enabled her to enter university and then leverage this capacity through weak ties with the university's decision-makers controlling the scholarships and employment of teachers.

The government tried to formalize building new weak ties in *Opinions on strengthening assistance for orphans 2006* (the Opinions), which was jointly issued by 15 ministries, including the Ministry of Civil Affairs. The Opinions specified detailed responsibilities and duties of multiple departments, including the departments of civil affairs, labour and social security, and housing administration, in job placement for young adults. However, almost none of the orphans had come into contact with the labour security department, the department for job placement, let alone other relevant departments.

Even necessary formalities were typically handled collectively by the welfare institution on behalf of the orphans. As adults, the orphans were supposed to be able to make contact with relevant departments themselves to establish a weak tie to acquire assistance. When asked why they were not willing to deal with these departments, the young adults answered: "We don't have any connection in these departments, and they simply won't provide any help for us". The leaders of the welfare institution, when interviewed, also confirmed this:

> "All of the Opinions issued by the authorities are principles only and can hardly be implemented at the grassroots level. Even when the welfare institution works with these departments, they are very reluctant to provide any support. There is no way for these children themselves to handle that."

Implications for policies to support young people leaving care

The case studies highlight the utility of the strong and weak ties framework for understanding the job-search experience of young adults leaving care. Four aspects of their social networks have policy implications: the security that young adults gain from having lived in a rural foster family; the multiple direct and indirect roles of the welfare institution before and after the young adults seek a job; the dependency on strong and weak ties to address disadvantage in the job market; and the importance of individual job capacity development and support.

The case-study analysis found that each of the young people had potential disadvantages in an open labour market, related to the quality and level of their rural education, disabilities, confidence from their history as rural foster care orphans and the limited resources (financial, information and connections) of their rural foster families. As a result, they were not able to simply rely on the same ties available to their peers in rural villages or cities, where they were entitled to return.

Connections and security from rural foster families

Most young people have strong ties with their family. The deep connections between family members mean that families tend to use all resources to provide support. This is particularly the case in China, where kinship relations and obligations are traditionally extremely important (Shang and Fisher, 2014a).

These expectations, which reflect strong family ties, also seemed to exist in foster care families. Compared to young adults in institutional care (Shang, 2003), the foster care case-study young people had foster parents with whom they had close ties, and they grew up in a village relatively free from discrimination because other foster care children also lived there. These experiences were important for preparing them for the job market and workplace, where they needed to be confident and adaptable with their workmates.

The strong family ties only had local effectiveness in job searching. Most of the young adults and their families said that this was because the families were in rural areas, with poor financial resources and limited social connections. The young adults with low skills were adequately supported by their families, who could help them find low-paid local or migrant worker jobs. Kang and Shu, for example, got help from their foster family strong ties when they looked for jobs. The more educated, ambitious young people had to look elsewhere for strong or weak ties to assist them in their job search. Here, the role of families as an intermediary to other ties was important, such as Mo's mother helping her get a temporary job at the welfare institution.

The attitude of the foster family whose responsibility it was to find the job also affected the effectiveness of the strong family ties for independence from the institution and the family. Kang and Shu's mother, for example, repeatedly mentioned that job placement was the welfare institution's responsibility. This probably affected the young people's attitude to their responsibility to find and keep a job.

These findings have implications for alternative care policy. Growing up in foster care seems to build strong ties between the orphans and the other foster family members, of which orphans in institutional care do not have the benefit. These ties helped them develop emotional and educational skills for adult life and job seeking. Young adults who have employment ambitions beyond the rural community need outside assistance to them and their foster parents to achieve their goals.

Multiple roles of the welfare institution

In addition to guardianship and service provision, the Datong institution also takes on responsibility for job placement for some orphans, which is beyond their statutory duties. The institution can advocate for the interests of young adults, taking the advantage of its status as a social organization and acting as an intermediary agent to help young adults find work through its informal and personal channels. The multiple roles fill the gaps in the capacity of the young people, their families and their rural communities highlighted earlier, and also recognize the emotional attachment and security that most of the young people feel towards the institution.

The sustainability of this approach and whether it supports empowerment and independence, however, are questionable. The institution has limited capacity, which is why it originally resorted to rural foster care. It would be overwhelmed if it arranged informal job searches for all young adults. Alternative approaches used internationally are to support the young person, family and community to prepare for transition to adulthood earlier in their childhood, so that their preferences, skills and capacity can be developed for independence. Options within this approach include information, training, community and workplace development, and other similar support.

Not all welfare institutions accept these responsibilities to prepare and support orphans to transition to adulthood, so the results of the Datong analysis cannot be generalized beyond benevolent institutions and directors. For example, in locations where the institutions for children and adults are separately administered, such as Beijing, the children's welfare institutions cannot influence the adult institutions to prioritize job placement.

Strong and weak tie dependency

The young adults in the case studies found their jobs through strong ties to their foster family and the institution, or weak ties that could act as intermediaries to the strong ties of the intermediary. Some orphans tried to find jobs through weak ties but failed, probably due to their lack of competitiveness in the job market and the lack of effective formal weak ties, such as outlined in the Opinion.

China's current formal job assistance channels for the young adult orphan group have failed to effectively replace or supplement the strong ties to the welfare institution. The economic transition and employment system reform have not addressed job assistance channels for young adults, except with an unimplemented policy statement. When young adults cannot get any help from formal job assistance channels, they must continue to rely on the accessible strong ties to the institution. It is foreseeable that with the improvement of the labour market, job search will rely more on weak ties than on strong ones. The general trend of the employment market requires the state to make relevant policies in time in order to rebuild or activate formal job assistance channels for young adults.

Job capacity development and support

The final implication from the cases is to develop and support the job capacity of young adults. Social networks have vital job-search functions, but they only supplement the job capacity of the young adult to find and keep a job. Their personal, family and community capacity influences the choice of strong or weak ties to seek job opportunities. The young adults with low capacity tended to acquire job opportunities through strong ties. Without weak ties, such as government job assistance channels, they relied on the strong ties with the welfare institution and foster families. In contrast, the young adults with higher capacity could rely on or build weak ties, for example, Fang and Hai.

Higher education levels and skills lead to higher competitiveness in the job market, allowing people to develop their strengths and empowering them to be discretionary and to have a say when they select jobs. Fang and Hai, for example, could overcome their disadvantages of disability, rural education and families without city connections. In addition, the connection to new groups made it easier to establish weak ties with others who hold social connections, and through these weak ties, establish more weak ties or intermediaries to strong ties. Information exchange and resource sharing with these weak ties increased the possibility of acquiring a preferred job.

Conclusion about social networks and employment

The experiences of these young people have implications for understanding the strength of strong and weak ties in job searching in China and implications for job support policy for young people leaving state care. The job capacity of young people starts with quality education, family support and community development. If they are supported to make choices about their future employment goals, they can become aware of their responsibilities to plan for their own independence within a competitive job market. This support during late childhood is a guardianship responsibility of welfare institutions towards the quality of their service provision during childhood. Access to vocational training relevant to their employment goals is a stepping stone to acquiring a preferred job.

In contrast to young people who grew up in institutional care, children who grow up in rural foster families have two strong tie networks: to their foster families and to the welfare institution. All young adult orphans can benefit during their childhood from their strong family ties to support their emotional and educational development. Families can continue to provide direct job-search assistance if the young adults' goals are for local low-skill jobs. They can also help with job-search costs, low-level job information and negotiating with government departments for job placement on behalf of young adults. In these respects, the welfare institutions can support foster families to provide this assistance and to instil these job-search expectations in the young people.

Welfare institutions can be reliable strong ties to find jobs through informal channels and act as intermediaries to advocate for the interests of young adults. Young adults with higher job capacity can also leverage weak ties through welfare institutions or by building new ones. The policy option of using formal weak tie support from government job support agencies does not seem to have been implemented.

Policy implications are that placing children in state care into foster families can have the benefit of developing strong ties. Support for these families from welfare institutions to maximize their education and employment skills would enhance this benefit. If welfare institutions helped families and communities to prepare young people for transition to employment and independence, they would be less likely to need to rely on the strong ties to institutions to find jobs. The implementation of government job-search assistance for young people in state care and other disadvantaged young people would also address this problem.

The strong and weak ties framework for understanding the job-search experience of young adults leaving care in China demonstrates that young adults in foster care use both strong ties and weak ties, depending on their job capacity and the relevance of the family and community ties to their job aspirations. Most of them are dependent on strong and weak ties to address the disadvantages that they have in the job market. Only those with high job capacity and high-level aspirations are able to leverage and build new weak ties to achieve their goals.

NINE

Housing pathways of young people leaving care

As discussed in earlier chapters, many of the young people still live in child welfare institutions in their adulthood. The impact of poor housing policy for young people leaving care potentially not only excludes them from housing, but also restricts their other social and economic opportunities, as introduced in Chapter Seven. This chapter uses the social exclusion framework to analyse the housing pathways of young people in state care who were trying to leave care at the time of the research. It considers their exclusion from the market, policy and society, and the interrelationship between these three aspects of exclusion due to their isolated childhood housing experience. It explores how the state manages their right to independent housing during their transition to adulthood and how their housing status affects other aspects of their adult life.

Without independent housing, many of the young people in care face multiple forms of social exclusion (Johnson et al, 2009). It affects not only health, education and overall well-being, but also self-identity and aspirations for social participation. Their expectations for future social relationships, their place in the community and their contribution to it can be stymied by their lack of housing options. Increasingly, too, the local governments in this research were concerned about the impact of its continued responsibility to house these young people into the foreseeable future.

Housing and social inclusion

The importance of the right to adequate housing and its key impact on social inclusion is recognized in international treaties and Chinese policy. The United Nations defines the right to adequate housing as 'each man, woman, youth and child have access to and retain safe house and community in peace and dignity' (UNHCHR, 2010), and calls on all countries to ensure their laws and policies on housing are appropriate for those most in need. The Second United Nations Conference on Human Settlements (Habitat II) held in 1996 passed the Habitat Agenda, which reiterated the commitment of states and governments to comprehensively and gradually fulfil the right to adequate housing (UNHCHR, 2010). It prioritizes the needs of people most likely to be excluded from housing:

> Some groups or individuals have a particularly hard time exercising their right to adequate housing as a result of who they are, discrimination or stigma, or a combination of these factors. To protect the right to housing effectively, it is necessary to pay attention to the specific situation of individuals and groups, in particular those living in vulnerable situations. These groups include women, children, slum-dwellers, homeless persons, persons with disabilities, displaced persons and migrants, indigenous peoples, etc. (UNHCHR, 2010)

Relevant to children who are orphaned and living with disabilities, the Convention on the Rights of the Child (UNCRC, 1989) enshrined four essential rights of children: the right to survival; the right to development; the right to protection; and the right to participation. Children's health, education and development and overall well-being are deeply influenced by the quality of their housing. According to clause 3 of Article 27 of the Convention:

> States Parties, in accordance with national conditions and within their means, shall take appropriate measures to assist parents and others responsible for the child to implement this right and shall in case of need provide material assistance and support programmes, particularly with regard to nutrition, clothing and housing. (UNCRC, 1989)

The right to housing security is also critical for people with disabilities. Social exclusion persistently prevents people with disabilities from exercising their right to adequate housing, including exclusion due to institutionalization, the absence of barrier-free environments and social discrimination. Young people with intellectual or psychosocial disabilities often have extremely poor access to housing security (Wiesel et al, 2015). It is a key social right recognized by states:

> States Parties recognize the right of persons with disabilities to an adequate standard of living for themselves and their families, including adequate housing, and shall take appropriate steps to safeguard and promote the realization

of this right without discrimination on the basis of disability, e.g. ensuring access by persons with disabilities to public housing programmes. (UNCRPD, 2008: Art 28)

Applying a multidimensional social inclusion framework implies that housing security is an important condition for young people's transition into their community and that the fulfilment of their right to adequate housing affects their realization of other rights, including economic security, social relationships such as intimate family ties and other meaningful social participation. With this framework, this chapter focuses on three topics: the right of young people in state care to independent housing in their communities for their transition to adulthood; the factors that influence access to independent housing, including barriers and facilitators; and the impact of housing conditions on their current and future expectations and social integration.

The qualitative research reviewed the data from the welfare institutions, interviewing young people in care, staff at the welfare institutions and social workers (see Chapter One). The chapter compares the outcomes of four different housing types of young people in care, with or without disabilities, in the four sites of Beijing, Taiyuan, Urumqi and Nanning. At each site, the researchers: spoke to young people in care, with or without disabilities, aged 19–25 years who no longer received state care; conducted in-depth interviews and focus group discussions with 48 young people in care, with or without disabilities, aged 16–40 years; and interviewed officials and professional workers closely associated with the support for children and young people in state care and foster care families. In addition to data from these four cities, the small-scale research in Datong City, Shanxi Province, which has a long history of foster care, was added to the analysis where relevant.

Housing systems and housing security for young people

The policy context of housing security for young people in care involves three systems: household-centred housing security (informal); the orphan basic living protection system; and the urban housing security system. Traditionally, Chinese housing security relies on family responsibility. Conventionally, when young people marry, the groom's parents are expected to offer a house to the couple. With urbanization and the commercialization of housing, such practices have adapted in various ways, such as parents purchasing apartments for children or paying the first instalment for the purchase. In the context of soaring house prices, this practice has become increasingly unsustainable. Parents often have to use all their savings to help their children secure housing. Young people who are orphaned and in state care do not have parents to fulfil this role, do not know their extended family and so do not have access to this housing security from a family. The social convention makes it difficult for young men in state care without access to housing to find a wife.

When the Chinese orphan basic living protection system was established in 2010 (see Chapter Two), the issue of the transition of young people in care to adulthood also became a concern (see Chapter Four). Various locations formulated general provisions about housing security for young people in state care. Young people in care mainly rely on the urban housing security system because the urban institution is their registered residence and they do not have access to family security. Yet, in the context of rapid urbanization and housing marketization, the welfare housing security system is undeveloped and provides inadequate support to groups with middle or low income.

The development of the urban housing system in China can be broken down into three phases: a welfare-based housing allocation system; the commercialization of housing; and the emergence of market economy-oriented housing security policies. Prior to 1979, housing was allocated by a state welfare-based housing system in urban areas, while household-based housing security persisted in rural areas.

During the welfare-based housing allocation phase (1950–79), state housing provision was based on decisions by the work units or institutions of employees. This system resulted in a serious housing shortage, poor-quality houses, inadequate maintenance and corruption in the allocation of houses. In addition to the state-owned housing, the family security system persisted, though the security was compromised. Although residents retained their privately owned property, they were no longer entitled to the land that the house was on.

In the reform phase of the housing allocation system (1979–98), the basis of the welfare-based housing system was gradually abandoned. In 1998, housing monetary reform marked the end of the welfare-based housing system and the establishment of the market-oriented housing allocation system. The development of the housing market began. From 1998 to 2007, the new housing security system witnessed full scale-up. At the beginning, a housing provision system focused on affordable housing was developed. Subsequently, along with soaring urban house prices, the policies gradually shifted their focus to low rental housing as the new priority for housing security. The state tried to promote the dynamic management of financially affordable housing and the limited acquisition of property rights. Housing security was incorporated into the scope of the government performance review (Li, 2008; Zhu, 2008). Inequalities in rural housing also changed, including safety, allocation and security of tenure (Wang et al, 2012).

Following 2007, investment in real estate became overheated and house prices rose to an unreachable level for average citizens. Inequality in housing grew (Fu et al, 2015). Unaffordable empty housing at market price sat alongside an insufficient supply of affordable housing in urban areas (Zhu, 2008) as the country shifted to a higher rate of urban than rural residents (Liu et al, 2015). A growing number of urban residents sought to return to welfare housing security. The emergent welfare housing security system now includes three approaches: affordable housing (commercial housing with government subsidization); low rental housing; and a rental allowance for housing. The government is most recently beginning to invest in public housing, contrary to international trends, perhaps because of the gap in provision in recent decades (Chen et al, 2014). The first two approaches to address the supply of affordable housing and low rental housing are insufficient to meet demand.

Young people leaving care struggle to find housing in this changing context. China is in transition from welfare to the commercialization of housing, yet the housing security system is still underdeveloped to protect people like young people leaving state care, who lack the personal or social resources to enter a commercial housing market. In major cities, market-based housing excludes most wage-earning young people unless their parents can support them to purchase a house. Young people leaving care can usually only rely on welfare support to enter the housing market.

Housing policies for young people leaving care

Young people leaving state care need independent housing in order to detach from welfare institutions and achieve independent living. This includes independent registered permanent residence, a place to live in the community close to their workplace and a residential space that supports independent social interactions and protects their personal privacy. Leaving care policies, including housing, were introduced in Chapter Four, and some of the young people and their housing experiences were initially discussed in Chapter Seven. The policies and experiences are further explored in this chapter.

In China, policymaking is largely delegated to government departments that formulate regulations as the basis for governance and administration. Government departments responsible for allocating affordable housing follow their own affordable housing allocation policies or those formulated by authorities at higher levels in the same sector. Not all welfare benefits articulated in official documents are actually provided in a particular location. Basic living protections and housing security policies for young people in care are not likely to be implemented unless they are also articulated in the local official documents on affordable housing allocations. In China, housing policies are highly decentralized, being formulated by local governments. The housing policies in Beijing, Taiyuan, Urumqi and Nanning are described here to illustrate the direction of housing policy change to support young people leaving care. They use the terms 'low rental housing' to mean government public housing and 'affordable housing' to mean government housing available to purchase for home-ownership.

Beijing housing policy

Housing security for young people in state care is incorporated into the policy documents of the Beijing Municipal Commission of Housing and Urban-Rural Development, which is the government authority responsible for housing allocation, the *Measures of Beijing on Management of Application, Review and Rental of Public Rental Houses 2011*. This means that state wards and other orphans are prioritized when they apply for affordable housing.

Opinions of Beijing People's Government General Office on Further Strengthening the Security for Orphans in the City (J.Z.B.F. (2011) Number 13)

A target group for housing security is any orphaned young person in Beijing. For orphans with housing property, the guardians are obliged to help them protect their property rights and maintain the property. Urban adult orphans without housing who do not live in a welfare institution are prioritized by the local government as the key target group of housing security if they meet the criteria for entitlement to urban low rental housing or other affordable housing. Rural adult orphans without housing who do not live in a welfare institution are included in rural dilapidated building renovation plans and prioritized in funding. Township or town governments and villagers' committees are to mobilize social resources and local villagers to help them build houses. Local governments are to include young adults in state care who are eligible for housing security into the urban housing security system and prioritize them while rationing public rental housing. Additionally, they grant rent allowances to those who are entitled to low rental housing, or support them to obtain other affordable housing, in order to help meet their need for housing following their placement in the community.

Measures of Beijing for Management of Affordable Housing (Trial) 2007

The target group for housing security with this policy is households, meaning that young people leaving care are usually not covered. The applicant must hold urban registered permanent residence in Beijing for at least three years and must be at least 18 years old. In households with one family member only, the applicant must be at least 30 years old. The applicant's household average per capita housing area and household income and assets must conform to the policies and criteria defined by the government. Priority targets for allocation are: households subject to housing demolition and relocation when land is acquired for building affordable housing or other key projects; households reallocated due to the reconstruction of old urban areas or the conservation of historic areas; and households with poor access to housing, as well as older people over 60 years old, people with severe disabilities or major diseases, key entitled group members, and ex-servicemen, but not other young people in state care.

Measures of Beijing for Management of Price-Capped Commercial Housing (Trial) (J.Z.F. (2008) Number 8)

Again, the target group for housing security with this policy is urban households, meaning that young people leaving care are not included. Urban residents' households with medium income and poor access to housing, rural households affected by housing demolition and relocation, and other households specified by the municipal government in Beijing are included.

Measures of Beijing on Management of Urban Low Rental Housing 2007

Although the target group for housing security in this policy is households, this can include young people leaving care if the household has an average per capita income, the household gross assets and

159

household per capita usable floor area conform to the specifications, and they meet one of the following circumstances: the household is subject to housing demolition and relocation; has family members with specific diseases or severe disabilities; has family members over 60 years old; is residing in houses defined as hazardous housing by the municipal government; and has at least two family members.

Measures of Haidian District on Placement of Adult Orphans

According to the policy in the inner-city district of Haidian, orphans of at least 18 years old are entitled to low rental housing and a lump-sum placement allowance of RMB150,000. The applicant must have a registered permanent residence of Beijing or have been raised by the welfare institution in Haidian District, with the capacity to live an independent life and capacity for paid employment. Adult orphans who remain unemployed are entitled to an allowance for low rental housing rent, heating expenses and property fees.

Measures of Beijing on Management of Application, Review and Rental of Public Rental Houses (J.J.F. (2011) Number 25)

The target group for housing security includes young people leaving care. Households on the waiting list for low rental housing, affordable housing or price-capped commercial housing are prioritized; households with family members over 60 years old, serious diseases or a history of major surgeries, severe disabilities, key entitled group members or ex-servicemen, model workers awarded by provincial or higher-level authorities, or adult orphans are prioritized. Adult orphans are also prioritized.

Taiyuan City, Shanxi housing policy

In Taiyuan, the need for housing by young people in care is not included in the measures for applying for low rental housing, and they are not prioritized as the target group in the provision of housing with low rent. Young people in care are only considered alongside any other affordable housing applicants when applying for low rental housing.

Measures of Taiyuan City on Application, Review, Public Announcement and Withdrawal of Low Rental Housing for Low Income Households 2009

The target group for housing security is any household meeting the criteria, which might include young people leaving care, such as low-income married households with poor access to housing. Provision of housing with low rent prioritizes households registered as a target group for low rental housing with orphans, older people or family members with serious diseases or disabilities, households eligible to minimum living protection, and other households in urgent need for relief.

Measures of Taiyuan City on Application, Review and Public Announcement of Affordable housing 2009

The target group for housing security is urban low-income households. No specific provisions for young people in care are included.

Urumqi City, Xinjiang housing policy

In Xinjiang, young people must rely on the general housing security system to address their housing needs.

Notice on Circulating the Opinions of Urumqi City on Strengthening Support for Orphans 2012

Adult orphans with the ability to live an independent life have access to different housing security provisions according to their financial capacities. Similar to the situations in other cities, the housing security types in Urumqi include public low rental housing and affordable housing. The state's subsidized housing policies are primarily targeted at low-income groups, including adult orphans and children with disabilities.

A major shortfall in the housing security policies is the exclusion of people with disabilities. Applicants must possess 'capacity to live an independent life' and 'full capacity for civil conduct', which consistently precludes people with disabilities from the right to adequate housing. With this definition, people with intellectual or mental disabilities are excluded from access to housing security. This clause was not evident in the policies of the other cities in this research. In principle, all cities have similar but slightly different policies, so it is unclear whether other cities implement their policy in a similar way, which may be likely.

Provisions of Urumqi City on Management of Application, Review and Rental of Public Rental Housing 2012

The target group for housing security might include young people leaving care if they meet the criteria of households with middle to lower income and poor access to housing, newly employed workers, and migrant workers in Urumqi City. If the applicants are married, they can apply as a household; if unmarried and newly employed, they can apply as new employees.

Provisions of Urumqi City on Management of Application, Review and Rental of Low Rental Housing 2012

The target group for housing security explicitly includes young people leaving care. Priorities are households with low income and poor access to housing. The applicants must be married or apply as a household. Provision of housing is through low rental, a rental allowance or a rental deduction. Young adult orphans who are registered as subjects of social support and relief by commerce and civil affairs departments, and who are aged less than 30 years and married, or over 30 years of age and unmarried, can apply for affordable housing independently. Second, young adult orphans who are registered as subjects of social support and relief by civil affairs departments, and unmarried people of at least 18 years of age who are the sole member of the household, enjoy minimum living protection and have full capacity for civil conduct, can apply independently. This provision can assist young people in care growing up in welfare institutions to apply for low rental housing.

Provisions of Urumqi City on Management of Application, Review and Rationing of Affordable Housing 2012

The target group for housing security includes young people leaving care in households with low income and poor access to housing. They must purchase the house as a household.

Nanning City, Guangxi housing policy

The housing security system was launched in Nanning City in 2003. Beginning from 2009, the city is implementing the policies on low rental housing security organized by the Nanning City Leading Group on Housing Security for Urban Low Income Households of the Nanning City Housing Property Administration.

Notice on Circulating the Detailed Methods of Low-Rent House Provision in Nanning City 2008

The policies target households with low income and poor access to housing; the applicants must be married or apply as a household. Orphans are provided with low rental housing, a financial housing allowance and rent reductions. Orphans with serious disabilities who are married are eligible to apply for low rental housing, but other orphans are not eligible.

The policies established the low rental housing security type with a combination of a rental allowance, the provision of low rental housing and rent deductions. The rental allowance refers to granting an allowance to households with low income and poor access to housing to apply for low rental housing in the market. Provision of low rental housing refers to the public provision of houses to households with low income and poor access to housing. The government charges them the low rental cost. Rent deduction refers to public housing rental agencies reducing the rent to the low rental housing cost for households with low income and poor access to housing.

Nanning has five standards for access to low rental housing: standards for low income; poor access to housing; the floor area of low rental housing; housing rental allowance; and housing rent. Many landlords choose not to lease houses to families with members who are old, weak, ill or with disabilities for fear that they may become ill or die in the houses. The policy stipulates that the government secure housing policy is to prioritize these households. Low-income households with poor access to housing and with family members who are seriously ill or have disabilities and no kin, ex-servicemen with injuries or disabilities, family members of a martyred soldier, or members who lost their ability to work can apply for housing with low rent, and the government should prioritize them in helping them secure housing.

This provision is relevant for young adult orphans, who might be included in these categories if they have disabilities because they also have no relatives. The categories include people who are seriously ill, which means major diseases, or family members with disabilities, which means an assessed level of disability in vision, mobility, intelligence, mental state, hearing or speech. According to this definition, young adult orphans who are physically healthy or have minor disabilities are not priority applicants for housing with low rent.

The housing security policy is primarily targeted at low-income households, with the two important eligibility criteria for low rental housing security being low income and poor access to housing. Low income is defined as the annual average per capita income being lower than 60% of the average per capita disposable income of Nanning urban residents in the previous year; poor access to housing is defined as the average per capita building area being lower than 60% of that of urban residents in the previous year. Since young people in care cannot generally marry without housing, most of them remain single, and those who have jobs generally have an income that is higher than the low-income standard, and thus are not entitled to housing security. Therefore, the housing security policy of Nanning City does not address their problems in accessing housing.

Summary of housing policies

Only Beijing has a fund for the housing of young people from state care (Wang, 2009). In other areas, the only recourse for young people leaving care is the general welfare housing security system, including preferential eligibility for local urban low rental housing or other affordable housing (Urumqi Civil Affairs Bureau, 2012). Nanning City also stipulates that city finance is responsible for subsidizing housing costs beyond the welfare housing security if the income of young people leaving care is less than the average annual salary of the city's urban employees (Nanning City People's Government General Office, 2013).

Except for Beijing, young people leaving care do not have preferential eligibility for housing and must rely on welfare institutions. Shanghai, Nanjing and Shandong have policies to support housing rental costs, but since housing is very expensive, affecting major interests, it often becomes a disputed topic in the community. As the welfare housing security system matures, young people leaving care might gain better access to subsidized or affordable housing. The follow-up research found that a few young people had already obtained low rental public housing in one site.

Social exclusion and young people's housing security

In addition to local policies, the second aspect of housing inclusion is the structural factors that influence the young people's access to independent housing. These structural considerations help explain young people's exclusion from housing through policy or market exclusion.

Housing support policy exclusion

The earlier policy description suggests that the housing security system in China is continuing to develop. Commercial housing in the market is the primary source of housing. In such a context, young people in care have problems obtaining housing independently. Although policy responses are beginning, at the time of the research, no substantial progress had been made to address the question of subsidized housing for most of the young people leaving care. Welfare institutions strive to help young people in care find state-subsidized housing, but since few of the policies specifically prioritize them, according to the directors of the child welfare institutions, most young people still have no access to additional housing security, except by remaining in the institution.

The Chinese welfare housing reform policies cover six aspects: promoting house deposit savings; preferential prices for housing purchases; rental allowances; constructing affordable housing; financial allowances to purchase housing; and low rental housing (Li, 2002). However, policy support is still very limited for the housing security of young people in care, as summarized previously. In addition to the omission of young people in care from policy design, the construction of state-subsidized housing is slow, and widespread corruption seriously hampers the implementation of government housing security policies.

For example, in the case of Taiyuan, the *Opinions on Strengthening Security for Orphans 2011* stipulated that for adult orphans entitled to subsidized housing security or other affordable housing, local governments should prioritize them when allocating low rental housing or rental allowances. The priority target group of low rental housing supply is urban families with low income and poor access to housing. Without a marriage certificate, young people leaving care are not a priority when they apply for low rental housing. Most adult orphans growing up in welfare institutions, particularly young men, cannot marry because they lack a wide social network, their income is low and they have no independent housing. Such housing priority policy forces young adult orphans into a paradoxical cycle: without a house, they cannot marry; without marriage, they cannot apply for low rental housing, which is the only housing that they could afford. In this policy context, it is rare that young people in care would have access to subsidized housing. They must participate in the market competition for private housing or stay in the welfare institutions.

Housing market exclusion

Most of the young people leaving care were in low-income jobs or unemployed because of the disadvantages they had faced during their childhood, being excluded by their status as orphans and segregated in institutional care, and without having adequate disability support, as discussed in Chapter Seven. Without government support, the young people with low incomes cannot afford market-based rent or house prices.

The only young people in the research cases who could afford market housing costs for rent or ownership were those with access to government housing support in Beijing and one young man with an inheritance for a deposit, Kang, who was also supported by the institution to buy an affordable house from the institution. Otherwise, the young people were excluded from the housing market. This exclusion is common to all low-income groups in urban China whose families cannot support their housing costs, not just young people leaving care.

The development of public systems for effective housing security to supply affordable housing for purchase and low rental housing is still weak in most cities for any low-income groups, including young people leaving care. For example, the 21-year-old young man Li, described in Chapter Seven, had a secure job at the institution, but was unlikely to find a higher-paid job in the community due to discrimination associated with having been a state ward and his hepatitis status. His income was low (after-tax monthly salary of RMB1,600) compared to his classmates from the community who had a monthly salary of RMB4,000–5,000. The young people with low-paid jobs could not forge the economic foundation sufficient for independent living away from the institution. Li described the relationship between his low salary and housing rental costs. The researcher asked how he would define his independence. Li replied: "I would have my own house out of the state child welfare institution, and I would be able to provide for myself. And I could save money and live individually".

Li and the researcher calculated whether Li's income could support his dream for independent living. From his after-tax salary of

RMB1,600, he would have monthly rent costs of over RMB1,000 for a one-bed apartment in the local area. Additionally, he would have to pay bills, a strata levy, daily necessities, food, transport, socializing costs and other essential expenses. Li's salary was far from adequate for affording independent housing.

In summary, most of the young people were excluded from the private and public housing markets because they were unemployed or in low-income jobs. Except in Beijing, neither the policies about leaving state care nor the housing policies adequately addressed their need for housing support. Most of them had no option but to remain in an institution.

Housing status of young people leaving care

The first part of this chapter reviewed the policies to address structural exclusions from housing security. The remainder turns to examine the experience of the young people trying to access housing. They recognized that a critical step in leaving care was to find independent housing. During their childhood, most children in state care either lived in group settings in welfare institutions or lived in foster families or other family-based care (see Chapter Two). Did that change when they became adults and how were the welfare institutions supporting them to secure independent housing? Most young people continued to live in group housing, even if they left the welfare institution (see Table 9.1).

Few of them had secured housing in the market as private renters and no one had purchased private housing in the market. The young people in private rental properties were all in Beijing and had the benefit of the government rental allowance; only one young person paid the market-based rent independently. Despite the housing welfare policies described earlier, few orphans had secured government affordable housing (4%) and none lived in government or welfare institution low rental housing. Only one young person secured housing with the support of their employer and another had purchased an affordable housing unit with the support of the institution. All the other young people in care relied on the welfare institutions unless they were attending school or lived with their foster family. The housing experiences of the young people in each of these housing options are described in more detail here.

Table 9.1: Housing status of the young people leaving state care

Housing option	Provider	Single room conditions	Payment	Percent
Group quarters	Welfare institutions	2–4 people	Free at welfare institution	56
Group quarters	Schools	6–10 people	Paid by welfare institutions, or schools charge reduced room rate	11
Private rental apartments	Private landlords	Varied conditions	Paid by young person, municipal government rental allowance	11
Housing in foster family	Foster families	1–3 people	Paid by welfare institutions, foster parents provide support	11
Low rental or free housing	Welfare institutions	Unit	Provided by welfare institutions	6
Group quarters	Employers	8–10 people	Employers charge reduced room rate or paid by young person	2
Affordable housing	Municipal government	Unit	Purchased by young person, government allowance supplement	2
Affordable housing	Welfare institutions	Unit	Purchased by young person, welfare institution allowance supplement	2
Low rental housing	Municipal government	Unit	Paid by young person, government allowance supplement	–
Low rental housing	Welfare institutions	Unit	Paid by young person, welfare institution allowance supplement	–
Private housing	Private owners	Varied conditions	Purchased by young person	–

Notes: Data for 2013. *N* = 54.

Group quarters provided by welfare institutions, schools or employers

Group quarters were the primary housing option for young people in state care, offered by welfare institutions, schools or employers (see Table 9.2). Most of the young people continued to live in dormitories at the welfare institutions. Some of them who worked outside the institution lived in dormitories provided by their employers during workdays and returned to the welfare institutions during weekends or holidays. Those who attended schools usually lived in the school dormitories, the cost of which was paid by the welfare institutions, and they also returned to the welfare institution during weekends or holidays.

Table 9.2: Young people living in group quarters

Alias	Sex	Age	Disability	Education	Employed or studying	Housing	Married	Alternative care	Place
Mao	M	40	Yes	Primary	Unemployed	Dormitory welfare institution	No	Institution	Taiyuan
Hong	F	37	Yes	No schooling	Employed at state child welfare institution	Dormitory welfare institution	No	Foster	Nanning
Ming	F	30	Yes	Junior primary	Employed at state child welfare institution	Dormitory welfare institution	No	Foster	Nanning
Jin	M	26	Yes	Technical college	Employed at massage clinic	Dormitory welfare institution	No	Institution	Taiyuan
Hu	M	24	No	Junior college	Employed	Dormitories at work and welfare institution	No	Institution	Nanning
Bao	M	23	Yes	Technical college	Employed part-time	Dormitory welfare institution	No	Foster	Beijing
Bo	M	22	No	Technical secondary	Casual work or unemployed	Dormitory welfare institution	No	Mixed	Taiyuan
Zeng	F	22	Yes	University	Student	Dormitory school	No	Institution	Urumqi
Li	M	21	Yes	Technical college	Employed at state child welfare institution	Dormitory welfare institution	No	Institution	Urumqi
Yong	M	18	No	Technical college	Student	Dormitory school	No	Mixed	Nanning

Notes: M = male; F = female.

Group quarters in welfare institutions vary in lodging arrangements and conditions, the two main types being dormitories and small group families. Some young people were particularly dissatisfied with living in group care, for example, if they lived in large dormitories or the rooms were very old and dirty. The young people still in education believed that their living conditions negatively affected their capacity to study. They hoped that they might enter university in other regions or leave the welfare institution for good after they graduate from college and begin to work. Some of the young people with disabilities relied entirely on the welfare institutions, where they continued to live. Welfare institutions provide them with basic living security, housing and jobs. They did not leave the institution and had no means to live independently or even marry.

The central government investment to upgrade facilities in child welfare institutions affected housing conditions. The comments about the conditions from the young people later in the chapter reflect this improvement. In Nanning, the state child welfare institution renovated a building in the institution and renamed it a youth dormitory. Eleven of the 12 young people in the research lived in this dormitory. The conditions were higher-quality, with each room housing two or three young people and having its own bathroom and balcony.

Some of the young people expressed satisfaction with the dormitory lodging arrangements, while also strongly exhorting the welfare institution to help them obtain independent housing. Especially as they grew older, sharing a single room became more antithetical to their social needs. This institutional housing could not meet their need for an adult life. Although the welfare institutions did not forbid the young people to continue living in group care, the conditions were not appropriate for adult life. They had no independent space for themselves, intimate relationships or social interactions. Most welfare institutions are located in remote areas far from urban centres, which is inconvenient for paid employment. For example, Bo was the 22-year-old young man introduced in Chapter Six on identity, who kept his orphan status quiet until he knew people well. He picked up part-time jobs in the local community but he still lived in the institution because he could not afford private rental with his limited earnings.

The institution staff spoke about how they helped by providing housing in the institution for young people who were not able to afford other housing, but they recognized that it was not convenient or suitable for well-paying jobs. The young people living in the institution held strong opinions about what should be done to provide them with better housing support. For example, Hu was the 24-year-old successful civil engineer who grew up in institutional care, introduced in Chapter Seven. Although he had found work and was a role model to younger teenagers living in the institution, he was discontented about his housing situation and what that meant for his future. He did not know how or when he could acquire his own home. It was an urgent problem for him to have his own private space that felt like his own home. He particularly emphasized that welfare institutions should coordinate with housing authorities to support them to obtain affordable housing to buy or low rental housing. He also suggested that the institution could help him pay the first instalment, as parents would, while he would pay subsequent instalments. He did not want to stay at the welfare institution because it was not his home. He said:

> "I need help. I have a job and can earn money. I hope to have my own independent space. But my salary is inadequate to pay rent, let alone the price of a house. So I have to continue residing in the welfare institution."

Some young people living in small family group care were still attending school, so they only came back to the institution on weekends. Zeng was the 22-year-old university student with disabilities introduced in Chapter Five, who had escaped an abusive family and adult welfare institution before she lived in the children's institution. Now that she was older, she lived in the university dormitory and a small family group apartment with six other young people at the welfare institution during term breaks. She said that she was content with her current living environment and facilities. However, she said that she "Wants to have a quiet home", and would consider how to move out of the welfare institution and live independently after she graduated.

Despite their social and economic constraints, many of the young people still living in group care were striving for independent housing, particularly the ones who were still studying or had grown up in foster care. Yong, the 18-year-old student living in the dormitory at his college, said that he had always planned to live in his own home. He expected to earn his own living after he graduated from college and move out of the welfare institution. He did not feel free in the welfare institution. He hoped that he would achieve his plan of independent housing by obtaining information about preferential housing policies and how to apply. He hoped that someone would provide occupational support and help him gather sufficient financial resources to meet the housing costs.

Apartments provided by welfare institutions

Many of the welfare institution managers view it as their responsibility to provide a home for the young people in care and view young people in care as their children. In Taiyuan, a senior worker said that the young people in care "Are deemed as children; when the children become adults of 18 years old, the institutions won't stop helping them or giving them allowances although the policy says no".

Some of the young people remain living in the welfare institutions, including those with mild disabilities or who are unable or unwilling to work in the community, as well as those who work in the community. They are provided with housing and a monthly allowance of RMB100 and petty cash of RMB50. Other young people remain the responsibility of the institution but they work in the community and live in a rental apartment outside of welfare institution; they also receive a monthly living allowance of RMB600. Some orphans who are successful in their career do not come back to collect the allowance, while those who are not successful voluntarily come back to claim the allowance.

In the first group are also young people who live in the institution, work and have established families but have no place to reside outside of the welfare institution. Some welfare institutions build additional houses containing single apartments on their land, which they give to the young people in their care who have married (see Table 9.3). The institution takes the traditional role of parents, where just like a family in which the young person has no dedicated house at the time of marriage, a separate room in the family's house is used for the married couple. The young people living in these institution apartments expressed deep gratitude for this fortunate arrangement. Although they and their children still reside and grow up in the welfare institution, they benefit from a secure, free family home.

In the research, the four married couples of Jing, Mei, Bing and Mo had stable jobs but lived in the institution. Their stories are told in other parts of the book. One of them, Bing, even held a position in a government public institution. However, due to housing costs, low wages and security, they lived in the old apartments provided by the welfare institution. Jing, the 38-year-old married mother, said:

> "We got married and live in the apartment provided by the welfare institution. The building is old. The director of the welfare institution had the building renovated to reinforce it. We have free lodging and dinner at the welfare

Table 9.3: Young people living in welfare institution family units

Alias	Sex	Age	Disability	Education	Employed or studying	Housing	Married	Alternative care	Place
Jing	F	38	Yes	Junior middle	Employed at massage clinic	Family unit welfare institution	Yes	Institution	Taiyuan
Mei	F	34	Yes	Junior middle	Employed at state child welfare institution	Family unit welfare institution	Yes	Institution	Taiyuan
Bing	M	28	No	Technical secondary	Employed	Family unit welfare institution	Yes	Institution	Taiyuan
Mo	F	28	Yes	Higher education	Employed	Family unit welfare institution	Yes	Foster	Datong

Notes: M = male; F = female.

Table 9.4: Young people living in private rental apartments

Alias	Sex	Age	Disability	Education	Employed or studying	Housing	Married	Alternative care	Place
Zhong	M	26	Yes	Technical secondary	Employed	Private rental	No	Foster	Beijing
Luo	M	23	No	Technical secondary	Employed[a]	Private rental	No	Mixed	Beijing
Guan	M	21	No	Technical secondary	Employed	Private rental	No	Mixed	Beijing

Notes: M = male; F = female. [a] Waiting for a government-arranged job.

173

institution, which can ease our burden.... My husband is working here, and the director is nice, accommodating us with room and board ... we each earn more than 1,000 yuan a month, and we have an amount of savings after expenses for food and my child's school. In consideration of our financial conditions, the welfare institution gives us a subsidy of more than 200 yuan every month."

Private rental apartments

The Beijing government provides young people leaving care with a housing rental allowance, as described in Chapter Four. Although rental costs in Beijing were the highest in the four research sites, several young people leaving care in Beijing were able to pay the market-based rent for an apartment appropriate for their work and living (see Table 9.4). In the other locations, their income was not high enough to pay market rent, they did not receive a subsidy and they continued to live in the free welfare institution dormitory.

In Beijing, the three young people who rented houses were young men aged between 21 and 26 years. None of them were married, one of them had disabilities and they were all employed. They had all grown up with some experience of foster care, either as the main form of alternative care or as part of a mix of care that they had received. Perhaps this exposure to living in the community with a foster family during their childhood meant that they were more likely to strive for this housing independence.

Luo, aged 23 years, was the young man who had lived in institutions and foster care. He had strong relations with his foster family, discussed in earlier chapters, and disliked living in the welfare institution. He wanted to live in the community, where he would know more people and find new opportunities. He used his own initiative to found a job and private unit on the Internet. He felt that his income was enough with the government subsidy to rent a place to live independently. He criticized the way in which the government's policy on leaving care was implemented. Although he knew how to find a job and place to rent, he said that many other young people who had grown up in institutional care did not have the capacity or support to deal with these basic affairs. He said that some young people who had left the institution, such as those with disabilities or with little education, were uncompetitive in the labour market. They wanted to return to the welfare institution but that option was no longer available to them. He felt sorry for their plight and thought that the government should give them more support in order to make their transition out of care succeed.

Housing of foster families

Children who grew up in foster families arranged by the institution can often live with the foster family before independence. The foster families are primarily located in rural areas, though a few foster families are urban residents. In rural areas, the foster care arrangements have explicit requirements about the standard of housing in foster family homes; generally, the standard must not be lower than the local average housing standard. Some urban foster families voluntarily raise children who were abandoned. They view the children as their own children and the children remain living in the families as long as it is feasible for the families. The research cases where the young people continued to live with their foster families involved those who were young, unmarried and mostly still studying (see Table 9.5).

When the young people in foster care reach an age for independence, they may leave the foster families and move into independent housing. Like other families, the foster parents consider how to help their grown-up foster children secure their first home. Some of the foster parents were considering giving their property to their foster children as the parents aged, though they were concerned about objections from their other children. Other young people with disabilities in foster care who did not have sufficient government support to achieve independence remained with the foster families as long as the institution continued to pay their living expenses, such as in Datong. This housing continuity in the community was threatened in locations where the policy position of the institution responsible for adults did not support foster care payments, such as in parts of Beijing, as described in Chapter Four.

Low rental public housing

After the housing policy reforms away from a welfare housing system towards the market, the availability of low rental public housing is very limited, as described earlier. None of the young people in the research had successfully applied for and secured low rental housing. In follow-up research visits, some welfare institutions had begun to assist young people to secure low rental housing, though they had not yet moved into the new units.

Table 9.5: Young people continuing to live with their foster family

Alias	Sex	Age	Disability	Education	Employed or studying	Housing	Married	Alternative care	Place
Ying	F	22	Yes	Technical secondary	Student	Foster family	No	Mixed	Beijing
Miao	F	21	No	Technical college	Student	Foster family	No	Other	Taiyuan
Shu	M	19	Yes	Primary	Employed part-time	Foster family	No	Foster	Datong
Jiang	M	19	No	Technical secondary	Unpaid intern	Foster family	No	Foster	Taiyuan
Pai	F	16	Yes	Junior middle	Student	Foster family	No	Mixed	Taiyuan
Yu	F	16	No	Technical secondary	Student	Foster family	No	Mixed	Taiyuan

Notes: M = male; F = female.

Table 9.6: Young people in affordable housing

Alias	Sex	Age	Disability	Education	Employed or studying	Housing	Married	Alternative care	Place
Kang	M	25	Yes	Higher secondary	Employed	Own subsidized house from welfare institution	No	Foster	Datong
Hui	M	21	No	Primary	Employed	Dormitory welfare institution	No	Institution	Urumqi

Notes: M = male; F = female.

Table 9.7: Young people with private housing

Alias	Sex	Age	Disability	Education	Employed or studying	Housing	Married	Alternative care	Place
Jing	F	38	Yes	Junior middle	Employed at massage clinic	Family unit welfare institution	Yes	Institution	Taiyuan
Miao	F	21	No	Technical college	Student	Foster family	No	Other	Taiyuan

Notes: M = male; F = female.

Affordable housing apartments

Affordable housing is built by the government to be available for low-income people to purchase for home-ownership. Although the housing is more affordable than market-priced properties, the average young person leaving care still cannot afford to purchase it. In the research, only one young man, Kang, aged 25 years, was purchasing an affordable home (see Table 9.6). When he was 17 years old, his parents died in an accident. The compensation for his parents' death totalled over RMB200,000 (£20,000). He used the money to pay the first instalment when he successfully qualified to purchase an affordable unit with the support of the welfare institution.

Another young man, Hui, aged 21 years, received a sum from a pension when his parents both died. With the pension and the support of the welfare institution, he paid the first instalment for affordable housing, though he had not yet obtained a house. Needless to say, Kang's and Hui's situations were rare and none of the other young people were likely to receive such a lump sum to secure a home. Most of the young people would only be eligible to apply for affordable housing when they reached 30 years old. That requirement restricted their marriage prospects, social connections and work possibilities until they reached that age.

Private housing ownership

The final housing option is private housing. In the major cities, the young people could not afford market-priced housing. In Taiyuan, housing in rural areas is cheaper, so private purchase is sometimes possible (see Table 9.7). The married woman with disabilities, Jing, was working and has a child. She said that although she lived in an apartment in the welfare institution with her family, she had purchased a very cheap house in a rural area for RMB20,000 (UK£2,000). She viewed it as security in case the welfare institution changed its policy and no longer allowed her to stay in the institution, meaning that she had an alternative place to live. The condition and location of the house were not appropriate for her to live in it, especially considering her disabilities, so she chose to stay at the welfare institution in the meantime.

Miao was a younger woman aged 21 years and still at college. She grew up in a foster family who regard her as their natural child and she had a strong sense of her self-identity through these close bonds, as described in Chapter Six. Their relationship was informal foster care that was formalized when that option became available. She planned to purchase a market-priced unit with the help of her parents when she began to work in the future.

Impact of housing constraints on social inclusion

The third part of the research about housing is about the impact of these housing constraints on the young people's social inclusion, including their independence, employment and social connections. This section illustrates the impact of these factors through the experiences of the young people. The link between housing and other social inclusion is also picked up throughout the other chapters. As discussed in Chapter Four, independent housing is a precondition for independent resident registration (*hukou*), which entitles people to public services in the location.

As canvassed in Chapters Seven and Eight, the housing location and economic security connection is critical for access to employment opportunities. In the research, some young people spoke about this association between where they lived and their jobs. Many of them who lived in the institutions also engaged in temporary odd jobs in the welfare institutions. Others had turned down or left jobs if the employers did not provide housing because they could not afford the housing costs themselves. The impact of housing on social connections and marriage opportunities were the two other links that the young people raised.

Social connections

Lack of independent housing had a significant impact on the social interactions of the young people in care. During the childhood of the young people who grew up in the institutions, their social interactions were with each other, in their schools, in their workplaces, with peers and with staff at the welfare institutions. Most of them continued to live in the welfare institutions when they became adults, and so did their children if they married. Their social relationships were confined to the small circle centred on the institution. The closed social relationships reduced their opportunities for employment and social interactions, accentuating a vicious circle of constraints on independent housing and marriage opportunities, as first raised in Chapter Six. For example, Li, the 21-year-old young man who worked in a full-time low-paid job at the institution and could not afford independent housing costs, concluded:

"I wish to live an independent life, too. But my income doesn't allow me to do so. After all, I've already grown up and am no longer a child; I feel inadequate in social interactions if I continue to reside in the state child welfare institution."

Marriage

The second impact of constrained housing choices on social inclusion is through marriage opportunities. In the absence of parents to provide or support the costs of housing for newly married couples, young people leaving state care are disadvantaged in what they can offer a potential partner. Most of them do not have independent housing. The young people said their housing situation had a profound impact on their considerations and practices in dating and marriage.

Young men who continued to live in dormitories at the institution, school or work were the most disadvantaged in finding a partner because their *hukou* (registered residence status) was viewed as 'households without house'. Even if they had not started an intimate relationship, this status affected their considerations about finding a partner. For example, Hu, the 24 year old with full-time employment who had grown up in foster care, was a successful model to other young people at the welfare institution. His academic performance was excellent and he had attended a good college. He had a good job after graduation, but his identity as being an orphan and living in the institution made him unconfident. He said:

> "As a child growing up in the welfare institution, I'm always not confident in myself, and so I'm not confident in taking a girlfriend as I have no assets. Although others told me I should be confident in myself, once I think of the future, such as the issues of housing and money, I lose my confidence."

These young men living in the institution compared themselves unfavourably to others when they were planning for marriage. Jin, the 26-year-old young man who had grown up in the institution and worked in a massage clinic, said:

> "As boys, we definitely must have a certain level of resources before making girlfriends.... You certainly hope other people don't discriminate against you.... No matter how

others are disadvantaged, they are in a better position than me. I have nothing. How can I interact with them with confidence?"

Jin was so worried about his status that he ended a relationship with his girlfriend during college. He viewed the problem of how to get married as a heavy pressure on him, though he still expected to "Get married when I'm 27, 28 or even 30 years old". Unlike Jin, other young people had given up on the idea of marriage. The two young women discussed in Chapter Seven, Hong and Ming, aged 37 and 30 years, respectively, who had grown up in foster care, said that they dared not marry because if the marriage did not last, then they would have given up their welfare security at the institution when their registration was transferred to their husband's *hukou*, and they would have no other way to support themselves and their children if their marriage failed. Despite having grown up in foster care, they had very little education, perhaps because of their disabilities, so their economic security was precarious.

Mao was the oldest person in the research, aged 40 years. He had lived his whole life in the welfare institution and school dormitory. He had had a girlfriend, but said that "I don't have the necessary conditions and capacity to marry, so for now, I don't consider marriage". Due to his disability, he had only attended primary school and did not have the economic means to marry. Like Hong and Ming, he was older, had little education and had disabilities. He blamed the isolation of institutional care for his dilemma (see Chapter Six).

Occasionally, the welfare institutions were able to mobilize their resources to support orphans to marry. Bing, the only man in the research to have married, was aged 28 years and lived in a family unit at the institution. After he was demobilized from the army and returned to the institution, he met a woman on the staff of the institution who wanted to marry him. Her parents agreed to the marriage but did not have money or a house, considered prerequisites for a wedding. The welfare institution supported the couple by offering them a one-bedroom apartment and gathering social donations for the expenses, furniture and electrical appliances for the wedding ceremony. *Xinhua News*, the most official news agency of the Chinese government, reported the wedding ceremony.

Compared to young people in care residing in welfare institutions, young people in care who grew up in foster families had greater confidence in their capacity to marry and control their future. Bao, aged 23 years, grew up in foster care and shifted back to the institution when he was in technical secondary school, which is the usual pattern for foster care in Beijing. He was involved in various recreation activities – magic, basketball, karaoke and football – with his friends or classmates in the community and the institution. He said that he did not find it difficult to interact with others. He felt happy in these activities, made new friends and strengthened his capacities. He expected to have a girlfriend when his situation was more stable. His vision was to marry within five years and engage in magic shows as a stable occupation.

Another younger adult with housing prospects, Hui, the 21 year old introduced earlier with an affordable housing deposit from his parents' pension payment when they died, also seemed more confident about his future marriage prospects than the other young people without his housing opportunities. For example, he said:

> "I'm now trying to find a girl to marry, and expect to get married at the age of 25.… [I hope the girl's] family condition is OK, and her parents are still alive. It's fine as long as the girl's family is not very poor.… [The girl should have a] relatively good personality."

Compared to the young people who lived in the dormitories and who did have not foreseeable housing options, Hui was evidently more confident about marriage and his capacity in controlling his future.

In summary, the impact of housing on social inclusion largely depended on where the young people had lived as children, where they currently lived, their age and their disabilities. The young people with the most positive horizons were those with higher levels of education who had lived in a family. The young people aged under 25 were most likely to be in this position. The older orphans who had only lived in an institution or had not received adequate education and disability support were most likely to have limited social connections and aspirations. Even the young people with higher education and a good job were socially disadvantaged if they did not have additional support to obtain independent housing.

Conclusion about housing security

Access to housing was one of the most important factors that enabled or prevented young people from leaving state child welfare institutions to start an independent adult life. Few of the young people in the study had achieved independent living, even those in paid employment.

Implications for housing policy are that unless responsibility for the housing needs of young people who have been excluded from familial social relationships during childhood is addressed across housing, education, child state wards and disability policy portfolios, the exclusion of these young people is accentuated even further into adulthood.

The position of most of the young people in state care was that they remained protected by a welfare housing system in the institution, but with few options apart from living in the institution. During their childhood, most of them had lived in the institution or in formal or informal foster families. A few had become state wards later in their childhood when their parents died. Chapter Six described the impact of growing up in institutional care on limiting their aspirations and capacity for an independent life. Institutional group care is also inappropriate for an adult life with social, economic and civil contributions in the community. The young people benefit from the security of access to the institution, which is one of the few welfare housing systems left in China, but it also traps them within a limited horizon. Leaving the welfare institutions means leaving this institutional welfare housing system and entering the market system, for which many of them have not received the economic or social support to build the capacity to succeed. In these circumstances, most of them chose to remain protected by the welfare-based housing system within institutional care, living in a dormitory or apartment provided by the welfare institution. Except for a few cases where the local policy subsidized housing, such as in Beijing, or they could access an inheritance, most of the young people could not enter the rental or ownership housing market.

The young people experienced market exclusion and policy exclusion. In the current Chinese political context, the housing market replaced welfare housing to take the dominant role in housing security. Public housing in the form of low-cost rentals, financial allowances or affordable housing for purchase has not yet developed as a major option in housing supply for effective housing security. Subsidized housing is primarily targeted at low-income households. Age, marital status and income level are the major criteria for access to such housing. For young people in care, age and marital status are often a vicious cycle in which the absence of housing prohibits their marriage, while non-married status makes them ineligible to apply for affordable housing.

Most locations do not have policies prioritizing young people leaving care for access to subsidized housing. In some areas where the policies do prioritize them, the policies are not implemented because of the absence of procedures and housing stock. Although staff at welfare institutions usually proactively support young people in care to obtain housing, they are stymied by the limited coordination and collaboration between government agencies and the lack of procedures to insist on prioritizing the needs of the young people that they are responsible for; hence, the issue of housing remains a difficult predicament to be addressed.

The efforts of young people in care to obtain housing in the market are obstructed by high house prices and rental costs, leaving few of them with any option but to remain living in the welfare institutions. Life as a young adult in a child or adult welfare institution restricts their social inclusion, including their social identity, inability to obtain independent registered permanent residence, choice of jobs, establishment of social networks, establishment of family life and development of intimate relationships.

The next chapter turns to the experience of children and young adults without parents or extended family who have grown up outside the formal responsibility of the state. It explores whether their future independence is relatively more positive that those of their peers in institutional state care.

TEN

State support for children in informal care

Children without known parents or extended family in China either become state wards under the guardianship and responsibility of state child welfare institutions or live in informal non-kinship relationships with members of the community. In this second case, the welfare institutions sometimes also come to learn of these children and intervene in direct or indirect ways with these informal care families. Some institutions formalize and financially support the community family relationships when the children come to their attention. In recent years, the state has more publicly recognized its policy responsibility to these children, as scandals even resulting in children's deaths have gained a profile in public media.

In January 2013, seven children died in a house fire in Henan Province. A local street vendor had used her house to shelter many children, perhaps as many as 100, found abandoned over at least two decades. She was well known to the local community and officials, who had not intervened and, in fact, had sometimes directed others to her to leave children in her care. While deeply regretting the fire and loss of lives, nationally, government officials, scholars and the general public also queried the issues raised by the disaster. Among them was the debate about government obligations to protect abandoned babies and children in informal care. Why had the officials allowed or facilitated the woman to care for so many children? What other protection was available for the children? What would have happened to the children if she had not cared for them?

This chapter examines the implications of these informal care relationships for children as they become young adults. These questions are important for the larger questions about good types of alternative care that benefit the well-being and outcomes for children and young people in care and as they prepare to leave care. This chapter considers the advantages and disadvantages of informal care compared to institutional care, the role of government in supporting or prohibiting informal care, and the implications for social policy change to support these traditional arrangements.

The research participants were young people aged 16 years or more from Taiyuan who had experienced informal care during their childhood (listed in Table A.4 in Appendix 1). Mixed qualitative methods were used. They included: a review of national, provincial and municipal policies and media about the informal care of orphans and abandoned babies; in-depth interviews with four young people in non-kinship informal foster care, directors of government adoption offices, directors of government foster care offices and leaders of foster care working groups; a focus group with informal care parents and a focus group with young people in institutional care; and telephone interviews with a married young woman who had grown up in informal care and her informal care parents who now lived in a different city to her. In addition, the researchers visited three families who were informal carers for interviews and to observe the living environment and the children's relationship with their informal parents.

Policy context of informal care

The Chinese government is gradually taking up responsibility for the support and regulation of the informal care of children without known family members. The policies are to protect children by regulating the quality of care by non-governmental organizations (NGOs) and through formalizing informal care by non-kinship carers, each described here.

Policies about the non-governmental care of children without families

In 2013, the Ministry of Civil Affairs (MCA) estimated that there were 878 registered and non-registered NGOs and community members that arranged alternative care for 9,394 orphans and abandoned babies in that year. One quarter of these children were informally fostered by community members (Xu, 2013). Over 60% were cared for by religious organizations, primarily Buddhist and Christian monasteries (MCA, 2013a, 2013b). In addition, many state child welfare institutions cooperate with NGOs, entrusting them to raise children who are state wards.

The MCA and local civil affairs departments regulate alternative care provided by these organizations. The *Interim Measures for Administration of Social Welfare Institutions 1999* provided for the establishment, management and legal liability of NGOs and individuals operating formal and informal child welfare institutions. It required that these organizations and individuals must operate in cooperation with local civil affairs departments at county or higher levels. This provision did not target individual citizens informally adopting orphans or abandoned babies, but an implication was that informal care arrangements were not adequate child protection.

The *Interim Measures for the Management of Family Foster Care 2003* indicated that the state officially recognized and promoted foster care organized by state welfare institutions (see Chapter Three). Although it did not directly cover children living in informal foster care, the policy recognized foster care as an alternative to institutional care, and that the approach could include government support to children already living in informal foster families in the community.

Another related policy from 2006 probably does not cover children in informal foster care because these informal parents do not have guardianship over the children. The *Opinions of 15 Ministries/ Departments including Ministry of Civil Affairs on Strengthening Relief for Orphans 2006* states that guardians of orphans shall implement their duties as guardians according to law and safeguard the lawful rights and interests of orphans. People's Courts are entitled to revoke the guardianship of those who fail to implement their duties as guardians or violate the lawful rights and interests of orphans. The Opinions aimed to protect the interests of orphans raised by extended families NGOs, but did not mention the protection of children in informal adoption.

The *Notice on Defining Minimum Caring and Living Standards for Orphans 2009* stipulates that the national standard minimum monthly allowance for orphans raised by NGOs or individuals was RMB600. It did not apply to children living in informal adoptive families without official recognition or a registered permanent residence, which is a further disadvantage for these children.

The *Opinions on Strengthening Safeguarding for Orphans 2010* from the General Office of the State Council called for the appropriate placement of orphans, including kinship care, state care in institutions, foster care and lawful adoption. The provisions focused on safeguarding the lawful rights and interests of orphans. These Opinions also did not include children living in informal care.

Policy reform to formalize informal non-kinship foster care

The main laws and policies to formalize de facto or informal adoption are the *Opinions on Issues Concerning the Implementation of Civil Affairs*

Policies 1984, Adoption Law 1992, Adoption Law 1999 and *Notice on Applying for Notarization for De Facto Adoption Established Prior to the Implementation of the Adoption Law 1993*. The reasons for each of these policies are described here.

Informal care of abandoned babies without lawful adoption is officially referred to in government documents as 'adoption of children on a private basis by domestic citizens'. It is a type of informal, non-kinship foster care – an approach to de facto adoption with a long tradition in China. In most cases, community members voluntarily raise abandoned children out of their sense of compassion or care for children, without entering into any legal procedures to obtain the guardianship of the children or register their citizenship. In this chapter, the term 'de facto adoption' is used to refer to such cases in order to follow the terminology in the legislation.

The state acknowledged the incidence of the informal care of abandoned babies in de facto adoption relationships prior to the implementation of the *Adoption Law 1992*. The *Opinions on Issues Concerning the Implementation of Civil Affairs Policies 1984*, issued by the Supreme People's Court, stipulated that:

> The adoption relationship shall be acknowledged if it is unanimously recognized by the relatives or the general public or testified by a certain organization that the foster parents have been living together with the foster children for a long period of time, even if the lawful procedure has not been completed.

Following the implementation of the *Adoption Law 1992*, the Ministry of Justice issued the *Notice on Applying for Notarization for De Facto Adoption Established Prior to the Implementation of the Adoption Law 1993*, in which it was stipulated that 'For a de facto adoption relationship established prior to the implementation of the *Adoption Law*, notarization can be applied for'. This Notice reiterates that prior to the implementation of the *Adoption Law 1993*, the state acknowledged de facto adoption relationships, that is, regardless of whether the adoptive foster parents met the conditions prescribed for adoption, the de facto adoption was acknowledged.

The *Adoption Law 1999* revised the law to recognize previous de facto adoption relationships that did not meet the criteria; however, prospective adoptive parents were still required to strictly conform to conditions. Parents who already had their own children by birth were not allowed to adopt abandoned babies. The revision meant that many parents already in de facto adoption relationships with abandoned children did not conform to the provisions for adoption, and the children's legal identity was not acknowledged by the state.

Despite the revision to the law, informal de facto adoption did not stop, of course. People still chose to raise abandoned children regardless of whether the adoption met the prescribed conditions. These children had no legal identity as citizens and were not allowed to be registered with a *hukou* as permanent residents. When they were young, they could be raised in their informal families without a registered permanent residence. However, public education is only provided to children with a registered permanent residence, so when the children reached school age, they were confronted with the obstacle of not having a *hukou* in order to access schooling. The children also faced many other challenges in accessing health and welfare services and support without a registered permanent residence. If community members cared for children without adhering to the official registration procedure, they and the government could not safeguard the children's lawful rights and interests.

The government issued a further notice to address this dilemma, the *Notice on Addressing Issues Concerning Informal Adoption of Children by Chinese Citizens 2008*. Parents who have already found children in the community and have the capacity to adopt can go through the procedure of adopting abandoned babies from social welfare institutions, without being constrained by the previous *Adoption Law* or by the fact that they must be childless. These parents can apply to register the permanent residence for an adopted child by presenting a *Notarization for De Facto Adoption* or *Adoption Certificate* in their local residence area government.

However, there are still many children living with de facto adoptive parents who cannot obtain registered permanent residence because the prospective adoptive parents or child do not meet the prescribed adoption conditions. For instance, children aged older than 14 years, the prescribed maximum age of adoption, at the time of the 2008 Notice were not included in the adoption procedures and were consequently denied access to registered permanent residence. The only way for these older children to gain a *hukou* would be to leave the informal de facto family and move to the institution.

One solution to this problem of children or families not complying with the requirements was to include them in formal non-kinship foster care instead. Before the national policy, the welfare institution in one of the research cities, Taiyuan, used this method to act in the children's interests. They formalized the informal care arrangements by transforming them into formal foster care and registered the children's *hukou* with the welfare institution, without requiring them to live in the institution.

In Taiyuan, some of the informal de facto adoption families voluntarily sought support from the welfare institution when it began to promote foster care in 2004, but the families did not meet the adoption requirements. The institution decided that it was in the interests of the children to include the families who had informally cared for these children for years within the foster care programme, provided that they met the conditions for foster care, even if they did not meet the conditions for adoption. The institution implemented supervision and evaluation according to the *Measures of Municipal Welfare Institution of Taiyuan for Management of Family Foster Care of Children 2004*, thus transforming the informal de facto adoption of children into non-kinship foster care supervised by the government. These children could then obtain registered permanent residence at the welfare institution and legal identity, the state became their lawful guardian, and the families received financial support to care for the children.

The MCA officially recognized that innovation in 2013. Following the 2013 fire disaster mentioned at the beginning of the chapter, the *Notice on Further Strengthening Work with Abandoned Babies 2013* from the MCA and other ministries reiterated the importance of regulating the informal care of abandoned children by NGOs and individuals on the basis of the *Notice on Addressing Issues Concerning Informal Adoption of Children by Chinese Citizens 2008*. The new Notice included provisions for circumstances involving the informal adoption of abandoned babies by individuals:

> In the case that the adoptive parents insist on raising the children on their own and meet the conditions for foster care, local child welfare institutions can sign agreement with them for foster care, and shall facilitate and supervise over them as per the *Interim Measures for Administration of Family Foster Care*. (MCA, 2004)

The remaining shortcoming of the approach is if the informal care families are ineligible for foster care, and in that situation, the Notice did not indicate how to protect the rights of these children.

The research participants in this chapter include children who had experience of the two types of care that are the focus of the policies described earlier: informal foster care (de facto adoption) and formal foster care when these de facto family relationships became overseen by the government. Informal foster care provided the children with a family environment, but without legal identity (citizenship and residency), because the parents did not have the right to guardianship. From 2004, when formal foster care was launched, the children who had their informal care converted to formal foster care not only obtained a legal identity, but also received support from the state. This included a living allowance, an allowance to the family for the foster care, free health care and education, and support for children with disabilities. In addition, the parents obtained temporary guardianship entrusted by the state. The childhood of these children was much smoother than other abandoned children facing similar situations without the opportunity to formalize their legal status and their family relationships.

Government support for formal and informal alternative care

The remainder of the chapter examines the case-study city of Taiyuan, which was one of the first places to formalize and support children in informal foster care arrangements. First, the policies in that city are examined and then the experience of the children and young people is analysed to understand the impact of these arrangements on their transition to adulthood.

Alternative care types

The types of alternative care practised by the municipal welfare institution included national and international adoption, state institutional care, and foster care. Formal foster care included a foster care programme of foster parents recruited by the welfare institution. In addition, the welfare institution supported three other types of foster care: provided by a NGO, non-kinship foster care and pre-adoption trial foster care. These last three types of foster care were each a transition from previous informal care to the de facto adoption of orphans and abandoned babies. From a legal perspective, the welfare institution treated these families the same as other foster care families supported by the welfare institution. The children's experience might be different to other children in state foster care, though, because they grew up in these families from early in their life, with their foster parents having always treated them as their biological children. Few of them were yet old enough to transition to full independence in their adulthood, so this study is not conclusive about the impact of that difference.

The first priority of the welfare institution when it receives a new child is to try to organize adoption. It aims to seek a stable and permanent family environment for children. National or international adoption is the preferred placement strategy. Every year, most new children obtain permanent placement via adoption. Before 2004, institutional care was the primary form of alternative care for the children in the responsibility of the welfare institution. Institutional care offered a basic living and therapy environment for orphaned children with and without disabilities. At the time of the research in 2013, over 130 children lived in the institution, including new children to be assessed and treated, children with disabilities receiving therapy, children with cerebral palsy or infectious diseases in need of additional care, children attending schools, and young people in care.

The welfare institution set up a foster care department in 2003. The Implementation Protocol for Foster Care of Children was developed, covering the implementation of foster care, responsibilities and obligations of families providing foster care, a management flowchart of foster care, and living expenses for children in foster care. In 2004, foster care recruitment was formally promoted to rural communities and urban families. By 2014, 460 children had lived in foster care and it had become the primary form of alternative care for the welfare institution in this location.

Support to informal care families

Once foster care was formally promoted to the local communities by the welfare institution in 2004 in order to recruit foster care parents, some informal foster parents also approached the welfare institution to ask for support for the children that were already in their care. These parents were encountering three difficulties caring for the children: first, the families were not eligible to adopt the children, so the citizenship of the children was not registered and they did not have a permanent local residence and could not attend school; second, the families were facing economic difficulties and could not afford the cost of treatment and therapy for the children with disabilities but they did not want to give up the care of these children; and, third, some of the informal foster parents were ageing or unwell and were increasingly unable to provide continuous care for the children.

According to the regulations, these children should have been sent to the welfare institution to overcome these problems. The welfare institution recognized that the children and informal foster parents shared deep attachment and affection, so, instead, it organized for the children to gain collective registered residence through the welfare institution, included the families in the formal foster care programme and provided them with subsidies for living, medical care and education. Only the children living in the informal foster families who could not continue to care for them shifted to live in the institution or another formal foster care family. In this way, most of the informal care families become formal foster carers.

From 2004 to 2014, the welfare institution supported 32 informal foster care families, caring for 13 boys and 19 girls. The children were aged 5–28 years. Most of the children had disabilities (60%); 20% of the children had cerebral palsy. Some children had not attended school due to disabilities – children with cerebral palsy, learning disabilities and other physical conditions. The other children entered local or special schools after obtaining registered residence from the welfare institution – two children in primary school; eight in high school (including two children at a school for deaf children); three in technical high school; two in technical college; one in university; and three had graduated from technical high school.

Impact of informal care on social inclusion

Comparing the impact on childhood and transition to adulthood of the children and young people whose informal foster care was formalized and young people who only grew up in institutional care is one way to understand the effectiveness of informal care (see Table 10.1). Does the social inclusion they experienced as children translate into stronger social inclusion opportunities as they reach the age when they are setting aspirations for independent adulthood? The experiences of these young people are compared on the dimensions of their identity, education, economic security and socialization.

At the time of the research, 18 state wards in the responsibility of the Taiyuan Child Welfare Institution were aged over 16 years (see Table 10.1 and Appendix 1). Most of them did not have disabilities, but some did, including cerebral palsy, surgery for cleft lip and palate, deafness, and congenital heart disease. Young people with disabilities had mainly grown up in the institution. Most of the young people had attended local schools, including some in tertiary education. Two of the women had married.

Table 10.1: Young people case studies of comparative institutional and informal care

Alias	Sex	Age	Disability	Education	Employed or studying	Housing	Married	Alternative care
Institutional care only								
Mao	M	40	Yes	Primary	Unemployed	Dormitory welfare institution	No	Institution
Mei	F	34	Yes	Junior middle	Work at state child welfare institution	Family unit welfare institution	Yes	Institution
Xue	F	30	Yes	Technical secondary	Student	Dormitory welfare institution	No	Institution
Jin	M	26	Yes	Junior college	Employed at massage clinic	Dormitory welfare institution	No	Institution
Liao	M	26	No	Technical secondary	Unemployed	Dormitory welfare institution	No	Institution
Xi	F	24	Yes	Junior college	Work at state child welfare institution	Dormitory welfare institution	No	Institution
Informal and formal foster care								
Miao	F	21	No	Junior college	Student	Foster family	No	Mixed
Min	F	21	No	Technical secondary	Homemaker	Private rental	Yes	Mixed
Ning	F	20	No	Junior college	Student	Dormitory school	No	Mixed
Jiang	M	19	No	Technical secondary	Unpaid intern	Foster family	No	Foster
Pai	F	16	Yes	Junior middle	Student	Foster family	No	Mixed
Quang	M	16	No	Junior middle	Student	Dormitory welfare institution	No	Mixed[a]
Miu	F	16	No	Technical secondary	Student	Dormitory school	No	Mixed

Notes: Data from Taiyuan. M = male; F = female. [a] Moved to institutional care.

Living conditions and identity

The families of the children who had grown up in informal care were all supported by the welfare institution by the time of the research. Most of the families had faced difficulties raising the children due to their economic constraints, including the costs of raising their children by birth. The families lived in the city suburbs and rural areas around the city. For example, three families on low wages or pensions were those caring for Miao, Jiang and Pai. Miao was a 21-year-old woman still living with her informal foster parents, who were sanitation workers in the city. Jiang was a 19-year-old young man living with his informal foster parents, who sold vegetables for a living. The informal foster mother of the 16-year-old school student, Pai, was retired and depended on an age pension.

Although the informal foster families generally faced economic constraints, they said that they considered the young people as the same as the other children in their family. The young people were also cared for by their foster siblings and other relatives in the extended family. For example, Miao, the 21-year-old student, said, "My foster parents have been good to me, carefully taking care of me and treating me just like their own children". Ning was another 20-year-old student who lived at the school dormitory during term time. Her informal foster father said that Ning and his other children look "exactly like biological sisters and brothers".

When the welfare institution formalized the informal care arrangements of these families as formal foster carers, the children and young people became state wards. This meant that they were eligible for collective registered residence in the welfare institution, and, each month, the welfare institution paid the foster families RMB600 as a living subsidy and about RMB260 for care for each child. These payments improved the living conditions of the foster families and the children in their care. Most of the fostered children knew their story, which they and their families said did not change their attitude and attachment to their foster parents. For example, Ning, the 20-year-old student, said: "I regard them as my birth parents", even after knowing her full story. Some of the children did not know their story because their foster parents did not tell them.

The starkest difference from the children living in the welfare institution was their understanding about social relations and their sense of belonging in a family. Most of the children in informal care had enjoyed a relatively stable family life in their informal foster family, with parents, siblings and extended kin relationships from when they were very young. They had positive views and expectations about kinship compared to the children growing up in the welfare institution. For example, Jiang, the 19 year old, demonstrated his extended kin relationships by saying: "I get money from relatives as a lunar New Year gift". Miao, the 21 year old, similarly said: "My mum gives me money as a lunar New Year gift every year. In her eyes, I have always been her child". Miao visits her extended foster family relatives by herself during the lunar New Year. In contrast, children growing up in the welfare institution had no opportunity to develop this side of a sense of belonging to a family or to hold an understanding of kinship.

Education

Until the foster care was formalized, the children had generally been refused free entry in local schools or had to pay sponsorship fees for school education because they did not have a local registered residence. This was especially difficult for the low-income families. For example, Miao's foster mother said:

> "We had to pay RMB1,000 [each school term] as a sponsorship fee for school education for Miao due to her lack of registered residence, but we were willing to pay it. After Miao graduated from the primary school, no middle school accepted Miao due to the lack of registered residence. Later, Miao obtained the collective registered residence in the welfare institution after going through many procedures at the local police station."

After she was registered, Miao was able to continue her education to a tertiary level and was still studying at a local junior college. Once the practice of formalizing foster care began, all the children gained collective registered residence, which enabled their access to school education. According to the welfare institution head responsible for the education of fostered children, children in informal care generally had satisfactory academic performance in schools because of the good quality of the informal foster care parental discipline in their early childhood. Many of the young people discussed the positive rewards of their experience of being urged by their informal foster parents to study hard. They said that their foster parents paid close attention to their education and enforced strict discipline about their study so that they developed good study habits and were aware of the importance of study. Growing up in a family had exposed them to community expectations about the importance of achieving well in education.

In comparison to the children growing up in the welfare institution, the children in informal foster care families were able to complete study more successfully. With the support of their informal family, these children usually completed compulsory school and many were still continuing into senior high school and tertiary education. In contrast, many of the children growing up in the welfare institution left school in junior high school or even in primary school (see Table 10.1). Children in the welfare institution relied on self-discipline because they had no family pressure or role models to follow or guide their study habits. For example, Mei was a 34 year old who had grown up in the welfare institution and left school before high school. She reflected that "Nobody would tell you what to do and how to behave, as parents would do for their children". Now that she had her own daughter, she was very strict with her child's study.

Employment

Most of the young people who had grown up in informal care were still young enough to be studying in schools or tertiary education and were not yet formally employed. The few who were employed were still in unstable jobs. For example, Jiang was aged 19 years and living with his foster family. He had graduated from technical secondary school and had a series of marginal sales jobs. As discussed in Chapter Seven, he wanted to open a small business. At the time of the research, Jiang was working during the day and studying at a technical college at night and on weekends. He was striving to improve his employment capacity so that he could take better care of himself and his foster family members. Jiang's foster mother was very supportive of his capacity to achieve those goals, but also recognized the employment barriers that he faced. She said:

> "Jiang has a strong character and always wants to be independent. After graduation from technical secondary school, he hunted for many jobs to earn his own living. He wants to find a good job to pay back society and the family, but there are very limited choices."

Young people who grew up in the institution faced similar challenges in employment from the fierce competition in the labour market. Their lack of social networks and poor education levels meant that it was difficult for them to compete, in addition to the discrimination they faced due to disability and their status as state wards, as discussed in Chapter Seven. It was difficult to find stable jobs and they changed jobs frequently. For example, Liao, a 26-year-old man without disabilities who grew up in the welfare institution, said: "I once did several jobs. Every time, I was fired after a short period of time". Liao's employment experience was similar to that of Jiang, but while Jiang continued to work and study, Liao was too discouraged to continue.

Some of the other young people in informal foster care who were still in education also spoke about their future employment goals. Miu was a 16-year-old student at technical secondary school who lived at the school during term time and returned to her foster family during vacations. She was ambitious to achieve further qualifications. She did not want to depend on the government or her family, and knew that she had to improve her performance to meet her goals. She said: "I want to receive further education after graduation from technical secondary school. That way, I can find a good job to pay back society and be more helpful to the community".

Some foster parents felt that the welfare institution should help their children find work. For example, Jiang's and Miao's foster mothers said that they hoped to receive assistance from the government to find employment positions for their children. In contrast, Ning's foster father thought that his 20-year-old daughter should be able to stand alone to seek future employment. This is an unusual position for a parent to take since families are often involved in helping their children with social connections to find a job if they can, as discussed in Chapter Eight. He said: "I'm unwilling to arrange jobs for Ning through personal relationships and acquaintances. I hope Ning can earn her own living. The stability of jobs is relative. Large cities will be a good choice for Ning".

Most of the young people in informal foster care expected that they would have to find jobs and grow their career through their own effort or with support from their family. For example, Jiang hoped to open a convenience store and emphasized that "I want to try my best and family support will be my last resort". The 20-year-old student Ning stridently claimed that "A person would be a loser if they had no career of their own. I want to grow a career through my own efforts by insisting on my dream". The ambitions of these young people were more independent, with a stronger sense of responsibility and possibility, than the ones in the institution.

The young people who had grown up in the welfare institution also had a strong desire for stable jobs but they were more passive and hoped to receive assistance from the government to find employment. For example, Jin, a 26-year-old man working in a massage clinic and still living in the institution, said: "We all hope to have stable jobs and happy families from an early age". Xi, the 24-year-old woman who also lived and worked in the institution, considered a stable job as a precondition for all other things. She said: "It will be better if there is a stable job. A job is the only hope. A stable job is a guarantee for marriage". They relied on the government to support them to achieve these goals, or, like Liao, they gave up if it was too difficult.

Economic security

Once the informal foster care families were supported by the welfare institution, although they were low-income households, the children in these families enjoyed sufficient economic security. Children in these families received RMB600 living allowance per month from the welfare institution and had their educational and medical expenses reimbursed by the institution. They usually received pocket money from their foster parents and relatives and gift money during the lunar New Year period. When they found a job, they could continue to receive the living allowance from the welfare institution in addition to their own income if it was a low-wage job.

Young people living in the welfare institution only received RMB100 for clothing and bedding articles and RMB50 for pocket money per month, in addition to lodging and meals. If they left the institution to work outside and paid rent for housing, they could receive the living allowance of RMB600 per month, like the young people leaving foster care. Only a few of the young people earned wages; the others relied on the pocket money from the welfare institution. Such low income only supported minimum living needs and was not sufficient for social contact, dating and other social interaction needs as adults.

Social relations

Young people growing up in informal care had a similar social context to other children living with their birth parents, including all the usual opportunities to build social networks. These young people were generally talkative, extroverted and optimistic in the research activities. They gave many examples of social connections that reflect those of other young people living in their family and local community. Ning, the 20-year-old student boarding at college, proudly said that she had many friends. Jiang, the 19 year old working and studying, said: "I make my friends at school, social occasions and in my workplaces. When I'm not busy doing part-time jobs, I usually play basketball with friends, talk with them or read books". Jiang's foster mother claimed that he was not discriminated against by others and said that: "Everyone is good to him and he has many friends". Of course, some of the young people were less extroverted and said that they were not good at engaging with other people due to family accidents, special family relationships or introversion.

In comparison with children growing up in the welfare institution, the young people in informal foster families had a higher level of socialization since they lived in a social environment similar to other children in the community. They had experienced how to accommodate themselves to social situations, had wider social networks and had a strong sense of self-identity. Children growing up in the welfare institution had limited contact with other people in the community and few opportunities to participate in social activities due to the closed living environment and the long distance from urban areas. Jing's story in Chapter Seven is an example of that. Limited living space and a narrow social network make them more sensitive to a feeling of inferiority. Xi, the 24 year old who had grown up in the welfare institution, said: "We are branded with the mark of the welfare institution".

Marriage

Most of the young people in informal foster care were still studying and were not ready to marry or start their careers. Only Min had married after graduation from technical secondary school. She lived in a private rental property with her husband and daughter. Her foster mother said that Min's husband was her classmate in technical secondary school. She said that he was a simple and honest man who took good care of Min, as did his parents. Like any proud mother of a newly married daughter, Min's foster mother said: "I'm so relieved because Min is happy". Other young people spoke positively about their hopes and opinions on marriage. Ning, the 20-year-old young woman, spoke about the rewards of marriage: "Marriage is a responsibility and also a continuation of love. Married people should not care only for themselves, but should take care of their wives, children and parents, and share all good things with family members".

Their hopeful expectations about marriage in the future contrast with the angst of many of the young people who had grown up in institutional care, as discussed in Chapter Seven. The link between marriage and housing discussed in Chapter Seven had the greatest impact on the young men. Their economic disadvantage hampered both. Although foster care seemed to lead to better economic prospects, it was not sufficient to overcome the housing and marriage link if the young person came from an economically disadvantaged foster family. For example, Jiang, the 19 year old who was studying and working, lost his foster father in a car accident several years before. He said: "My [foster] parents were both workers until my father died. Now, 70% of family income is earned by my older sister and brother-in-law and 30% by me".

His foster mother reiterated that arranging a marriage for Jiang would be difficult: "We do not have adequate money to support his marriage, but if there is any suitable girl, we will try our best to help him get married". She had a house that the government would offer compensation for under a compulsory acquisition, but she could not decide whether to hand the house to Jiang since she was worried about dissatisfaction from her other birth children. Young men like Jiang, with collective residential registered status, still faced the embarrassment that they were excluded from property inheritance and other practical problems even though they had been cared for as biological sons by their foster parents since they were babies. Consequently, their difficulties in marrying were similar to other children in institutional care.

Both the young people in foster care and institutional care experienced similar barriers to marriage, though they were worse for those in institutional care, as discussed in Chapter Seven. Young women were more likely to marry and young men would struggle because of the additional employment and housing expectations of them. Women without disabilities were the most likely to marry. Over recent years, six women from the institution had married with migrants from other places or peers in the welfare institution. Although their husbands did not have high incomes, they had happy families since their husbands were generally honest.

In contrast, men struggled to find partners. Only one man from institution, Bing, had ever married. He had joined the army and later worked in a stable job at a public institution, which contributed to his capacity to marry. Similarly, young men in informal foster care had to postpone marriage until they could find stable employment and housing.

Challenges of transition for young people leaving informal care

The children who grew up in informal foster care were treated like other family members and had achieved better social inclusion through the development of life skills, education, employment and social interaction. However, they still faced many challenges in their transition to adulthood, including their collective legal status as state wards, the economic disadvantage of their foster families and disruption to the informal care relationship, each discussed here.

Legal status as permanent 'orphans'

The formalization of the foster care relationships of most of the young people in this sample began between 1992, when the original *Adoption Law* was promulgated, and 1999, when the revised *Adoption Law* was implemented. Without a registered residence during their early childhood, schools had refused them entry or insisted on sponsorship fee payments. Although they gained collective registered residence later in their childhood, their legal guardianship was still managed by the welfare institution. A limitation of this status is that their relationships with their foster parents were not protected by law, which would affect their eligibility for care in the future and their rights to family property inheritance. It also inhibited the marriage eligibility of the young men, as discussed earlier.

High-risk families

Many of the informal foster families now supported by the welfare institution were at high risk from economic constraints and ageing foster parents. Many of the foster parents were aged over 65 years by the time the children reached teenage years. These families were vulnerable to accidents and illness due to ageing. If their foster parents died or became chronically ill, the young people were at risk of having to shift to the welfare institution. This risk of discontinued foster care added emotional pressure on the young people and their families.

Some of the children and young people in the foster families also provided care to their foster parents. For example, Pai was a 16-year-old student who lived alone with her foster mother after the mother's son died in a car accident. They lived on the mother's retirement pension and Pai's living subsidy from the welfare institution. However, Pai's foster mother needed additional care herself and took daily medicines. Before going to school each day, Pai packed and labelled the medicine to be taken three times a day to remind her foster mother to take the medicines. This reciprocal care is typical of filial obedience but also made them each vulnerable to change in the future availability of each other.

The welfare institution was aware of these risks in several of the formalized foster families and paid more attention and provided additional support to them. In this way, the institution hoped to preserve the family stability, though they were ready to accept children back into other forms of alternative care if the foster care relationship could not be sustained.

Impact of disruption to foster care

A few of the young people who had previously lived in informal care had to shift to the welfare institution when the informal foster care ceased after family accidents or disruption. The loss of their informal families had severe emotional impacts on some of them. For example, Quang was aged 16 years old and had grown up in informal foster care. His foster father had first cared for him and continued to do so after he remarried when Quang was five years old. The new couple raised Quang for 10 years. However, when his foster parents separated after an emotional breakdown, Quang was sent back to the welfare institution because neither of them could continue to care for him. This change was emotionally disturbing for him because of the many losses during his childhood, first as an abandoned baby, then after his foster parents' separation, resulting in the loss of the opportunity to continue to live in a family home. Quang's teacher said that he had only average academic performance, said very little in class and had little communication with classmates.

Two other young people in the sample were in similar situations. Now living in the welfare institution, they were often depressed and paid little attention to their studies. These children, who had experienced foster care and once enjoyed good care from foster parents in a family home, were less able to adapt to life in the welfare institution. In contrast, children who had only grown up in the welfare institution had accommodated themselves to the life there and had never experienced the feeling of home.

Conclusion about informal foster care

Informal foster care provided in a family and social environment is more conducive to the social inclusion of children without parents than institutional care. When the welfare institution formalized the alternative care relationship, the support from the institution to the foster families and children contributed to the basic rights and interests of the children to economic security, education, health care and social participation. The children growing up in such alternative family environments showed no obvious differences from other children in ordinary families. Policy to formalize and support these families represents a successful step in recognizing the children's rights.

The comparison of the transition of young people in informal foster care and institutional care demonstrated that young people in informal foster care had greater advantages in economic security, access to education, social interaction and independence during their childhood, which improved their aspirations for their future. Children in foster families enjoyed a secure social environment and stable living conditions similar to children in ordinary families, as well as care and guidance from family members and relatives, providing models of social behaviours and positive emotional adjustment. In contrast, children who grew up in the welfare institution were generally more sensitive, with a feeling of inferiority and a poor sense of self-identity. This was due to their closed living environment, stigma as an orphan and the lack of expectations and guidance about their education and future independence.

Although the children in informal foster families experienced stronger social inclusion than children in the welfare institution, they still faced problems with property inheritance and emotional security. Compared to other children in other families, they were not formally adopted by foster families and were not legally recognized as family members of the foster parents.

Future social policy could continue to strengthen support for the community practice of families taking in children since the advantages over institutional care are demonstrated in the good practices in Taiyuan. If families wish to provide alternative care, they could be encouraged to adopt the child or register for foster care. Discussion about policy responses to questions about registration status, guardianship and financial support should consider the interests of the child, including implications for future independence. These families might be encouraged to adopt if the adoption procedures were simplified, they received support to go through adoption procedures and they received financial assistance for the disability support needs of their children after adoption. The recent changes to the guardianship laws in 2014, discussed in Chapter Two, might make that more feasible. Chapter Eleven turns to examine the impact of another form of alternative care on the transition to adulthood, family group care.

ELEVEN

Growing up in institutional family group care

In addition to formal foster care in families, some state child welfare institutions also provide alternative care in family groups with a paid house mother on the site of the institution. This type of alternative care raises questions about whether this grouping is sufficient to simulate the benefits of family-based care in relation to outcomes for children when they are growing up, and the impact on their transition to adulthood. As an intermediate step of a smaller family grouping but still within an institution, with a paid house mother, is this sufficient to achieve the social inclusion expected for other children who grow up in the community with their birth or foster family?

The chapter examines the experience of seven young people in one city who had lived in this arrangement. It considers the differences for these young people during their childhood and as they prepared for possibilities to leave the family group care in the institution.

Approach to alternative care at the institution

The Urumqi Children's Welfare Institution is the only welfare institution for children in the city. It was founded in 1947. At the time of the research in 2012, it had 184 staff and more than 300 children. The children were from many ethnic groups because the region is diverse, with a large Chinese Muslim minority. Most of the children had communicable diseases or disabilities (90%), mainly cerebral palsy and learning disabilities. A few children with disabilities at the institution were not state wards. Their families were paying for them to receive therapy services and special education while they lived at the welfare institution. This unusual practice for child welfare institutions helps families remain intact and provides the child with access to disability support not otherwise available in the community. Some other welfare institutions are beginning to develop this practice in order to try to reduce the number of families who leave their children to become state wards so that they receive the treatment they need.

The welfare institution mainly provides family-based alternative care, including formal and informal foster care. It also provides family group care at the institution, which simulates family households in apartments built at the welfare institution. At the time of the research, the institution had 22 family group homes, each with paid staff in a mother role to the children. In addition, the welfare institution had more than 70 foster families.

The welfare institution also has a kindergarten for children with disabilities for day care, special education and therapy training both for children who are state wards in any of the forms of alternative care and for children with disabilities who live with their own birth families in the community. The welfare institution is unusual in that it provides free special education and therapy for children with disabilities who live in low-income families in the local community. In this way, the children who are state wards have the opportunity to interact with children with disabilities who live with their families, and children with disabilities in the community have access to support. Any food served in the institution is halal in order to respect the Chinese Muslim staff and children.

Family group care is the most expensive type of care at the institution. Unlike foster care in the community, the children live in an artificial community at the institution. The supervision, standards, training and other requirements of the house mothers are higher in family group care. Most group care was supported by charity organizations to cover the additional costs. It was not a common type of care in Chinese child welfare institutions. The additional costs raise questions about the comparative advantages of family group care compared to institutional and foster care, which are explored in this chapter.

Characteristics of the young people in family group care

The research focused on how the young people in family group homes prepared for adulthood. It included in-depth interviews with two young women and five young men aged 16 to 22 years (see Table 11.1). Liu and Zhou were interviewed together and others were interviewed alone. Zeng, Li and Wang had acquired disabilities. Zeng lived at her university dormitory and the others still lived in their family group homes. Li had lived briefly with a rural foster family for one year.

The characteristics of the young people in family group care were different to the typical profile of children entering state care. First, they all entered the welfare institution when they were children and

Table 11.1: Young people in the institutional family group care case studies

Alias	Sex	Age	Age became state ward	Disability	Education	Employed or studying	Housing	Married
Zeng	F	22	16	Yes	University	Student	Dormitory school	No
Li	M	21	5	Yes	Technical college	Employed at welfare institution	Family group care	No
Hui	M	21	18	No	Primary	Employed	Family group care	No
Wang	M	19	10	Yes	Technical secondary	Student	Family group care	No
Liu	F	18	17	No	Junior middle	Student	Family group care	No
Zhang	M	16	12	No	Technical secondary	Student	Family group care	No
Zhou	M	16	11	No	Primary	Student	Family group care	No

Notes: Data for 2012 from Urumqi. M = male; F = female.

teenagers, rather than babies. Only one young man, Li, had entered the welfare institution at the age of five years; the others were all aged between 10 and 18 years when they entered care (see Table 11.1). Most of them were state wards because their parents had died or were unable to support them as a result of significant family tragedies. Some of them even came from wealthy families. They held different opinions of family group care depending on why they entered the institution, as illustrated here.

The second difference to other state wards was that only Li had entered the institution before 2000. After 2000, the facilities and processes at the institution had been greatly improved and the living standard was similar to that of the average urban households in the cities. Families with significant misfortunes, however, were usually living in poverty or with below-average income. For the children from these families, the relatively high living standard at the welfare institution influenced their sense of satisfaction and their evaluation of their living conditions when they entered state care. Hui, for example, was aged 21 years and had only finished primary school. He was from a poor family and had entered the welfare institution when he was nearly 18 years and had had several jobs. He said:

> "I'm from Hubei. We were poor when I was young. I discontinued my education at the junior high school and then went out with my parents to work in Guangzhou. I did many jobs including working at a woollen mill and a leather bag factory and I learned electrician skills."

When his parents died, he came to the welfare institution, where his material living standard was higher than before. The change for him was that he no longer had parents and that his only brother was cared for elsewhere. He said that he was satisfied with his life at the welfare institution and was working hard.

The third difference between these young people and other children in state care was that they were living in family group homes within the welfare institution, instead of congregate institutional care. Within the family group home, they had a paid carer who they identified as the family group home mother and they treated the other members of the household as their siblings.

Fourth, these young people did not have severe disabilities. Li and Wang, who had hepatitis B, and Zeng, who had burn scars, did not have communication or functional difficulties. The other young people did not have disabilities. Fifth, although they lived at the welfare institution, they attended local schools with other children from the community because they were all relatively older when they entered the institution and they did not have disabilities that precluded them from enrolling in mainstream schools. This history meant that they already had experience of forming strong social ties during their childhoods.

Combined, the characteristics of the young people, their circumstances while they were growing up and their family group home living seemed to mean that their trajectories into adulthood were different to the other young people living in institutional care. Understanding the impact of each of these factors is important to draw implications for the relative benefits of family group care. Their experiences in transition to adulthood are described in terms of self-identity, the characteristics of the group home conducive to childhood development and challenges to experiencing a socially inclusive young adulthood.

Self-identity

Chapter Six introduced the concepts of self-identity and the impact of forms of alternative care on the opportunities for children and young people to develop a strong sense of who they are and their aspirations for the future. The young people in family group care in this sample seemed to each hold a relatively positive sense of self-identity, from their confidence about living in a family group home, their capacity to face the earlier traumas in their lives and to form strong future goals, and their motivation to try to achieve their plans.

Positive evaluation of living in a family group home

Zeng was aged 22 years and had lived in state care from when she was 16 years. Introduced in earlier chapters, she said that "The child welfare institution is paradise". She had survived harsh domestic violence when her father had fired a gas cylinder in a quarrel with her mother, who died in the fire. The right side of Zeng's body was badly burned. Her father was imprisoned and she was first sent to an adult welfare institution. However, a manager of the civil affairs bureau noticed her during a work inspection and approved her transfer to the child welfare institution. She said:

> "I had stayed at an old people's home, where I had a bad time…. There were old people and people with mental

disorders at the old people's home. They seemed abnormal. Although my skin was injured by fire, I'm still a normal person. I felt my future was ruined there."

Zhang was aged 16 years and became a state ward when he was 12 years. He said that family group care was a very good style of alternative care because the house mother provided good care for the children. He refused an offer of adoption because he had settled into his life in the family group home at the welfare institution. Wang, aged 19 years, agreed, saying: "I think this is a very good environment for living". The other young people living in family group care, such as Li, aged 21 years, described the care staff and institution as "not bad", indicating their acceptance of the living conditions as satisfactory, though not ideal. Li was the only child in the case studies to have lived in family group care from a young age. Earlier in the book, examples of his dissatisfaction with institutional care were discussed, such as his heartbreak when a younger child in the family group was adopted and he no longer had any means for continued contact.

Facing past traumatic experiences

All children at the welfare institution, including those in family group care, had difficult events in their childhood, which typically included serious traumatic experiences. Part of the process of forming their self-identity was how they faced their traumas, and whether they felt overshadowed by their experience as a victim or whether they became resilient and confident. These young people in the family group homes frequently mentioned their past experiences in the interviews. Li, the 21-year-old young man who had entered the welfare institution at five years, was cynical about his early childhood experience, though it did not upset his current goals, as discussed here. He said simply of why he was a state ward, "I was abandoned", without any further emotional description. When asked about his identity, and 'Who am I?', he said:

> "I can't be anybody else but Li.... The name is not important to me and, in fact, I can use any name since I don't have a family. I think the name means nothing to me but a symbol on my ID card."

In a different reaction, Zeng, the young woman who had experienced family violence until she was aged 16 years, detailed why she had entered the welfare institution, with clear emotional insight: "The conflict between my parents led to an accident – a gas cylinder explosion. Then my mother died and my father became a prisoner. That is, as you can see, I'm a victim".

The stigmatized identity as state wards or children with disabilities was a constant occurrence for many of the young people. For example, the carers would say 'This is a child from the welfare institution' when they sought support, such as at a hospital. 'I am a child from the welfare institution', had become the early self-identity recognition for many of the young people, with the associated negative impact that might have. Despite this, many of them seemed to have established a positive attitude towards their futures, as discussed later.

Positive life goals

Like the aspirations of the other young people in alternative care that are important for self-identity in transitions to adulthood discussed in Chapter Six, the young people living in family group homes seemed to have a clear sense of their social identity, what they wanted to achieve and the social relations they wanted to gain. They also sought to be like other young people who had grown up in their birth families. Asked about the social position they wanted, they reiterated this desire to be like others: "an ordinary worker" (Li), "a normal person" (Hui) and "a common person" (Wang).

Zhang was a 16 year old who had become a state ward when he was aged 12 years. He was attending a technical secondary school in the local community. He was confident in his self-identity and future:

> "I am a very confident person…. I can become a boss, a musician or a basketball star…. I can become an influential person, for example, a philanthropist or a star…. I want to be confident and not to give up."

Wang was a 19-year-old man who had become a state ward when he was aged 10 years because the woman who had informally adopted him in the community was unable to take care of him due to her own age-related support needs. Wang was still at technical secondary school and expected to start his career and then to get married. He was ambitious and said: "I've never thought about a stable job because that kind of job may be too boring. I want to create my own career".

Li, the 21 year old, was also ambitious. He had graduated from technical college and was working at the welfare institution. He also expected to create his own career so that he could become a responsible man, able to support his own family, saying: "I've never imagined how high I would reach … but I just think that I'll become independent and get married and that I'll support my family independently by doing any kind of job".

Most of them (five out of the seven) were still in education. When asked what kind of people they would like to become in the future, their goals were different to those of the young people who grew up in institutional care. They had ambitious expectations beyond an average life. Many of their answers were focused on a professional career, in business or senior technical professions:

> "I want to run my own 4S store after my graduation." (Wang, 19 years)

> "I want to run my own auto-repair shop after my graduation." (Zhang, 16 years)

> "I think the outside world is wonderful…. My future career can be in four phases: a single store, a city-wide chain of stores, a province-wide chain of stores and a nationwide chain of stores." (Hui, 21 years)

> "I think my current life is already very good." (Zhou, 16 years)

Motivation to work towards goals

Compared to the young people living in institutional care in Chapter Six, the young people in family group care also seemed to have the motivation and to understand that they needed to apply themselves to achieve their goals. They spoke about how their approach to their goals was to improve their skills and enrich their knowledge through hard study in order to find good jobs or achieve their goals. For example, two of the young men who were at technical secondary school said:

> "I'll learn more skills when I have opportunities." (Wang, 19 years)

> "I enjoy going to school, and I like my auto-repair courses…. I'm proud of myself for having chosen this right

specialty because now the auto-repair trade is so popular."
(Zhang, 16 years)

Li, the 21-year-old graduate from technical college, had studied hard. He proudly said: "I had a very good school performance between the third year of junior high school and senior high school". He was concentrating on improving his health and curing his hepatitis B. His ambition was to be promoted by preparing for the examination to become a civil servant or to join a public institution. He had clear plans:

> "I'm considering how to pass the examination for this fixed position for a stable income and then to develop my second career. And I think that I should be able to get it [to achieve my life goal] with both of these incomes."

The young people spoke proudly of their educational and vocational achievements, which greatly strengthened their self-identity. When asked what achievements they were proud of, they said: "Passing all the examinations" (Zeng, 22 years, at university); and "At a provincial skills competition in 2010, I won an Award of Excellence. Not bad, huh' (Hui, 21 years).

The young people who had lived in family group care had all experienced physical or psychological trauma before becoming a state ward. They had generally faced their traumatic experiences and were reconciled to their current status, as victims, state wards and young people with disabilities. Most of them seemed resilient and confident in their self-identity. With this confidence, they had goals, dreams and substantial commitment to applying themselves through study and career development. The fact that they generally had a resilient, positive outlook on their economic future from living in family group care, after their own families in their earlier years, implies that the form of alternative care, at the least, did not harm them and probably contributed to their well-being. Some of them with disabilities and health conditions still felt discriminated against, as described further later.

Characteristics growing up in family group care

The second aspect of differences between family group care and other institutional care is the characteristics of the care, including the care style, resources, therapy, education and opportunities for social interaction during childhood.

Care style of family group homes and house mothers

The first characteristic was that although the family group homes were located at the institution, the children lived in small households. Each family group lived in a separate apartment, with a house mother and seven to eight children of different ages. The material living conditions in the family group homes were comparable with those in average local households. The group was a family-like environment for the children, and the house mother took care of their living and development needs. For example, Zhang, the 16-year-old student, said: "I'm deeply impressed by my house mother, who gave me the most meticulous care and treated me as her own son when I came here in 2008. I always spend the Spring Festival time with her family".

Since the young people were older than the other children in the house, they also cared for their younger siblings within the family group. Mutual care and love was a positive factor during their childhood. One of the benefits of this form of care was the continuity of relationships between the house mother and the children during their childhood. Zhang, for example, had had the same house mother for the four years since he had become a state ward and trusted that strong relationship to continue, though Li's emotional distress when a household member was adopted, described earlier, also demonstrates the limits to this continuity.

Relatively secure financial conditions

The second factor in the quality of the family group care was the relatively high financial and other resources available to the children in the family group home. After expenses for their food, they received more than 50% of the state-provided basic living allowance for their own personal use. The children who received charity donations for their education had even more money at hand.

Children who are state wards generally have well-developed savings habits, as found in the full research sample of young people in all forms of alternative care. The children in the family groups did not need to use much money while they were at the welfare institution, so they deposited their spare money with their house mother or teacher and drew the money back when they needed it. This procedure developed their habit of saving.

Li and Hui were both working at the age of 21 years. They each had a low monthly wage of more than RMB1,000. As they lived in family group care at the welfare institution with free room and board, they basically did not need to spend any money. Li said that the biggest expense in each month was "going out with my friends".

The welfare institution covered all their expenses, including their education and living costs. Some schools waived part of the school costs as appropriate. For example, Li had a tuition fee waiver when he was at senior high school, and Zeng had a room cost waiver during her university education. Zeng received financial support from the institution and a foundation grant for her living costs. She said: "I have a monthly living allowance of 960 yuan, consisting of 460 from the welfare institution and 500 from the foundation…. This amount covers all things such as medical costs and clothing costs".

Except for Zeng living at the university, all the other young people in this sample went to local schools and lived in the family group home at the welfare institution. As local school pupils, they had very little extra expenses. Zhang, who was 16 and at technical school, said: "My house mother keeps my money and I take it from her when I need it…. I spend 150–200 yuan per month, mainly for things such as guitar books and English books".

The advantageous financial conditions relative to the children in institutional care, together with the tight family group care financial management, contributed to developing good financial habits in the young people. They did not strongly feel any immediate material shortage, and they had good savings habits during their childhood. However, the next section notes that once they reached adulthood, they did not receive sufficient financial support to live in independent housing.

Active medical and therapy services

The third characteristic of the family group care was that the young people with disabilities, health needs and injuries received health and disability support. While their support needs were likely to be ongoing, the welfare institution actively made medical arrangements for them. The medical and disability support from the institution reassured them. Li and Zeng said:

> "I still remember the time when our teachers and the president were very concerned about my disease, and, in fact, I was deeply moved."

> "When I went to apply the external medicine, all of my teachers would provide support and help."

Managing their conditions also affected the confidence of some of the young people. Zeng thought that her burn scars were the main cause of her diffidence. Managing their health and disability support needs sometimes also affected their mental health. They were also sometimes subject to social and employment discrimination. Zeng believes that her scars were an important factor that hindered her employment.

Their diffidence and their experiences of discrimination influenced their immediate and future plans in ways that they tried to minimize in order to avoid further social exclusion. Like the other young people in institutional care, they chose to continue to rely on the institution for the first step in their employment in order to overcome these disadvantages. Zeng said: "I simply think that my life is not stable since I have to run about, and I just want a stable life". Li told several stories about the cumulative psychological impact of discrimination from having hepatitis B:

> "I don't know when I was infected.... I felt depressed by the disease all the time, from primary school to junior school and to senior school.... And then I know this is an incurable disease. I've been using medicine all the time, without any special effect as a matter of fact. The doctor told me to take good rests and keep in a good mood.... I have such a [compromised] personality possibly because of the circumstances. I think that my disease has greatly influenced my personality and many of my other things.
>
> In fact, at the time of my graduation, I considered staying and working out there. But, yes, many recruiting companies marginalize those with certain diseases. They don't mention discrimination but, in fact, they do so. In fact, alas, they always have good excuses to refuse you."

Despite the extra resources of family group care that these young people had grown up with, they still described negative experiences and feelings of exclusion similar to other children who had grown up in congregate care in the institution.

Inclusive education environment

The fourth characteristic of family group care that was conducive to social inclusion was the inclusive education experience that they had all encountered. Any state wards at the institution could attend the local school if they achieved a high enough standard. The children in family group care were among the most successful cases in the institution, which explains why they were in the local school. Perhaps this was because most of them were old enough to have attended school before they became state wards. They said, they had not been marginalized in their education since becoming state wards and they had all completed their compulsory education. They all received cost waivers from schools and subsidies from other organizations. Even Hui, who was 21 and only completed compulsory minimum education, was pleased with the inclusive education. He said that, "At school, there are many preferential treatments, including tuition waiver for me due to my special conditions".

Li, the young man who had been a state ward the longest, since he was aged five years, also mentioned the fee waivers at his senior high school"

> "I was given education cost waivers.… When I was in the third year of junior high school … the teacher suggested that I try to enter the senior high department of the same school, where I could have a tuition waiver. We at the welfare institution were really happy with this good news. I took the teacher's suggestion because I thought that the cost for senior high school might not be so low as that for the compulsory education, and I passed the admission exams. And so, I paid almost nothing for the three years of my senior high school."

A foundation cooperates with the institution to fund extra education subsidies for some of the children, enabling them to access additional education on skills and hobbies that is often only available to children from middle-class families. Zhang, the 16 year old who was still at his technical secondary school, said: "I go to the vocational school on weekdays, and on weekends I go to the guitar and English classes that are paid by … the Foundation".

Decisions about education were made with the help of the welfare institution, such as selecting subjects and specialities after senior high school education. Taking a parenting role, the opinion of the welfare institution managers about education and career choices was dominant, taking into account the interests of the young people. A consideration was how to best use the limited resources of the welfare institution to support their education. This parental role from the institution was explicitly described some of the young people. Li said:

> "Except the welfare institution, I don't have any relatives still alive. And most of my acquaintances are peers, who are living with their parents and are unable to take care of me. It's impossible for me to ask them for help even if they are my best friends."

Inclusive social interaction

The final characteristic of family group care contributing to their social inclusion was that the young people had all experienced inclusive social interaction. They felt that the compassion towards orphans from the community had helped them develop trust to overcome their family traumas and build a positive attitude towards life. The primary relationships of the young people in family group care were with their peers and the house mother. Other friendships and relationships were with other workers and managers at the institution, their schoolmates, and their teachers.

Their adult friends were all associated with service support from either their time at the institution or from before becoming a state ward. Zhang, the 16-year-old student, had a close relationship with his house mother and said that he was reassured that other adults also looked out for him: "One of the adults always reminds me to turn to him whenever I have any difficulty or need". Zhou, the other 16 year old, mentioned a police officer who provided a lot of help for him when he was a street child. After he became a state ward, the policeman still kept in regular contact with Zhou and he told the policeman about any concerns he had. Li retold the deep impression it made on him that his teacher and classmates celebrated his birthday when he was at the senior high school. He said: "I was really moved". These interactions with adults and friends in and outside the institution were additionally important in the absence of any extended family relationships.

Like other young people, their social participation included interaction with friends, mostly in leisure and recreational activities, such as Zeng: "We went climbing or playing, and then ate outside".

Their limited resources restrict what they do, but they make do with free or low-cost activities, as Li explained:

> "we simply can't afford any tour [in the school holidays]. Some of my former classmates are students at the … university not far from here. Sometimes, in the afternoon, I go to visit them. And I go there in the summer time to play basketball or something else."

While the young people described many inclusive social opportunities, they also reflected that they sometimes still felt that they were treated differently to other young people. They described how they sometimes had to pretend not to be sensitive to other people's patronizing reactions to their status. They tried to present themselves as having had normal experiences and not needing additional help. Wang explained: "When I feel most helpless, I'll rely on myself to get out from it".

Most of them encountered discrimination and they tried to avoid this by keeping their orphan status unknown to others, as Hui said: "Keeping the secret". They said that the discrimination was usually not marginalization or exclusion. Perversely, it was the excessive compassion and inclusion that they felt constrained them, so that was why they were not forthcoming about their orphan status. Hui descriptively explained: "I just fear those weird looks. I don't like those compassionate eyes or the like. I don't wish to see them. I wish that I looked as normal as other people".

As a result of the different way they were treated, although they participated in many social activities and did not have any communication barriers, they found it difficult to find a sense of belonging in social activities that were specifically arranged for them. Sometimes, their reaction was to withdraw from these situations so that they did not have to deal with the strange way they were treated. They were particularly reluctant to participate in charity events organized at the institution. Wang, the 19-year-old student, bluntly said: "'I don't like to participate in social activities". Similarly, Zhang, only 16 years old, said: "I don't like to participate in those activities because there is too much noise". They especially disliked the one-off or temporary social activities where they were required to participate. Li had decided that "A single get-together doesn't have any influence. I think, however, fixed or regular activities are meaningful". At least they seemed to have developed the capacity to exercise their own choice about which activities they were prepared to participate in.

These benefits of family group care during their childhood meant that the young people had greater social inclusion experiences as they were growing up compared to the children in the dormitories. They formed stable, family-like relationships with their house mother and the other children in the household. Their financial and other resources were relatively better because of the efficient cost management in the family group home, and the savings habits that it encouraged. The institution was still able to support them with free medical and disability support, though the young people with disabilities felt some discrimination towards them. They all attended local schools and tertiary colleges so they had the benefit of quality education and friendships at school. They also had other relationships with adults, though these were all support-based. They particularly disliked and avoided relationships and social events based on compassion, which they found patronizing and excluding.

Challenges of the transition from family group care

Growing up in family group care seemed to have many benefits for the young people compared to congregate institutional care. Once they reached young adulthood, they faced new challenges as they prepared for the possibilities of independence, including health, therapy, education, employment, economic and housing security, social participation, and marriage.

Health and therapy

The shortage of medical and therapy resources compromised the quality of care and capacity for inclusion of the children in state care, especially those with disabilities, irrespective of whether they were in family group care or not. While there were some therapy facilities within the welfare institution and therapy centres in nearby rural foster sites, the house mothers and foster parents both complained that they did not receive sufficient training or support to administer the therapy to the children in their care. A single house mother was responsible for the care of all the children in her household, including all daily care. They frequently commented that they did not have sufficient time for therapy and other specific care for the children. It seemed to be that once they reached teenage years, young people with disabilities were only provided with housing, food and clothes, but not with additional therapy and medical treatment.

Education

The house mothers believed that the young people, especially those with disabilities, were marginalized from education and medical services. Except in the special education centre and rehabilitation centre built within the welfare institution, they had limited access to community and social resources. This city had few comprehensive special education schools and the special education centre at the welfare institution did not have sufficient or qualified teaching staff. Some of the children with learning disabilities, mental illness or other serious disabilities had no supportive programme of personalized education.

Without necessary support, some of the young people in family group care in transition from the compulsory nine school years did not have sufficient direction to continue with education or work. Liu, aged 18 years, and Zhou, aged 16 years, were still at junior high school and primary school despite their older age and age-appropriate social needs. Neither of them were formally identified as having learning disabilities. They expressed their frustration and lack of interest in learning in this environment, which was irrelevant to their social needs and life stage. Liu said: "I used to have a very good school performance, but not now. I no longer wish to learn".

Further education was an easier choice for the young people in family group care who had done well at school. Zeng, the 22-year-old woman with disabilities at university, recognized that her choices were simpler, saying: "For school education, you just need to achieve a good school performance; while for a job, you have to consider a lot of things".

Some of the young people who were ready to leave school were in a dilemma about whether to pursue further education or just find a low-paid job. Some chose to look for a job because they did not have a good educational record. Wang, the young man with disabilities who was aged 19 years and still at technical secondary school, said: "I'm not going to a university because I don't have a firm enough foundation for it, based on my previous vocational school education, and my correspondence technical secondary education curriculum was too narrow".

Other young people leaving school chose to move straight to a job because of their financial situation, such as Li, the 21 year old with disabilities who had finished technical college and worked at the institution. Zhang, who was younger, aged 16 years and still a student at a technical secondary school, was more determined to leave school and get training experience through a job itself. He said: "I want to find a job because I think it's a waste of time to continue my education. And, I can also learn more things at an auto-repair shop, where I can learn faster".

Employment

The young men living in family group care were more likely than the young women to want to find jobs and to take up technical and trade jobs. They were more specific in their career plans. For example, Zhang, the student aged 16 years, said: "I want to run my own auto-repair shop after my graduation". Hui was already working and his ambition was that "I want to become an electrician ... learn by doing, and then apply for the certificate". Zhou said: "I want to become a soldier and serve in the army all the time". Li, the 21 year old with hepatitis B, was slightly older than these teenagers and had already experienced a lot of short-term employment. He was relatively conservative about his future choices compared to his peers:

> "When I was in Shenzhen, they asked me to stay there ... but I didn't think I was capable enough to work there.... I'm not very interested in this [work at the welfare institution].... The pay is too low for me to continue working here. I remain here just because sometimes I feel happy and have a sense of achievement when I see [the children] making progress bit by bit. However, when I think about my future, I feel.... Just think about some of my university classmates, who easily got interesting jobs, with good pay right after graduation because they had competent parents. They didn't need to visit job fairs and didn't need to consider about many things. But we had to seek for job opportunities. I've visited many job fairs, mostly for the lowest positions."

The young people leaving family group care faced considerable difficulties finding employment, the same as other young people in congregate institutional care. Their marginalization from the labour market and society disadvantaged them in job seeking and, in turn, opportunities for independence. They felt that their difficulties in employment lay in their lack of social networks. Li, the 21 year old who worked in the institution, said: "I think the most important are the knowledge and skills you have, followed by your personal connections". Hui, who was the same age and employed in short-term jobs, agreed: "The most significant is your educational background, followed by your social experiences". Zeng, who was still studying at university, thought that she would encounter employment discrimination due to her facial burn scars.

Like the other young people in institutional care, their disadvantages in competition with peers in the labour market were due to: their lower confidence; their lower education levels and interpersonal skills, which restricted the range of their job choices; and their marginalization from employment opportunities, particularly the young people with disabilities. Living in family group care had not improved their employment prospects. They recognized that they needed a good job to be able to live independently and wanted support from the welfare institution to enact that, as several of them commented:

> "[I need help] to find a job or to receive training on how to get a job … and receive recruitment information, for example, what companies are recruiting and what pay they offer … and interview techniques." (Hui, 21, in casual employment)

> "I think they can provide something like information about industries and training on job application planning." (Li, 21, employed at the institution)

> "I wish to find a job and I need recruitment information. I prefer to be recommended to a company." (Zeng, 22, university student)

> "I need to be told about when they will conscript [to the army], how to apply for it and any advice." (Zhou, 16, school student)

Housing security

The children who grew up in family group care or institutional care did not have private spaces or places to protect their privacy. They were even more eager to live somewhere where they had private space when they reached young adulthood. Family group care was still in a large group of children, without private space, and not suitable for young adults. Li, the 21 year old employed at the institution, said: "In fact, I'm eager [to live alone] because I'm already old enough. Always living in the institution may affect many of my social activities. It isn't convenient". This desire for a private, independent home was even more explicitly described by the young women: Zeng, aged 22 years, said that "I want a quiet home", and Liu, aged 18 years, said that "I want to stay alone without disturbance". As a housing security policy was not available for state wards (see Chapter Nine), housing was an insurmountable challenge for most of the young people.

Social participation

The young people in family group care did not speak about having many difficulties in social participation, though their social relationships are narrowed by the lack of opportunities for most of them to participate outside the institution and school. The young people with disabilities were particularly socially restricted by accessibility, discrimination and few social opportunities, preventing them from participating in social activities and community integration.

The institution did not prioritize social participation as a policy imperative for children and young people or respond with appropriate arrangements to promote this right. Instead, it focused on safety and their basic needs rather than their development needs. Li, who had lived in the institution and family group care since he was aged five years, explained that during his childhood in the welfare institution, the staff "Might not let you out very often when you were young, for they were afraid that something [dangerous] might happen". The family group house mothers said that it was impossible for them to have the time to take into account the social participation needs of the children.

The restrictive social environment in the institution hindered their access, and community groups rarely offered to arrange continuing social opportunities. Some volunteer services and NGO programmes occasionally extended the social activities of state wards, but it was often a one-off activity, in isolation from other children and without the elements of community integration that would stimulate meaningful relationships, especially as they grew older.

The young people in family group care themselves either did not know about their social participation rights or they did not prioritize them in the discussions. They were more concerned about practical economic security questions, such as education and employment, which were essential to gaining independence. Occasionally, they realized the importance of social participation when they referred to the link between their narrow social group and their lack of connections to find a job or marriage partner in the future. In the area of social participation, they were not able to differentiate between their constrained social environment and their confidence in social interaction. They accepted that they were required to participate in certain social activities organized for the institution but they did not feel a sense of satisfaction with them. Neither did they use social participation as an opportunity to speak out about their own circumstances.

Marriage

None of the young people living in family group care were married, but they held strong views about love and marriage. The young men, such as Li, the 21 year old, emphasized that they needed resources and security before they could find a partner. He said: "A man needs to become capable enough before dating a girl". The young women were more concerned about the emotional and social capacity necessary for marriage. Zeng, the 22-year-old university student, was at a loss about her experience, saying: "I don't think it's easy to find a good man. Considering that a marriage may last for a lifetime, I have no idea about how to find a husband".

This lack of confidence and sense of uncertainty of themselves put them in a dilemma about the ideals and reality of their marriage prospects. Li had a girlfriend in the past but he broke if off when he graduated from school. He said:

> "I proposed the break-up.… I thought that she was from an inland city and it's impossible for her to settle down in this city. And it's also impossible for both of us to work outside together since her parents wanted her to go home."

He hoped that he would have sufficient independence and security by the time he was aged 30 years so that he was ready for marriage. He said:

> "You don't want others to look down on you.… If I made a marriage proposal in my current condition, the girl's parents may … however bad conditions they have, they would be better-off than me. Since I have nothing, how can I talk with them? Even if we were both still in love with each other, the resistance from her parents would separate us."

Hui, aged 21 years, hoped to marry at about 25 years. He was determined that his partner's parents must be alive because, otherwise, "There would be nobody to take care of our future child". These ideas were consistent with current expectations about the age of marriage and the mutual contributions from extended families.

Conclusion about family group care

Family group care seemed to have several advantages over other institutional care, though compromises relative to foster care remained. The children who grew up in this form of care had generally become state wards as children rather than as babies and were less likely to have disabilities. Most of them had memories, positive or traumatic, from their former families. Their placement in family group care probably reflects practice decisions within the institution – family group care was a newer form of institutional care, when the institution had more resources.

Once they reached young adulthood, they were more likely than other young people in institutional care to have education achievements and social relationships outside the institution because of the type of education that they had attended. However, their social networks were not strong enough to enable them to find well-paid jobs or housing. This was also the case for young people who had grown up in formal or informal foster care, but at least those young people had wider social networks and role models that gave them other options (see Chapters Eight and Ten).

These findings have implications for policy and practice about supporting state wards to be more likely to have the capacity to successfully plan for their future independence. All state wards, irrespective of the form of alternative care in their childhood, struggled to secure housing. Policy changes discussed in Chapter Nine to prioritize their access to affordable housing would alleviate their difficulties. In some provinces, the housing priorities exist in policy but are not implemented. Similarly, the young people said that they needed support in how to find work and how to make decisions about whether to enrol in further study to facilitate entry into higher-paying jobs. The young people in family group care had better education than other children in institutional care or rural local schools, so their capacity to undertake tertiary training was greater.

More generally, these young people were still disadvantaged socially because they had not grown up in a family in the community. This weakened their social networks, social skills and understanding about how to live independently. They formed goals to achieve independence but lacked the role models and adults in their lives to assist them to do that. In the absence of such relationships, at the least, they would need formal support to help them in that transition.

TWELVE

Policy implications for young people leaving care in China

China, like other countries, is changing its policy and implementation to better support young adults leaving state care. The Chinese and international communities are sharing understanding about good practice in alternative care while children are growing up, particularly by prioritizing long-term family-based support. They are also changing alternative care practices to support children during their childhood and as they reach young adulthood, so that they are prepared emotionally and practically to live independently as adults in the same ways as their peers, away from state control. As yet, opportunities to learn from the Chinese experience have been scarce (Pinkerton, 2011).

Children in state care in China are almost always children whose families cannot be found, either because their family members have died or their families have left them in a public place without any way for the state to find the family. This differs from state care in other countries, where most children in state care are children who have been forcibly removed from their families because of the risk of harm. In the future, this is likely to change as the reasons for children becoming orphaned reduce and the child protection system develops to care for children removed from abuse in their families.

This book reviewed these policy and practice changes in China for the generation of young people who grew up in state care over the last 20 years, when alternative care was beginning to shift away from institutional care and recognize the rights of children and young people to an inclusive childhood and adulthood. It examined whether social inclusion was experienced by that generation of young people leaving care and whether current policies support inclusion for children who are growing up in state care now.

Experiences of young people leaving care

The book explored whether the Chinese government supports these children and young people in state care to achieve social inclusion in their young adulthood and experience their rights to transition towards independent living in the same way as their peers in their communities.

It considered this question from the perspective of the young people, looking back on their childhood, their current experiences and their future plans for independence.

Social inclusion in childhood

The social inclusion of children who grew up in state care depended on where and with whom they lived during their childhood. Child welfare institutions, which are responsible for children in care, prioritize adoption over other forms of care, so children who are adopted are able to live in a family and social context in the same way as their peers – they have immediate and extended family relationships, attend a local school, and live and move about in their local community.

Some institutions also provide long-term family foster care to replicate these family conditions with children for whom adoption cannot be arranged, such as some children with disabilities. Many of the children spoke of deep family ties to their foster family members. They pointed to their reciprocal obligations with their parents and other relatives once they left home, such as visiting, caring and emotional and practical support. Others noted the limits and inequities they felt compared to their foster siblings. The paid foster care relationship was usually an open one that children and other family members knew about, and some children experienced this as different to the unconditional bonds in the family towards their siblings.

Other children had lived in multiple living arrangements, such as in their birth family, informal foster family, institutional care and foster care. Some of these conditions were positive and contributed to their social inclusion during their childhood, such as early and continuous bonds with adults in family-like roles. Other conditions were harmful and disruptive to their well-being, such as violence and rejection, in the extreme.

Half the children had grown up in institutional care and had no memories of family-like relationships. Their social inclusion was limited to bonds with peers in the institution, some adult carers and volunteers, and sometimes school relationships. Children with disabilities were least likely to have wider social experiences. At worst, some of the children with disabilities were excluded from education in the institution and the local community, and had only participated in therapy instead. These childhood experiences of family relationships, peer friendships and education not only affected their social inclusion during their childhood, but also laid foundations for later capabilities and social networks in their transition to adulthood.

Social inclusion when leaving care

Most of the young people did not receive sufficient support to leave state care and achieve social inclusion and full citizenship alongside their peers in the community. All young people in China face greater competition in job and housing markets than before the economic reforms that started 30 years ago. Young people who were state wards face greater barriers because of their childhood experiences and their limited social connections to leverage their opportunities. Most of the young people had not left care and did not know how they might achieve it. Some of them were still in education, so dependence on their foster families or the institution was to be expected at their age and stage of acquiring education and training for later independence.

Others, though, had left education and were hampered by barriers at three levels: the economic changes in the job and housing markets; their restricted social inclusion during their childhood; and the limited practical support from the child welfare institution and other parts of government.

The social context of their childhood limited or facilitated opportunities for independence in their young adulthood. A wider social network during childhood, especially one that extended to the city, meant that they were more likely to have connections for training, employment, housing and intimate relationships. In contrast, young adults with deeper social exclusion during their childhood were less likely to have these connections. Some exceptions were young people who had grown up in institutional care but had been able to arrange employment from vocational training connections or introductions from institution staff.

Education

Reasons for restricted educational attainment during childhood depended on where the child had grown up and whether they had disabilities. Some children only had access to education in the institution, so they did not have contact with peers in families who expected high performance. Even if they had gone to a local school, many of them had failed to thrive due to the stigma they felt and discrimination they faced from some children, teachers and the community. Children with disabilities were less likely to have attended any education or education that anticipated their capacity for open employment. Children in rural foster care were often disadvantaged by the relative poor quality of the education available in their local community, especially if they chose to move to the city and compete with city-educated young people for employment.

Employment

Some of the young people had found secure employment related to their training and qualifications. They were generally young people who had secure relationships with their foster families, who supported them to pursue education and quality work. Young people who grew up in institutions and gained quality employment were generally those that received practical support from the welfare institution to find a job or had disability-specific occupational training for people with vision impairments.

However, most of the young people in the institutions did not have secure employment. They often lacked the education and social skills to know how to find and keep a job. Lack of employment had serious consequences for the young people and the institutions.

Housing

Even the young people who had grown up in the institution and had jobs remained living there because their income level was insufficient to make other choices, with few exceptions. Those without a job did not have enough income to live outside the institution. Only in Beijing were some young people supported to live in private rental properties. Some young people who had grown up in foster care were forced to live in a welfare institution when they became older than school age and they wanted to continue education or did not have a job, if the local policy did not support adult foster care. This was most likely if they had disabilities because they did not have the economic means to live independently and the foster families did not have the financial support to continue to care for them.

Policies to support leaving care

Until recently, Chinese policy to support state wards when they reached adulthood concentrated on managing the transition of government responsibility. If the same government organization was not responsible for child and adult welfare, the arrangements were about transferring financial responsibility and the living place of the young person.

Welfare institutions are the only remaining government institution with responsibility to provide lifetime benefits, and the level of welfare support, including health, housing and disability support, is much higher than for other disadvantaged groups. The child welfare policy is a continuation from the pre-reform era, so it does not have a cut-off date when support stops. Children, foster families and institution staff have no signal about an end to government support at a particular age or level of readiness for independent adulthood. Most of the young adults who grew up in care are now neither prepared nor supported to leave the responsibility of the institution.

Due to this policy anomaly of unlimited secure child welfare for children with no family contact, it is difficult for most young people to ever achieve the position of readiness to leave the security of the institution, financially, emotionally and socially. This is particularly so for young people with disabilities, who are more likely to have been deprived of adequate education and who are more likely to expect to have ongoing health and disability support needs.

If the state does not support children, teenagers and young adults in ways conducive to leaving care and achieving socially inclusive independence, the state will continue to care for them throughout their adulthood, irrespective of the preferences of the young person or the state. Over the last 10 years, some cities have shifted towards a broader conceptualization of responsibility to assist state wards to leave care. The change has also been driven by the practical concern that state wards remain one of the last groups of people for whom the state remains responsible their entire life. Changes to support independence include improving the quality of care during childhood, choices about the characteristics of the care and leaving care policies.

Material environment

Material conditions in state child welfare institutions have improved over the last two decades as more central government resources have been allocated to state wards and policies have focused on child well-being. The quality of material care within welfare institutions and the foster care programmes they operate has generally improved, especially the living conditions and schooling. Entering state care now means that the most basic security of children's lives and development are usually met. Whether they live in the institutions or foster families, they are guaranteed daily necessities, basic medical care and financial support. The welfare institutions cover the costs of their education if they are qualified for admission to school or education at the institution. Some welfare institutions organize job opportunities and housing support when the young people finish their education.

However, even in the institutions that offer practical support during childhood and for young people to leave care, whether the institution has provided adequate emotional, social and psychological support during childhood is more problematic, especially for children growing up in congregate institutional care. Until children, foster families and staff have the confidence and security that young people will be adequately supported to achieve independence like their peers, they are unlikely to commit to the difficult steps of preparing for and achieving a socially inclusive life in the community. While material conditions help children and young people to survive, neither welfare institutions nor foster families can provide enough motivational and social support to them if they do not have recourse to reliable policies, rules and professionals to facilitate independence.

Alternative care options

The type of alternative care that children experience during childhood is relevant to achieving later independence. Children who leave care through adoption are most likely to be treated like and achieve the same independence as their peers. The state shifts the primary caring responsibility to the adoptive parents to nurture the development of the child, eventually towards independent adulthood. Other children have the benefit of long-term foster care, which is conducive to permanence and stable family relationships and social connections in their community.

The young people in this study who grew up in long-term foster care were more likely than children in institutional care to have the social, educational and motivational experiences conducive to forming and achieving goals for independence. Most of the foster care programmes are too new for children to have reached the age for independent living, but in places with the earliest foster care, such as Datong, young people have gained employment and live in the foster care village where they grew up or they have moved to the city for further training and job opportunities (see Chapter Eight). The availability of adoption and long-term foster care is increasing in most parts of China, which is consistent with the policy goal of successful transition to independent adulthood.

However, in many cases, the forms of family-based alternative care were not sufficient to ensure the readiness of young people to leave care and the conditions to make it possible. Their capacity for independence has become increasingly compromised by wider social and economic changes, such as a competitive job market and rising housing costs in the cities. Many of the foster care programmes are in rural communities because the alternative care costs are lower there. Yet, economic and social opportunities when they grow up are limited in rural communities. If the young people want to return to the city, the fewer education resources available in rural foster care communities mean that, like their rural peers, many of the children who grew up in foster care do not have education levels sufficient to compete in city job markets. Their parents and extended family do not have the resources and connections to find work for them or pay for housing in the city.

Children with disabilities

Children with disabilities are the most disadvantaged in their access to alternative care options that would support them towards independence. Children with disabilities are least likely to be adopted. Some children with disabilities remain in institutional care and are refused access to long-term foster care or adoption, especially if they have infectious diseases. Some children are not eligible for education in the institution or community on the grounds of their disabilities, despite China's commitment to inclusive education. The United Nations has criticized China for this breach of the 2008 Convention on the Rights of Persons with Disabilities.

When young people with disabilities reach adulthood, they are more likely to be sent to an adult welfare institution for segregated lifetime support, irrespective of whether they have grown up in foster care or institutional care. A small number of welfare institutions that are responsible for child and adult support, such as Datong, allow the young adult with disabilities to continue to live in foster care.

In theory, young people with disabilities who have been supported to prepare for paid work can gain employment and live independently. The examples in this study were few, partly because many of the children with disabilities in long-term foster care tended to be younger than those in institutional care. Other young people with disabilities were working in welfare institutions or disability-specific jobs arranged by the Disabled Persons' Federation (DPF). The DPF supported people with vision impairments to gain massage therapy training and a job in a DPF massage clinic, which was sufficient for a reasonable income and job security. This model has implications for welfare institutions to collaborate with the DPF for vocational training and employment support.

Implementing quality alternative care and leaving care policies

Some cities have also introduced policy changes about transition to independence that explicitly support young people to leave care, including housing, employment and income support. In the locations where the policy was implemented, some young people successfully left care because they had a job with reasonable income and had secured housing. The most developed example is Beijing, which includes financial contributions for income support during education and transition to employment, referrals to jobs and housing, and financial support for private or public housing. Shanghai is another example with affordable housing for young people leaving care. The quality of these policies is due to the fact that these cities have more resources available for welfare support, which is less likely to be possible in inland provinces. Even in the locations with good written policies, the quality and consistency of implementation varies. Young people with disabilities again seem to be least likely to benefit from these changes.

In addition to the support that most young people need from their family to find employment and housing and to make social connections to achieve independence, children who have grown up in state care are likely to have other social and emotional needs due to their personal and social history. Unless these young people have long-term foster care or other close adult relationships, welfare institutions are unlikely to manage this support need. Internationally, peer support social and web networks are important for bridging some of these social gaps (Stein, 2014).

Employment preparation, vocational training, job referral or placement, and employment support are irregularly implemented. Exceptions are where welfare institution staff and managers make a personal commitment or the local DPF is particularly committed to implementing support. The study did not find local examples where the parts of government responsible for employment policy and implementation took responsibility for supporting state wards to prepare, find and stay in paid work. In the cities with policies on leaving care, job placement was a responsibility of local districts. However, some young people argued that the placement procedure was too complicated, time consuming and slow, and only referred to poor-quality jobs. More successful were young people who had found jobs through graduating from secondary technical schools with job placements settled by the schools.

The Chinese central government has made resource commitments to improving the quality and type of alternative care for children in state care so that they might grow up with aspirations for independence. Some provincial and municipal governments have also passed policies on leaving care to support employment and housing, and provide financial support to enable that transition. Widespread implementation of these policies and supplementary social support will be vital if children entering care and the foster families and workers who support them are to have the security of knowing that they can plan to achieve a socially inclusive adulthood. Policies and support for children with disabilities in state care have the furthest to shift before their rights to an inclusive future are likely to be realized.

The national policy that already prioritizes adoption recognizes that a socially inclusive childhood, in a family, in the community, is the greatest predictor of an independent adulthood. Extending that recognition to other long-term alternative family care options and practical support to prepare and plan for transition to adulthood is the next policy step. Engaging other government agencies and community members in accepting their joint responsibilities to include young people in state care is a more difficult task. The successful examples in this book of the joint efforts of young people, foster families, welfare institutions, other government institutions, educational institutions and employers may help to accelerate that policy commitment. Sharing these policy experiences with other countries may also contribute to the global development of policy to improve the lives of young people leaving care.

References

Anghel, R. (2011) 'Transition within transition: how young people learn to leave behind institutional care whilst their carers are stuck in neutral', *Children and Youth Services Review*, 33(12): 2526–31.

Beijing Civil Affairs Bureau (2009) 'Notice on issue relevant to measures of Beijing on placement of adult orphans growing up in child welfare institutions' (JMFF Number 217) and 'Notice on circulating the measures of Beijing on placement of adult orphans growing up in child welfare institutions' (JMFF Number 102).

Bian, Y. (1994) 'Guanxi and the allocation of urban jobs in China', *The China Quarterly*, 140: 971–99.

Bian, Y. (1997) 'Bringing strong ties back in: indirect ties, network bridges, and job searches in China', *American Sociological Review*, 62(3): 366–86.

Blaxland, M., Fisher, K. and Shang, X. (2015) 'Transitional and developmental challenges for Chinese social policy', *Asian Social Work and Policy Review*, 9: 1–2.

Cai, Y. (2003) 'Labour market, social network and occupational achievement: the reemployment of redundant women workers in the transitional period', *Journal of Huazhong Normal University*, 52(5): 155–62 (in Chinese).

CDPF (China Disabled Persons' Federation) (2007) 'Statistical analysis report for China's Second National Sample Surveys on Disability (Conference)', International Forum for Disabled Population and Development, 10–12 December.

Chen, J., Yang, Z. and Wang, Y.P. (2014) 'Review of "The new chinese model of public housing: a step forward or backward?"', *Housing Studies*, 29(4): 534–50.

Chen, L. (2009) 'Nanning's practical exploration for the development of moderate generalized preferential child welfare', China Child Welfare Policy Research and the Fifth Session National Forum for Directors of Child Welfare Institutions, Wuhan, 22–23 October.

Chen, X.M. and Chen, Y.A. (2008) *The status analysis and strategies study of children with disabilities in China*. Beijing: Huaxia Press.

Chen, Y. (2012) 'Do networks pay off among internal migrants in China?', *Chinese Sociological Review*, 45: 28–54.

Cui, R. and Cohen, J. (2015) 'Reform and the hukou system in China', *Migration Letters*, 12(3): 327–35.

Cui, L. and Qin, Y. (2000) 'A study of social support to children in foster care and their subjective well-being in SCAB', Shanghai Charity Foundation and *Xinmin Evening News*, Shanghai, pp 156–66.

Cui, L. and Wu, M. (2000) 'A study of life satisfaction of children in foster care in SCAB', Shanghai Charity Foundation and *Xinmin Evening News*, Shanghai, pp 140–6.

Cui, L. and Yang, Z. (2002) 'A study of social development of children and foster caring in SCAB', in Q. Yan, S. Wang and X. Shang (eds) *Social welfare and vulnerable groups*, Beijing: Chinese Social Science Press, pp 147–55.

Dowling, M. and Brown, G. (2009) 'Globalization and international adoption from China', *Child and Family Social Work*, 14(3): 352–61.

Erikson, E.H. (1968) *Identity, youth and crisis*. New York, NY: Norton.

Fisher, K.R. and Li, J. (2008) 'Chinese disability independent living policy', *Disability and Society*, 23(2): 171–85.

Fisher, K.R. and Shang, X. (2013) 'Access to health and therapy services for families of children with disabilities in China', *Disability and Rehabilitation*, 35(25): 2157–63.

Fisher, K.R. and Shang, X. (2014) 'Protecting the right to life of children with disabilities in China', *Journal of Social Service Research*, P560–72.

Fisher, K.R., Shang, X. and Xie, J. (2011) 'Support for social participation of children and young people with disability in China', in B. Carrillo and J. Duckett (eds) *China's changing welfare mix: Local perspectives*. London and New York, NY: Routledge, pp 193–210.

Fisher, K.R., Shang, X. and Xie, J. (2015) 'Global South–North partnerships – inter-cultural methodologies in disability research', in S. Grech and K. Soldatic (eds) *Disability in the Global South: The critical handbook*. New York, NY: Springer.

Fisher, K.R., Shang, X. and Blaxland, M. (2016) 'Disability and welfare services', in B. Carillo, J. Hood and P. Kadeza (eds) *Handbook of welfare in China*. Cheltenham: Edward Elgar.

Frazer, H. and Marlier, E. (2007) *Tackling child poverty and promoting the social inclusion of children in the EU: Key lessons*. Brussels: European Commission.

Fu, Q., Zhu, Y. and Ren, Q. (2015) 'The downside of marketization: a multilevel analysis of housing tenure and types in reform-era urban China', *Social Science Research*, 49: 126–40.

Goodkind, S., Schelbe, L.A. and Shook, J.J. (2011) 'Why youth leave care: understandings of adulthood and transition successes and challenges among youth aging out of child welfare', *Children and Youth Services Review*, 33(6): 1039–48.

Granovetter, M. (1974) *Getting a job: A study of contacts and careers.* Cambridge, MA: Harvard University.

Gui, Y., Gu, D. and Zhu, G (2002) 'The impact of social network on job seeking: the case of redundant workers in Shanghai', *World Economy Summory*, 3: 45–51.

Gui, Y., Lu, D. and Zhu, G. (2003) 'Social network, cultural system and job searching behaviours', *Journal of Fudan University (Natural Science)*, 3: 16–28 (in Chinese).

Harder, A.T., Köngeter, S., Zeller, M., Knorth, E.J. and Knot-Dickscheit, J. (2011) 'Instruments for research on transition: applied methods and approaches for exploring the transition of young care leavers to adulthood', *Children and Youth Services Review*, 33(12): 2431–41.

Heaser, H. (2016) 'Korean Australian adoptee diasporas: a glimpse into social media', PhD Thesis, UNSW, Australia. Available at: http://handle.unsw.edu.au/1959.4/56917

Hillan, L. (2008) 'Welcome to adulthood: supporting young people in care', *Children Australia*, 33(2): 48–50.

Hills, J., Le Grand, J. and Piachaud, D. (eds) (2001) *Understanding social exclusion.* Oxford: Oxford University Press.

Hobcraft, J. (1998) 'Intergenerational and life-course transmission of social exclusion: influences of childhood poverty family disruption, and contact with the police', CASE paper 15, London School of Economics.

Jiang, X. (2005) 'An exploration and analysis of the application of law on China's foreign-related adoption', *Global Law Review*, 6: 737–42 (in Chinese).

Johnson, G., Natalier, K., Bailey, N., Kunnen, N., Liddiard, M., Mendes, P. and Hollows, A. (2009) *Improving housing outcomes for young people leaving state out of home care,* Australian Housing and Urban Research Institute Positioning Paper Number 117. Melbourne: AHURI.

Johnson, K.A. (2016) *China's hidden children: Abandonment, adoption, and the human costs of the one-child policy.* Chicago, IL: University of Chicago Press.

Kamerman, S.B. (2002) 'Social exclusion and children: background and context', Institute on Child and Family Policy at Columbia University.

Keller, S., Strahl, B., Refaeli, T. and Zhao, C. (2016) 'Researching care leavers in an ethical manner in Switzerland, Germany, Israel and China', in P. Mendes and P. Snow (eds) *Young people transitioning from out-of-home care, international research, policy and practice.* London: Palgrave Macmillan, pp 241–61.

Kogan, I., Matković, T. and Gebel, M. (2013) 'Helpful friends? Personal contacts and job entry among youths in transformation societies', *International Journal of Comparative Sociology*, 54: 277–97.

Levitas, R., Pantazis, C., Fahmy, E., Gordon, D., Lloyd, E. and Patsios, D. (2009) 'The multi-dimensional analysis of social exclusion', research report for the Social Exclusion Task Force. Available at: http://webarchive.nationalarchives.gov.uk/+/http:/www.cabinetoffice.gov.uk/social_exclusion_task_force/publications/multidimensional.aspx

Li, B. (2002) 'Social exclusion theories and Chinese urban housing reform system', *Social Science Research*, 3: 106–10.

Li, P. (2008) 'Policy analysis of Chinese housing system', *Journal of Public Management*, 3: 47–57.

Lin, J. and Si, S. (2010) 'Can guanxi be a problem? Contexts, ties, and some unfavorable consequences of social capital in China', *Asia Pacific Journal of Management*, 27(3): 561–81.

Lin, N., Vaughn, J.C. and Ense, W.M. (1981) 'Social resources and occupational status attainment', *Social Forces*, 59: 1163–81.

Liu, T.-Y., Su, C.W. and Jiang, X.-Z. (2015) 'Is economic growth improving urban? A cross-regional study of China', *Urban Studies*, 52(10): 1883–98.

Liu, Y., Li, Z. and Breitung, W. (2012) 'The social networks of new-generation migrants in China's urbanized villages: a case study of Guangzhou (case study)', *Habitat International*, 36(1): 192.

Malvaso, C., Delfabbro, P., Hackett, L. and Mills, H. (2016) 'Service approaches to young people with complex needs leaving out-of-home care', *Child Care in Practice*, 22(2): 128–47.

MCA (Ministry of Civil Affairs) (1996-2012) *China Civil Affairs' Statistical Yearbook*. Beijing: China Statistics Press.

MCA (2004) 'Interim Measures for Administration of Family Foster Care'. Available at: http://www.mca.gov.cn/article/zwgk/tzl/200711/20071100004024.shtml

MCA (2006) 'Opinions of the MCA and other fourteen ministries on strengthening relief for orphans'. Available at: http://www.gov.cn/zwgk/2006-04/14/content_254233.htm

MCA (2013a) 'The Minister of Civil Affairs on orphan security: the investigation of private adoption after Lankao fire incident – an interview with Li Liguo, Minister of Civil Affairs'. Available at: http://www.MCA.gov.cn/article/zwgk/mzyw/201303/20130300424491.shtml

MCA (2013b) 'It is urgent to increase the capacity of caring for orphans in China comprehensively: responding to Henan Lankao 1.4 fire incident from the relevant Official of the Ministry of Civil Affairs'. Available at: http://www.mca.gov.cn/article/zwgk/mzyw/201301/20130100404905.shtml

McLean, K.C. and Pasupathi, M. (2012) 'Processes of identity development: where I am and how I got there', *Identity*, 12(1): 8–28.

Mendes, P. (2009) 'Globalization, the welfare state and young people leaving state out-of-home care', *Asian Social Work and Policy Review*, 3(2): 85–94.

Mendes, P. and Snow, P. (2014) 'The needs and experiences of young people with a disability transitioning from out-of-home care: the views of practitioners in Victoria, Australia', *Children and Youth Services Review*, 36: 115–23.

Mendes, P. and Snow, P. (eds) (2016) *Young people transitioning from out-of-home care, international research, policy and practice.* London: Palgrave Macmillan.

Mendes, P., Johnson, G. and Moslehuddin, B. (2011) *Young people leaving state out-of-home care: Australian policy and practice.* North Melbourne, Vic: Australian Scholarly Publishing.

Micklewright, J. (2002) *Social exclusion and children: A European view for a US debate*, Innocenti WP 90. Florence: UNICEF.

Ministry of Health (2012) 'China's birth defects prevention report 2012'. Available at: http://www.moh.gov.cn/wsb/pxwfb/201209/55840.shtml

Munro, E.R., Pinkerton, J., Mendes, P., Hyde-Dryden, G., Herczog, M. and Benbenishty, R. (2011) 'The contribution of the United Nations Convention on the Rights of the Child to understanding and promoting the interests of young people making the transition from care to adulthood', *Children and Youth Services Review*, 33(12): 2417–23.

Murphy, E., Clegg, J. and Almack, K. (2011) 'Constructing adulthood in discussions about the futures of young people with moderate–profound intellectual disabilities', *Journal of Applied Research in Intellectual Disabilities*, 24: 61–73.

Nanjing Ribao (2008) 'Interim provisions of Nanjing on management of older orphans in state child welfare institutions'. Available at: http://www.guer.org/thread-12340-1-1.html

Nanning City People's Government General Office (2013) 'Opinions on strengthening the welfare provision for orphans, Nan Fu Ban (2013)', Number 6. Available at: http://www.nanning.gov.cn/ Government/jcxxgk/zcwj/nnzb/nnzb2013/2013ndwq/201301/ t20130110_66303.html

Nanning City Social Welfare Institution (2000) Annual work summary of Nanning Social Welfare Institute. Unpublished field research report.

Nanning City Social Welfare Institution (2004) Annual work summary of Nanning Social Welfare Institute. Unpublished field research report.

Nanning City Social Welfare Institution (2009) Annual work summary of Nanning Social Welfare Institute. Unpublished field research report.

Pinkerton, J. (2011) 'Constructing a global understanding of the social ecology of leaving out of home care', *Children and Youth Services Review*, 33(12): 2412–16.

Qian, L. (2014) 'Consuming "the unfortunate": the violence of philanthropy in a contemporary Chinese state-run orphanage', *Dialectical Anthropology*, 38(3): 247–79.

Ran, D. (2005) 'Qingdao issued the opinions on placement of adult orphans'. Available at: http://news.sina.com.cn/o/2005-06-24/10346259173s.shtml

Ruan, D. (1993) 'Interpersonal networks and workplace controls in urban China', *The Australian Journal of Chinese Affairs*, 29: 89–105.

Selman, P. (2012) 'The global decline of intercountry adoption: what lies ahead?', *Social Policy and Society*, 11(3): 381–97.

Shang, X. (2003) 'Protecting children under financial constraints: the case of Datong', *Journal of Social Policy*, 32: 549–70.

Shang, X. (2008a) *A study of the condition of orphans in China*. Beijing: China Social Sciences Academic Press (in Chinese).

Shang, X. (2008b) *Chinese vulnerable children protection system*. Beijing: Social Sciences Academic Press (in Chinese).

Shang, X. (2009) 'Interviews with young people with disabilities and directors of SWCIs in China', unpublished working report, Social Policy Research Centre, UNSW, Australia.

Shang, X. (2012) 'Looking for best practice in caring for disabled children: a case of socialized foster care in China', *Asia Pacific Journal of Social Work and Development*, 22(1/2): 127–38.

Shang, X. (2013) *Study on family experience of children with disabilities in China*. Beijing: Social Sciences Academic Press (in Chinese).

Shang, X. and Fisher, K.R. (2014a) *Caring for orphaned children in China.* Lanham, MD: Lexington Books.

Shang, X. and Fisher, K.R. (2014b) 'Social support for mothers of children with disabilities in China', *Journal of Social Service Research*, 40(4): 573–86.

Shang, X. and Fisher, K.R. (2016) *Disability policy in China: Child and family experiences.* Abingdon: Routledge.

Shang, X. and Katz, I. (2014) 'Missing elements in the protection of children: three cases from China', *Journal of Social Service Research*, 40(4): 545–59.

Shang, X. and Wang, X. (eds) (2013) *Leading research on child welfare and protection in China: 2013.* Beijing: China Social Sciences Academic Press (in Chinese).

Shang, X. and Wu, X. (2003) 'The changing role of the state in child protection: the case of Nanchang', *Social Service Review*, 77(6): 523–40.

Shang, X., Fisher, K.R. and Xie J. (2011) 'Discrimination against children with disability in China: a case study in Jiangxi Province', *International Journal of Social Welfare*, 20(3): 298–308.

Stein, M. (2014) 'Young people's transitions from care to adulthood in European and post-communist Eastern European and Central Asian societies', *Australian Social Work*, 67(1): 24–38.

Stepanova, E. and Hackett, S. (2014) 'Understanding care leavers in Russia: young people's experiences of institutionalisation', *Australian Social Work*, 67(1): 118–34.

Su, L. and Meng, D. (2013) 'Strong ties or weak ties: the use of social capital in the employment of university students', *Journal of Huazhong Normal University*, 52(5): 155–62 (in Chinese).

Sun, X. and Bian, Y. (2011) 'The participation of Chinese American scientists in China and their social network: the re-examination of strong ties and weak ties', *Society*, 31(2): 194–215 (in Chinese).

Tang, Y. (2007) 'A study of social network and university graduates job searching', *Journal of Chongqing Institution of Technology (Social Science)*, 7: 89–92 (in Chinese).

The General Office of Shanxi Provincial People's Government (2011) 'Opinions of the General Office of Shanxi Provincial People's Government on Strengthening the Implementation of Orphan Protection Work' (Office of Shanxi Government [2011] No.66). Available at: http://www.shanxigov.cn/xxgk/zfgb/2011nzfgb/d16q_5268/szfbgtwj_5270/201109/t20110902_101574.shtml

Trimble O'Connor, L. (2013) 'Ask and you shall receive: social network contacts' provision of help during the job search', *Social Networks*, 35: 593–603.

UNCRC (United Nations Convention on the Rights of the Child) (1989) 'United Nations Convention on the Rights of the Child'. Available at: http://www.un.org/chinese/children/issue/crc.shtml

UNCRPD (United Nations Convention on the Rights of Persons with Disabilities) (2008) 'United Nations Convention on the Rights of Persons with Disabilities'. Available at: http://www.un.org/chinese/disabilities/default.asp?navid=12andpid=714

UNGACC (United Nations Guidelines for the Alternative Care of Children) (2009) 'United Nations Guidelines for the Alternative Care of Children'. Available at: https://www.unicef.org/protection/alternative_care_Guidelines-English.pdf

UNHCHR (Office of the United Nations High Commissioner for Human Rights) (2010) 'Fact sheet number 21, the right to adequate housing', Office of the United Nations High Commissioner for Human Rights. Available at: http://www.ohchr.org/Documents/Publications/FS21_rev_1_Housing_en.pdf

Urumqi Civil Affairs Bureau (2012) 'Notice on Issuing Opinions of Urumqi on Strengthening the Implementation of Orphan Protection Work' (Office of Urumqi Government [2012] No.439). Available at: http://mzj.urumqi.gov.cn/bmwj/189323.htm

Urumqi City Coordinating Committee for People with Disabilities (2002) 'Urumqi City interim provisions of people with disabilities to enjoy a number of preferential policies'. Available at: http://www.cdpf.org.cn/zcfg/content/2003-01/01/content_30316145.htm

Wang, H. (2009) 'Beijing: adult orphans can receive lump sum allowance of RMB 150,000'. Available at: http://www.china.com.cn/news/txt/2009-03/06/content_17387396.htm

Wang, H., Su, F., Wang, L. and Tao, R. (2012) 'Rural housing consumption and social stratification in transitional China: evidence from a national survey', *Housing Studies*, 27(5): 667–84.

Wang, L. (2016) *Outsourced children: Orphanage care and adoption in globalizing China*. Redwood City: Stanford University Press.

Wang, W. and Viney, L.L. (1997) 'The psychosocial development of children and adolescents in the People's Republic of China: an Eriksonian approach', *International Journal of Psychology*, 32(3): 139–53.

Ward, H. (2011) 'Continuities and discontinuities: issues concerning the establishment of a persistent sense of self amongst care leavers', *Children and Youth Services Review*, 33(12): 2512–18.

Wellman, B. (1988) 'Structural analysis: from method and metaphor to theory and substance', in B. Wellman and S.D. Berkowitz (eds) *Social structures: A network approach*. Cambridge: Cambridge University Press, pp 19–61.

Wen, R. (2009) 'Adult orphans in Beijing can receive lump sum allowance of RMB 150,000', *The Beijing News*. Available at: http://finance.sina.com.cn/g/20090307/06125944414.shtml

Wiesel, I., Laragy, C., Gendera, S., Fisher, K.R., Jenkinson, S., Hill, T., Finch, K., Shaw, W. and Bridge, C. (2015) *Moving to my home: Housing aspirations, transitions and outcomes of people with disability*, AHURI Final Report No.246. Melbourne: Australian Housing and Urban Research Institute.

Wu, L., Han, X. and Gao, X. (2005) *Foster care: Motivations and outcomes: An in-depth analysis of the 'Beijing Model'*. Beijing: Social Sciences Academy Press (in Chinese).

Xinjiang People's Government General Office (2011) 'Opinions of Xinjiang People's Government General Office on strengthening the welfare provision for orphans, Xin Zheng Ban Fa (2011)', Number 59. Available at: http://www.cdpsn.org.cn/policy/dt206l32627.htm

Xu, J. (2013) 'Starting from systematic, standardization and specialization, to continuously improve the civil society's ability of raising children', a speech at the seminar of Raising Children by Chinese Civil Society, 26 October, Beijing. Available at: http://www.chinacatholic.org/fics/children/26371.html

Yu, W. (2013) 'Older orphans in Chengdu are "trapped" in welfare institutions', *Chengdu Economic Daily*, 7 February. Available at: http://cd.qq.com/a/20130702/002317.htm

Zhang, C., Li, M. and Lu, D. (2004) 'Social network analysis: an important method for sociological study', *Gansu Social Science*, 2: 109–11 (in Chinese).

Zhao, Y. (2002) 'The social capital in re-employment: effectiveness and limitation', *Social Science Study*, 4: 43–54 (in Chinese).

Zhao, Y. (2003) 'Social network and reservation wages of job searchers – with re-employment of laid-off workers as an example', *Sociology Study*, 4: 51–60 (in Chinese).

Zhu, Y. (2008) 'Analysis of Chinese housing security policies – social policy perspective', *Public Administration Review*, 4: 89–114.

Appendix: Characteristics of young people participating in the research

Table A.1: Young people in institutional care

Alias	Sex	Age	Disability	Education	Employed or studying	Housing	Married	Place
Mao	M	40	Yes	Primary	Unemployed	Dormitory welfare institution	No	Taiyuan
Jing	F	38	Yes	Junior middle	Employed at massage clinic	Family unit welfare institution	Yes	Taiyuan
Mei	F	34	Yes	Junior middle	Employed at state child welfare institution	Family unit welfare institution	Yes	Taiyuan
Xue	F	30	Yes	Technical secondary	Student	Dormitory welfare institution	No	Taiyuan
Bing	M	28	No	Technical secondary	Employed	Family unit welfare institution	Yes	Taiyuan
Ping	M	27	Yes	–	Employed at state child welfare institution	Dormitory welfare institution	No	Nanning
Jin	M	26	Yes	Technical college	Employed at massage clinic	Dormitory welfare institution	No	Taiyuan
Liao	M	26	No	Technical secondary	Unemployed	Dormitory welfare institution	No	Taiyuan
Hu	M	24	No	Technical college	Employed	Dormitories at work and institution	No	Nanning
Zeng	F	22	Yes	University	Student	Dormitory schoolb	No	Urumqi
Li	M	21	Yes	Technical college	Employed at state child welfare institution	Family group care	No	Urumqi
Hui	M	21	No	Primary	Employed	Family group care	No	Urumqi
Yao	M	20	Yes	–	Unemployed	Dormitory welfare institution	No	Nanning
Wu	M	20	No	Junior middle	Unemployed	Dormitory welfare institution	No	Nanning
Jian	M	19	No	Junior middle	Student	Dormitory welfare institution	No	Taiyuan
Wang	M	19	Yes	Technical secondary	Student	Family group care	No	Urumqi
Liu	F	18	No	Junior middle	Student	Family group care	No	Urumqi
Yong	M	18	No	Technical college	Student	Dormitory school	No	Nanning
Ling	F	18	No	Higher secondary	Student	Dormitory welfare institution	No	Nanning
Lan	M	17	Yes	Technical secondary	Unemployed	Dormitory welfare institution	No	Nanning
Hua	F	17	No	Junior middle	Student	Dormitory welfare institution	No	Nanning
Zhang	M	16	No	Technical secondary	Student	Family group care	No	Urumqi
Zhou	M	16	No	Primary	Student	Family group care	No	Urumqi
Jie	M	16	Yes	–	Employed at state child welfare institution	Dormitory welfare institution	No	Nanning
Focus group participants*								
Xiao mei	F	-	-	-	-	Dormitory welfare institution	No	Nanning
Xiao ling	F	-	-	-	-	Dormitory welfare institution	No	Nanning
Written materials participant*								
Long	M	35	No	-	-	Dormitory welfare institution	No	Taiyuan

Notes: 2013, M=male; F=female. *In Nanning an additional 6 girls and 2 boys participated in focus groups; characteristics were available for 2 girls only. In Taiyuan one man chose to write about his life rather than participate in an interview. **Family group care before university.

Table A.2: Young people in foster care

Alias	Sex	Age	Disability	Education	Employed or studying	Housing	Married	Place
Hong	F	37	Yes	No schooling	Employed at state child welfare institution	Dormitory welfare institution	No	Nanning
Ming	F	30	Yes	Junior primary	Employed at state child welfare institution	Dormitory welfare institution	No	Nanning
Hai	F	29	Yes	Master degree	Employed	Private rental	Yes	Datong
Deng	M	29	Yes	Junior middle	Unemployed	Dormitory welfare institution	No	Nanning
Mo	F	28	Yes	Higher education	Employed	Family unit welfare institution	Yes	Datong
Zhong	M	26	Yes	Technical secondary	Employed	Private rental	No	Beijing
Kang	M	25	Yes	Higher secondary	Employed	Own subsidized house from welfare institution	No	Datong
Bao	M	23	Yes	Technical college	Employed part-time	Dormitory welfare institution	No	Beijing
Fang	M	20	Yes	Technical secondary	Intern	Dormitory employer	No	Datong
Shu	M	19	Yes	Primary	Employed part-time	Foster family	No	Datong
Jiang	M	19	No	Technical secondary	Unpaid intern	Foster family	No	Taiyuan

Notes: Data for 2013. M = male; F = female.

Table A.3: Young people moving between institutional care and foster care

Alias	Sex	Age	Disability	Education	Employed or studying	Housing	Married	Place
Jiu	M	25	No	Senior secondary	Student	Dormitory welfare institution	No	Beijing
Luo	M	23	No	Technical secondary	Employed[a]	Private rental	No	Beijing
Xin	M	23	No	Technical secondary	Employed[a]	Dormitory welfare institution	No	Beijing
Hen	M	23	Yes	Technical secondary	Student	Dormitory school	No	Beijing
Wei	M	23	No	Technical secondary	Student, part-time job	Dormitory school	No	Beijing
Ying	F	22	Yes	Technical secondary	Student	Foster family	No	Beijing
Bin	M	21	No	Technical secondary	Student	Dormitory welfare institution	No	Beijing
Guan	M	21	No	Technical secondary	Employed	Private rental	No	Beijing

Notes: Data for 2013 from Beijing. M = male; F = female. [a] Waiting for a government-arranged job.

Table A.4: Young people in other forms of care – kinship and non-kinship care or institutional care after parents died

Alias	Sex	Age	Disability	Education	Employed or studying	Housing	Married	Place
Xi	F	24	Yes	Technical college	Employed at state child welfare institution	Dormitory welfare institution	No	Taiyuan
Zi	M	23	No	Technical college	Army	Dormitory army	No	Taiyuan
Bo[a]	M	22	No	Technical secondary	Casual work or unemployed	Dormitory welfare institution	No	Taiyuan
Miao	F	21	No	Technical college	Student	Foster family	No	Taiyuan
Min	F	21	No	Technical secondary	Homemaker	Private rental	Yes	Taiyuan
Yue	F	21	No	University	Unemployed	Dormitory school	No	Taiyuan
Ning	F	20	No	Technical college	Student	Dormitory school	No	Taiyuan
Miu	F	16	No	Technical secondary	Student	Dormitory school	No	Taiyuan
Pai	F	16	Yes	Junior middle	Student	Foster family	No	Taiyuan
Yu	F	16	No	Technical secondary	Student	Foster family	No	Taiyuan
Quang[a]	M	16	No	Junior middle	Student	Dormitory welfare institution	No	Taiyuan

Notes: Data for 2013 from Taiyuan. M = male; F = female. [a] Moved to institutional care.

Table A.5: Chinese education levels referred to in the tables

Level	English	Chinese
	No schooling	
Primary	Junior primary	初小
	Primary	小学（初小和高小）
Secondary	Junior middle/junior secondary	初中
	Higher secondary	高中
	Technical secondary	中专（中等专业学校）
Higher education	Technical college	大专
	University	大学，大本

Index